Reactionary Democracy

Aurelien Mondon is a senior lecturer in Politics at the University of Bath. His first book, *The Mainstreaming of the Extreme Right in France and Australia: A Populist Hegemony?*, was published in 2013 and he recently co-edited *After Charlie Hebdo: Terror, Racism and Free Speech* (2017).

Aaron Winter is Senior Lecturer in Criminology at the University of East London. He is co-editor of *Discourses and Practices of Terrorism: Interrogating Terror and Historical Perspectives on Organised Crime and Terrorism.*

Reactionary Democracy

How Racism and the Populist
Far Right Became Mainstream

Aurelien Mondon and Aaron Winter

VERSO
London • New York

First published by Verso 2020
© Aurelien Mondon and Aaron Winter 2020

The moral rights of the authors have been asserted

1 3 5 7 9 10 8 6 4 2

Verso
UK: 6 Meard Street, London W1F 0EG
US: 20 Jay Street, Suite 1010, Brooklyn, NY 11201
versobooks.com

Verso is the imprint of New Left Books

ISBN-13: 978-1-78873-423-3
ISBN-13: 978-1-78873-422-6 (HBK)
ISBN-13: 978-1-78873-424-0 (UK EBK)
ISBN-13: 978-1-78873-425-7 (US EBK)

British Library Cataloguing in Publication Data
A catalogue record for this book is available from the British Library

Library of Congress Control Number
2020932048

Typeset in Minion Pro by Hewer Text UK Ltd, Edinburgh
Printed and bound by CPI Group (UK) Ltd, Croydon CR0 4YY

For Alex, Alexandra, Matthew and Shane.

Contents

Acknowledgements

We would like to thank the many friends, relatives, colleagues and students who helped us with this project through their time and energy, intellectual and political engagement and example. There are too many of you to name, but you know who you are and we hope you also know how grateful we are for your support.

Introduction

Confronting the great resurgence of white supremacist organizations and seeing the rhetoric and beliefs of these groups surface as part of accepted discourse in every aspect of daily life in the United States startles, frightens and is enough to throw one back into silence . . . These days white racism can let it all hang out, hold nothing back.

bell hooks, 1995

bell hooks's words sound even truer today than they did in 1995. The mainstreaming of the far right has not only legitimised its politics, but also strengthened systemic racism and emboldened racists of all kinds. In recent years, the election of Donald Trump, the vote for Brexit and Marine Le Pen's accession to the second round of the French presidential election with over 30 per cent of the vote have marked a new level in the resurgence and rise of far-right politics. This is not limited to the three cases central to this book – the United States, France and the United Kingdom: the Lega in Italy and the Freedom Party of Austria both entered governing coalitions on the back of strong electoral performances, even though both failed to hold on to power for long. The rightward turn of former mainstream parties in central Europe also has compounded this effect among far-right parties vying for power in much of Europe. Despite its relatively high living standards, Scandinavia has not been spared this trend; and recently Spain, which had so far resisted it, has witnessed the rise of its own far-right party, Vox. Outside Europe and the United States, the far right has also made gains with Jair Bolsonaro's victory in Brazil, and has continued to influence politics in Australia, for example. Far-right violence has also become increasingly common, from daily microaggressions and racist incidents to terrorist attacks such as the one in Christchurch on 15 March 2019, where fifty Muslims were killed.

All this has led to the publication of countless books and articles about the far right, racism and, more recently, 'populism'. Countless hours of news reports, opinion pieces, documentaries and films have covered these events, discussing and analysing the phenomenon more broadly. All of this, we argue, has contributed to the hyping of far-right ideas, and played a key role in their legitimisation. Indeed, it is no longer outlandish to warn of the potential return of fascism.[1] This appears to have somewhat shattered the comfortable denial afforded by the spurious post-race narrative, which holds that racism is something of the past, defeated by the forces of liberalism and liberal democracy, and that it could only ever be found in individualised and pathologised pockets of the most extreme right. Of course, this was always little comfort to those at the sharp end of more covert, systemic racism, those left to face daily discrimination and oppression deeply rooted in our political system. Yet, things have worsened in recent times. We argue that the rise and mainstreaming of the far right not only distract us from existing systemic racism, but legitimise its cruder expressions by giving them platforms. This has served to place concerns about systemic racism further in the back of the liberal mind, as it focuses instead on the extreme and far right. We argue that liberal democracies have become consumed by a fight for survival against a threat they have themselves nurtured, to divert attention away from their inability to respond to the inequalities and growing number of historical crises fuelled by capitalism and its innate conflict with liberal-democratic ideals of liberty and equality.

In this context, we ground our understanding of current events – specifically the mainstreaming of racism and the far right – in history and wider power structures. Contrary to the idea that progress is unidirectional or unavoidable, we argue here that what we witness today cannot be understood in a linear fashion whereby movements, ideas and ideologies move gradually towards 'the end of history'. Instead, we maintain that the history of racism and the far right, from their inception to the forms they take in the present, should be seen in the same way as other ideologies and social formations: in constant, messy, contested and adaptive evolution, and subject to wider social

---

1   See Jason Stanley, *How Fascism Works: The Politics of Us and Them* (New York: Penguin Random House, 2018); Ugo Palheta, *La possibilité du fascisme: France, la trajectoire du désastre* (Paris: La Découverte, 2018); Enzo Traverso, *The New Faces of Fascism* (London: Verso, 2019).

forces and contingencies. We explore how common sense and popular will ('the will of the people') are constructed to defend certain ideas. This is not an exercise in pointing the finger at particular culprits, but, rather, an in-depth exploration of how power is constructed through processes and narratives.

Yet, the larger aim of this book is to provide the necessary clarity and focus to understand this threat more holistically. At a time when we are beset by multiple crises – economic, social, environmental – we believe that it is essential that we do not become side-tracked by the forces of reaction. This can only lead to further harm being done to the more vulnerable and racialised groups they scapegoat and target in a strategy of distraction and deflection – and will delay actions that are urgently necessary to address these crises on a global scale, as they force us to return to narrow and destructive nationalist politics. To this end, we cannot rely on the 'mainstream' as essentially virtuous and wait passively for things to fix themselves. It has become obvious that solutions will come at a clear cost and will demand radical change – something our current model, and the elite shaping it, have preferred to ignore and even prevent to protect their interests. While this book is aimed at a broad audience, we expect that many of those who will have the opportunity to read it will also have the space to think and act. To them we say: apathy is a political choice, and a reactionary one. Things do not have to be this way.

This book builds on our research, bringing together the various strands of enquiry and analysis we have developed over the years. Our interdisciplinary background is not only a strength, but in fact essential to reaching a more complete understanding of the situation. Research on the far right and associated fields has grown tremendously in recent years, raising questions and concerns about our role as researchers in the coverage we provide to such ideas. That increasing attention has been paid to these parties, movements and ideas is to be commended: they are not only a fact of social life, but also a threat to many. However, recent trends in academia, under the pressure of the neoliberalisation of research, have led to a number of problematic developments. Claims that the study of politics and society can be conducted just like any other scientific research have led many to ignore their own standpoint, privilege and accountability with respect to the matter they study. We do not believe that objectivity in research can be achieved. We do not hide the fact that we take sides: racists and anti-racists are not equivalent, and we do not stand in the middle or above as objective bystanders. We recognise both our ideological standpoint and our privileged positions. We are clearly and unashamedly anti-racist researchers. Does that make us less objective researchers than those who uncritically state their objectivity in order to push reactionary agendas under the guise of science? Does that make us more biased than those who refuse to acknowledge their ideological standpoint or privilege (institutional, racial and/or gendered)? We do not think so.

We also believe that access to public discourse and our ability – shared by politicians and the media – to shape it through our work comes with responsibility and accountability. Having said that, we do not claim to speak for everyone suffering from racism or the far right. Nor do we purport to speak for the 'left-behind' who have been used to justify the legitimisation of racism and the far right as some sort of democratic wish. We see such a construction as both flawed and ideological: a diversion away from a unitary class struggle towards an elite-driven race struggle. Instead, our book targets this very elite who occupy similar institutions of privilege to our own, whether in the media, academia or polity, but who use it to legitimise and rationalise both racism and classism, reaffirming systems of power, privilege and inequality. Instead of blaming the rise of poverty and alienation on immigrants or racialised others, or the rise of racism primarily on the working class, we turn our focus to those with the means to set the agenda and have their voices heard, their politics implemented, and their selfish and narrow interests defended.

It is in this context that our book tries to caution against certain tendencies, whether it be the framing of reactionary ideas as democratic or the limitations of our democratic imagination to liberal, hegemonic forms at the expense of more radical critique. Instead, we offer ways to develop better frameworks, practices and mechanisms in studying and combating ideas and movements that undermine the very core of what democracy should be. This is why we titled our book *Reactionary Democracy*: we believe there is more to democracy than what is currently on offer. Democracy is not necessarily progressive, and will only be so if we make it. What we call 'reactionary democracy' is the deployment of the concept of democracy and its central understanding of power (*kratos*) being held by the people (*demos*) for reactionary ends. We argue that the resurgence of racism, populism and the far right is not the result of popular demands, as we are often told, but instead the logical conclusion of the more or less conscious manipulation of the concept of 'the people' to push reactionary ideas in the service of power. This serves to re-enforce existing inequalities and divert us away from real concerns and radical alternatives to the current system. In this move, the far right is used as a decoy, diverting our attention away from new political imaginaries: our only choice is between an increasingly resented status quo and the far right. This, in turn, has legitimised the far right as an alternative, strengthening its hand and leading us into a vicious circle. It does not have to be this way: more progressive paths are available. However, embarking upon them necessitates a careful and thorough deconstruction of the hegemonic discourse – what is understood as mere common sense in our politics, but we believe is currently preventing us from thinking beyond the liberal–populist dichotomy. This book therefore identifies discourse and discursive practices as central to any political project. Only by understanding how meaning is constructed and expressed, and how ideas are constructed as popular and 'common sense', can we develop a better understanding of the systemic forces underpinning the exploitative and discriminatory basis of the current system.

This book seeks first of all to develop an analytical framework through which to understand the operation of racism in the current context. The first two chapters are dedicated to providing a comprehensive way to understand and combat racism in our contemporary societies. Racism is commonly understood in a monolithic, archaic and illiberal manner – which is one of the reasons why many academics, politicians and commentators shy away from the term and deny it. The association of the concept with fascism and Nazism, but also with the biological politics and policy, which our societies are supposed to have overcome in the twentieth century, make it difficult for some to acknowledge that we do not live in post-racial societies, and that racism still underpins our structures and institutions. Too often, this ideology is considered to be fixed (as is fascism). While liberalism has been allowed to evolve and shed some of its more negative aspects throughout its history, racism is commonly considered immutable.

Thus, building on a wealth of literature, Chapters 1 and 2 develop a framework for understanding the place and role of racism in contemporary societies. We argue that, in order to understand racism today, it is essential to separate its various articulations, distinguishing what we call liberal and illiberal racisms. While the borders between the two are fuzzy, the existence of illiberal racism in opposition to liberal racism is essential to the perpetuation of a system built on discrimination and privilege, ensuring its mainstream acceptability. Chapter 1 focuses on illiberal racism, describing at length how it operates, but also how the contemporary far right has evolved from it. Chapter 2 turns to liberal racism. After providing a brief definition, we explain how it is legitimised through the perverted use of progressive struggles such as those for women's rights, LGBTQ+ rights and free speech. Finally, we turn to some of those who have helped legitimise and mainstreamed this reactionary understanding of equal rights and liberty, illustrating how the process can take place.

Chapter 3 turns to the issue of mainstreaming, exploring how racism has become increasingly common and potent in our public discourse. The chapter starts by providing a definition of mainstreaming. We attempt to move away from looking solely at electoral politics and performance to gauge the advance of far-right politics. Instead, we create a framework that takes a more holistic approach and engages with ideas and discourse, which we see as crucial to hegemonic control. We then turn to examples that illustrate the process, demonstrating that there is more than one way in which far right ideas can be mainstreamed – each necessitating more than a successful far right party, and relying also on the active involvement of elite discourse.

Finally, Chapter 4 seeks to challenge the narrative which blames the resurgence of the far right and racism on 'the people'. In recent years, and particularly since the rise of populism as a concept ubiquitous in political analysis, it has become commonplace to hear that the rise of the far right is the result of popular demand, and that the elite – the media, academics, politicians – are merely responding to democratic demands by veering to the right, and thereby providing huge platforms to these ideas and their proponents. Thus, this chapter also seeks to challenge the way in which the idea of 'public opinion' is conceptually constructed – a move which, we argue, underpins a relatively new and narrow understanding of democracy. We then turn to questioning and critiquing another prominent narrative, which has placed the blame for the rise of the far right not only on 'the people', but more precisely on the working class. This allows us to understand fully the role played by recent populist hype in obscuring what is really at stake in the rise of the far right and the strengthening of reactionary democracy.

While, in our view, support for the far right has been exaggerated, this does not mean in any way that the threat it represents is not real. The politics it pushes do have real consequences for the lives of many, and particularly for those less privileged and already subject to various forms of discrimination and oppression. Warnings about the return of fascistic politics should not be brushed off as exaggerations; the signs are clearly worrying, and have serious implications for those whom it targets and for democracy itself. Yet, neither should such warnings be used to ignore, detract from or accommodate systemic, mainstream racism. We argue that what we describe as populist 'hype' has led to the legitimisation of far right ideas and their normalisation, as shapers of public discourse have appropriated and repackaged them increasingly brazenly. At the same time, it has delegitimised the concept of 'the people' that is central to the very idea of democracy. The blame for the rise of the far right has been placed on their shoulders, while exonerating a supposedly powerless elite who has felt forced to send its 'people' down a dark road. Only through a holistic understanding of the situation, including that of the role played by liberalism in the perpetuation of racism, inequality and injustice, can we combat the far right effectively.

In addition to the central analytical aims, we provide a number of conceptual tools and frameworks. These are designed to be deployed to understand both the transformation and application of racism in a variety of contexts in which far-right discourse has been normalised, and the mainstream is failing to offer a real alternative. To illustrate this, we will be using examples drawn from three case studies. These were chosen based on our areas of expertise, but, more importantly, for their capacity to operate as lenses through which the process of the mainstreaming of racism may be understood, as well as how to combat it. Throughout the book, we refer to a broader literature. We do not expect readers to be familiar with these texts, but encourage those interested in particular points to engage with writers we are particularly indebted to.

As Wendy Brown wrote about 'neoliberalism's stealth revolution', the role of political theory – and, we would add, of any critical academic enquiry – is to formulate

> a critique – an effort to comprehend the constitutive elements and dynamics of our condition. It does not elaborate alternatives to the order it illuminates and only occasionally identifies possible strategies for resisting the developments it charts. However, the predicaments and powers it illuminates might contribute to the development of such alternatives and strategies, which are themselves vital to any future democracy.[2]

This is what we hope this book achieves.

---

2   Wendy Brown, *Undoing the Demos: Neoliberalism's Stealth Revolution* (New York: Zone, 2015), p. 28.

CHAPTER ONE

Illiberal Racisms, Extremism and the Discursive Reconstruction of the Far Right

In western societies, it is commonly thought that the defeat of Nazism and segregationist Jim Crow laws, together with the end of colonialism and passing of the Civil Rights Act, signalled the defeat of racism. These events are thought to represent the victory of the new, post-war or post–civil rights egalitarian liberal order, which would eventually inform the so-called post-racial narrative that emerged decisively with the end of Apartheid and Nelson Mandela's election victory in 1994, and culminated with Barack Obama's in 2008. Both were powerful symbols, as they became leaders of countries with long and notorious histories of racism. On the day after Obama's election, Richard Cohen wrote in the *Washington Post*: 'It is not just that [Obama] is post-racial; so is the nation he is generationally primed to lead.' Cohen quoted former president Lyndon B. Johnson, who had overseen the passing of the Civil Rights Act, declaring: 'My fellow Americans, we have overcome.' In an iconic editorial cartoon, Riber Hansson showed Obama walking up to the White House past a downcast Klansman leaning on his cross, a pile of spent matches at his feet.[1] The idea that the United States had overcome racism with the election of Obama was not surprising, as the phenomenon remained deeply misunderstood. According to Eduardo Bonilla-Silva and Victor Ray, most mainstream social analysis, and most Americans themselves, view racism as 'individual-level animosity or hatred towards people of colour', associated primarily with its most explicit historical manifestations and representations, such as 'Archie Bunker-type rhetoric, Klan rallies or overt racial behaviour like hanging a noose from a tree.'[2] This is similar to what Alana Lentin terms 'frozen racism'. According to Lentin,

---

1 Riber Hansson, 'Obama and Resigned KKK Member', *Cagle Cartoons*, 2008.

2 Eduardo Bonilla-Silva with Victor E. Ray, 'Getting Over the Obama Hope Hangover: The New Racism in "Post-Racial" America', in Karim Murji and John Solomos, eds, *Theories of Race and Ethnicity: Contemporary Debates and Perspectives* (Cambridge: Cambridge University Press, 2015), p. 59.

Frozen racism serves its concomitant motility because, by freezing so-called 'real racism' in historical time, we allow discrimination and abuse to continue polyvalently under the guise of purportedly post-racial arguments about cultural incompatibility, secularism versus religion, or sovereignty and security.[3]

The situation is similar in Europe, where Nazism and fascism are frequently referenced as a stain on its history, but also as part of a story of overcoming and defeating racism and hate. Of course, manifestations of crude racism remain a reality in the post-war and post–civil rights eras, but they are usually constructed as a remnant of the old order or a return of the repressed, out of time and out of line with the contemporary liberal order and consensus. As such, they are often used as examples of what is right and wrong, what we had in the bad old days, and what we should be grateful for in imperfect but ultimately post-racial times. This was the case, at least, until the most recent resurgence and manifestation of illiberal trends. We argue that it is precisely this liberal narrative which frames our times, constructing racism as illiberal, tied essentially to the past and extreme right. It is constructed as antithetical to our contemporary liberal-democratic politics, and thus as concealing more acceptable and coded articulations of racism, central to the liberal system. The term 'articulation' is used here to highlight not simply how these are types of racism, but the ways in which they act together and are expressed in society. However, before turning our attention to liberal racism, it is essential that we first examine the way illiberal racism has come to be posited as the continuation of traditional forms of racism, limiting our understanding of racist practice to exceptional and outdated modes of politics, beliefs and social relations. Again, this is not to deny the historical and contemporary threat of the extreme right; but it is important to examine how it is often used to deny and diminish the significance of less overt, more deeply embedded systemic racisms.

---

3   Alana Lentin, 'Racism in public or public racism: Doing anti-racism in "post-racial" times', *Ethnic and Racial Studies* 39:1 (2016), p. 3.

RACISM: A BRIEF HISTORY OF A BAD IDEA

To clarify what we mean by 'liberal' and 'illiberal' racisms, we must first provide a brief overview of what we will call here 'traditional racism'. While the term is not perfect, we can differentiate it from the liberal and illiberal articulations central to our argument, even though it is linked closely to the former as a point of reference and core to the process of discursive reconstruction. We call it 'traditional' as it is also widely considered in the mainstream as the canonical form of racism. First, it is crucial to recall that, while racism is a reality both for those who suffer and those who benefit from it, race is a human invention. Therefore, contrary to what is often claimed in traditional racist theories, it is neither natural nor immutable, and does not come down to us from time immemorial. While it is difficult to know exactly when racism emerged as an idea, and debates are ongoing in the field, what is clear is that it is a modern idea that is intricately linked to the advent of our contemporary world, notably through colonialism and the formation of the nation-state system.

In popular culture and discourse, many tend to associate racist ideas and practices with particular evil periods, regimes and practices in history, such as slavery, colonialism, Nazism and the Holocaust, or Jim Crow segregation. But it is important to stress that traditional theories and articulations of racism, from which illiberal racism emerged, were not on the fringe or considered extreme. They were often produced by the scientific establishment and policies of the political elite, informing the management of racialised populations and their empires.[4] The concepts and theories were themselves racist, in that they presumed the authority of the white European, as 'racially' superior, not only to define the other (racialising them as central to the process), but to dominate them based on the justification contained in their own 'ideas' and constructions. The other was not a subject of knowledge or agent of action, but an object. For Michael Banton, 'Physical differences between peoples have been observed throughout human history; all over the world people have developed words for delineating them. "Race" is a concept rooted in a particular

---

4   Angela Saini, *Superior: The Return of Race Science* (London: 4th Estate, 2019).

culture and a particular period of history which brings with it sugges-
tions about how these differences are to be explained.'[5]

The term 'race' entered the English language in the sixteenth
century to refer to family, lineage and breed, and the term 'racism' was
first introduced to the *Oxford English Dictionary* in the early 1900s as
a form of supremacy and superiority based on human differences. It
defined racism as 'the theory that distinctive human characteristics
and abilities are determined by race'. It was synonymous with
'racialism', defined as the 'belief in the superiority of a particular race'.
The term only became widespread in the 1930s, when it was used to
refer to the policies advocated and implemented by Nazi Germany.[6]
Yet it would be mistaken to think of it as limited to these 'extreme'
cases. Historians and sociologists of race and racism have charted the
origins and development of racism through the theorisation of race
and racial differences in Europe, and among the intellectual
establishment, since the sixteenth century.[7] In his work, Banton
identifies three useful paradigms through which 'race' has been
constructed historically, demonstrating the development of the
concept, its racist rationale and implications – including the practices
it justified – as well as its power and its contingency.

The first paradigm is that of *race as descent*. This theological
explanation for racial difference holds that the 'two races of man',
black and white, or African and European, have either unified origins
(monogenesis) or different origins (polygenesis), developed in later
race science in the eighteenth and nineteenth centuries, as well as
different and unequal moral capacities. The most well-known iteration
of this can be found in the Curse of Ham. This biblical story was used

---

5   Michael Banton, 'The Idiom of Race: A Critique of Presentism', *Research in Race
and Ethnic Relations* 2: 21–42 (1980), p. 39.

6   Robert Miles and Malcolm Brown, *Racism* (London: Routledge, 2003).

7   This overview is not exhaustive, and does not address a multitude of theories,
scientific developments and debates, shifts in language and terminology such as 'ethnicity',
or later scholarly analyses. For these we recommend Les Back and John Solomos, eds,
Theories of Race and Racism: A Reader (London: Routledge, 2000); Michael Banton, *Racial
Theories* (Cambridge: Cambridge University Press, 1987); Martin Bulmer and John
Solomos, eds, *Racism* (Oxford: Oxford University Press, 1999); David Theo Goldberg, ed.,
Anatomy of Racism (Minneapolis: University of Minnesota Press, 1990); George
Frederickson, *Racism: A Short History* (Princeton: Princeton University Press, 2002).

in the sixteenth and seventeenth centuries to justify slavery, and to reassure colonial settlers that their skins would not turn black. Colonial powers argued that 'blackness' came from the times when Ham, Noah's son, was cursed by his father, in a bizarre moral tale in which his descendants would become slaves and be marked with darker skin.[8] Older examples of the use of theology for the purposes of racism is the anti-Semitic claim that Jews were the murderers of Christ, and the 'blood libel' charging Jews with murdering Christian children for their blood.

However, while these biblical and theological justifications for racism maintained some purchase and an ongoing foundational influence, racism as we understand it in the modern context crystallised with the emergence of the Enlightenment in the eighteenth century. It was through Enlightenment ideals and science that racist theories developed, spread and really gained hegemonic power. As a more humanistic and universal vision of society developed in parts of Europe, science and reason came to replace or complement older ideas. While the Enlightenment is often described uncritically as the origin of our progressive modern world, and used to demonstrate the west's 'civilisational superiority', it was also inextricably linked to the rise of racism as a new pretext for domination by the white man. The biological classification of human beings through a number of pseudoscientific theories provided a much stronger and more permanent explanation for the exploitation of other races than Christianity had: redemption and conversion became impossible.[9]

Here is where Banton's second paradigm comes in: that of *race as type*. This first example of race science was based on the work of Carolus Linnaeus and Georges Cuvier in particular, which held that the different races were the product of polygenesis – of representative specimens, types and subtypes belonging to geographically specific contexts. Their rates of progress in culture were also thought to be different.[10] The third paradigm is *race as subspecies*, based on the work of the Social Darwinists, which placed biology at the centre. While

---

8   Frederickson, *Racism*, pp. 43–4.
9   Ibid., p. 64.
10   Banton, 'Idiom of Race', pp. 54–6.

allowing for adaptation and the evolution of peoples, it informed debates and conclusions about their superiority and inferiority, and different rates of progress. Charles Darwin's work (through its perversion) was seminal for Herbert Spencer's notion of the survival of the fittest, and for his cousin Francis Galton's theory and advocacy of eugenics.

One of the most prominent theorists to lay the groundwork for modern forms of racism was the French anthropologist Comte Arthur de Gobineau. His book *An Essay on the Inequality of the Human Races* (1853–55) provided the framework that became central to the Nazis' understanding of racial inequality. De Gobineau separated human beings into three races: members of the 'white race' (also known as *ariane*) were leaders at the origin of all great civilisations; members of the 'yellow race' were hardworking but lacking imagination; and members of the 'black race' were infantilised and unable to thrive without the domination of others. De Gobineau was pessimistic about the future, as he believed that democracy had already led to miscegenation, and thus decay. Contrary to the idea of rebirth at the heart of fascist and Nazi ideologies, it was already too late.

It is not surprising that the development of racial thinking began as nations developed into distinctively political entities in sixteenth-century Europe. As borders and citizenship became political realities, delimiting people between races also became easier – something most clearly found in the German Romantic notion of (and naturalising conflation between) blood and soil. With the new political systems forcing upon their people a more delineated political space, the division hardened between a nation's own citizens and foreigners. Through the construction of an historical legacy and destiny, it was increasingly held that distinctively French, British, German and Italian national characters had been nurtured by long-shared histories – a myth which remains anchored in our political identities to this day.

While the development of nationalism as a political construct remained somewhat open, since it was possible for some to be 'naturalised', racism prevented passage between races. This proved particularly powerful as empire-building led to a competition between European 'enlightened' nations (as a civilisational bloc) to colonise, 'civilise', dominate and exploit those whom 'white' western racial constructs had positioned as inferior, primitive and/or savage. In time, it would also be deployed within Europe by the Nazis against internal enemies. Until the Second World War, these constructs and discourses were used openly to provide a logic for official, state-sanctioned practices that sought, in varying degrees, to exclude, dominate, separate, exploit and/or eradicate the other. Examples of such practices include slavery, colonisation, ghettoisation, segregation, immigration bans, the colour bar, ethnic cleansing and genocide. In the wake of Nazism and the Holocaust, in 1948 the UN would pass the Universal Declaration of Human Rights, guaranteeing that *everyone* is entitled to all the rights and freedoms set forth in this Declaration, without distinction of any kind, such as race, colour, sex, language, religion, political or other opinion, national or social origin, property, birth or other status.'[11]

This would present a challenge to traditional racism, and to European colonialism and American segregation which continued. Following the passing of the US Civil Rights Act (1964) and Voting Rights Act (1965), the International Convention on the Elimination of All Forms of Racial Discrimination condemned racism, defining it as 'any distinction, exclusion, restriction or preference based on race, color, descent, or national or ethnic origin that has the purpose or effect of nullifying or impairing the recognition, enjoyment or exercise, on an equal footing, of human rights and fundamental freedoms in the political, economic, social, cultural or any other field of public life.'[12]

While many of these racist ideas and practices have since been cast aside, traditional forms of racism persist today, most clearly apparent in mimetic movements of neo-fascists, neo-Nazis and confederates in the United States, all of which continue to embrace these ideas uncritically. We have also witnessed the return in recent years of certain scientific assumptions and theories reminiscent of traditional racism. In the 1990s, debates about IQ and the 'bell curve'

---

11   United Nations, *The Universal Declaration of Human Rights* (1948).
12   Part 1 of Article 1.

started to re-emerge in academia.[13] They were widely rejected, but ever since, and particularly in the context of the current reactionary backlash, a growing movement has sought to return to this debate, and eugenics and race science more broadly, to its position as an area worthy of study.[14] But this has taken place in a setting in which such ideas are no longer accepted by society at large; instead, they occupy a space in apparent opposition both to power and social norms.

ILLIBERAL RACISM

Illiberal racism is grounded in the present, but is often identified and defined with reference to the past. It is thus intricately linked to 'traditional' racism. It is described by its illiberal, absolutist or totalitarian character, and appears to be in conflict with the contemporary liberal social and political order (or at least with its self-perception and representation). Yet it occupies a place which is also different from that of traditional racism, as it is grounded in our world rather than in the one we have convinced ourselves we left behind after the end of the Second World War, decolonisation and desegregation in the United States. Illiberal racism, compared to the traditional racist ideas and movements it is derived from, has thus internalised this new context, even though it may not have accepted it entirely, as we can see in examples of Holocaust denial, which can occur in both mimetic movements and illiberal racism.

It places unequivocally and openly 'white' populations as superior to all other races and places. The traditional others, the targets of this racism, include black people, Asians, Arabs, Jews and other racialised groups who are minorities in white dominant societies or live outside their borders. Its targets are often perceived and represented in visible physical terms, such as skin colour and physical features, and in

---

13   Richard J. Herrnstein and Charles Murray, *The Bell Curve: Intelligence and Class Structure in American Life* (New York: Free Press, 1994).

14   Chris Baynes, 'University College London Launches "Eugenics" Probe after Controversial Conference Secretly Held on Campus', *Independent*, 11 January 2018; Richard Adams, 'Cambridge gives role to academic accused of racist stereotyping', *Guardian*, 7 December 2018; Angela Saini, 'Why Race Science Is on the Rise Again', *Guardian*, 18 May 2019; Saini, *Superior*.

essentialist and total terms as monolithic and innately inferior to 'pure' white Europeans, who constitute the normative standard in this construction. There are rarely distinctions made or differences acknowledged within racialised groups, and assimilation into white societies or a loyalty test to gain acceptance is not possible, unlike in more modern liberal racism. Moreover, illiberal racism can take the form of explicitly racist speech acts (racist insults, conspiracy theories, threats), and of discrimination, harassment and violence (hate crime and terrorism). It may even take the form of nostalgia or support for re-establishing traditional racist practices that have become unacceptable, such as slavery, colonialism, genocide, segregation, bans on miscegenation. These impulses can readily seep into mainstream politics.

In the post-war period that consigned traditional racism to the dustbin of history, the new order has been discursively construed as one of global cooperation and neoliberal economic globalisation. Cooperation, equality, diversity and multiculturalism are often promoted (within the constraints of capitalism), and the existence of racism is denied in a shallow, self-serving manner. This has served to replace global inequalities established by colonialism through neocolonial trade practices, economic and business practices, and labour and resource exploitation. In this context, the regressiveness of the extreme right has served as a convenient counterpoint to justify the new world order based on (neo)liberal liberty and equality, in a process resembling the caricaturing of forms of communist totalitarianism which made the 'end of history' seem like the best possible alternative.

The marginalisation of the extreme right was reinforced as formal and explicit state racism declined and formal institutional racism has become subject to legal prohibition, and is thus more coded and more easily denied. High-profile individual examples of success on the part of black people, such as Barack Obama's election, have been used to suggest that racism is no longer a barrier to power and achievement. The racist backlash has been derided as from another time, and useful as a representation of bad, illiberal racism because of its seeming randomness and apparently individual nature – a key function of liberalism. The latter separates illiberal racism from wider beliefs, structures and institutions, confining it to aberrant and arbitrary acts perpetrated by abnormally hateful, mentally ill or even evil individuals. This, in turn, allows society as a whole to maintain deniability in relation to racism, and a veneer of liberal tolerance. Moreover, the historical construction of racism and extremism as illiberal threats to the post-war liberal-democratic order and consensus emerged at the same time. Both used the Nazis and fascists in Europe, but also the Ku Klux Klan in the United States, and Communism, as enemies and terms of reference. The framing in Paul Hainsworth's key text in the field, *The Politics of the Extreme Right: From the Margins to the Mainstream*, is telling here:

> Historians and political commentators will look back upon a century of extremism, in which fascism and intolerance figured prominently, and to devastating effect. Total war, Holocaust, ethnic cleansing and scapegoating of 'the Other' have marked the past hundred years of Western 'civilization'. The mid-point of the century, of course, witnessed the defeat of Nazi and fascist forces and signalled – in the West – the victory of liberal democratic ideas, rooted in pluralism, multi-partyism, a renewed assertion of dignity of the individual and a respect for human rights.[15]

With the Second World War and the defeat of Nazism, the west was redeemed and offered a blank slate, regardless of systemic racist practices that still persisted.

THE EXTREME RIGHT, THE FAR RIGHT AND ILLIBERAL RACISM

A brief terminological clarification is essential here. Terms such as 'extreme right', 'far right' and 'radical right' have been used over the years, sometimes interchangeably, to describe a myriad of movements and parties, from mimetic iterations of fascism and Nazism to nationalist parties with no ties to such historical ideologies. There is a lack of consensus, not only on the appropriate terminology, but also

---

15   Paul Hainsworth, *The Politics of the Extreme Right: From the Margins to the Mainstream* (London: Pinter, 2000).

on which features should be used to define such a disparate ideological family. If anything, all of this tells us that the way in which we understand and define such phenomena is not fixed across different historical and political contexts and disciplines. The weight of history, the lack of founding texts, and the varied origins of such parties and movements have made their study far more complicated than that of other traditional political tendencies.[16] These differences can reflect changes to the movements in question, in their relationship to the mainstream or centre, in what is considered acceptable political discourse, and in the function of such terminology (or in scholars' analyses or objectives).

Our aim here is not to come up with a decisive way to describe a very wide range of parties, movements and ideas; but we should make clear how we are using each of the relevant terms. We use the term 'extreme right' for those movements and activists who express 'illiberal' articulations of racism and engage in violence, whether verbal or physical. We use 'far right' to describe movements and parties that espouse a racist ideology, but do so in an indirect, coded and often covert manner, notably by focusing on culture and/or occupying the space between illiberal and liberal racisms, between the extreme and the mainstream. Of course, this separation between mainstream, far- and extreme right is a product of historical and ideological processes and constructions; but we believe that, for our purposes, it provides a particularly effective framework.

THE EXTREME AND FAR RIGHT: BETWEEN
ORGANISATION AND INDIVIDUAL

While the study of the extreme right tends to focus on organisations and movements, the late twentieth and early twenty-first centuries have seen an increasing emphasis on the individual. This has contrasted with a persistent focus on Islam when terrorist attacks are carried out in its name, in which the perpetrator – however loose

---

16 For terminological debates, see, among others, Cas Mudde, *Populist Radical Right Parties in Europe* (Cambridge: Cambridge University Press, 2007); Paul Hainsworth, *The Extreme Right in Western Europe* (Abingdon: Routledge, 2008).

their adherence to or knowledge of the religion might be – is attached to a global threat, and to all of those who are, or are thought of as, Muslims. With the extreme right, on the other hand, there seems to have been a more or less conscious trend towards separating the individual crossing liberal boundaries, through terrorist attacks or clearly racist acts, from the organisations which support such politics but denounce their logical illiberal outcomes.

While an in-depth study of extreme-right terrorism is not the purpose of this book, it is essential to acknowledge that the apparently individualistic nature of extreme-right attackers is often central to their framing as mere happenstance, rather than as a more widespread ideology representing a systemic or coordinated threat. This strengthens the polarised distinction between extreme, far and mainstream right; violent actions are represented as aberrations, thus affirming post-racial narratives, while whiteness is represented as innocent in a context where Muslims are automatically labelled 'terrorists'. The discourse individualising acts of violence from the right is further complicated by populism and the mainstreaming of the far right. The way in which 'populism' euphemises and mainstreams racist far-right ideas as 'the will of the people' also implicates the wider public in these ideas. This makes it difficult to maintain the discourse of individualisation when an attack occurs and the perpetrator cites ideas about immigrants or Muslims that the media represents as 'populist' and popular. Lines between extreme right, far right, mainstream, as well as illiberal and liberal, thereby become blurred.

In recent years, the 'lone-wolf' trope has become increasingly popular to describe extreme-right attacks, leading some commentators to lament the double standards within analyses of terrorism.[17] Attacks seemingly conducted in the name of Islam have generally come to be treated as automatically terroristic in nature, by both politicians and the media. Extreme-right attacks, meanwhile – even those with clear and

---

17   See, for example, Aysel Morin, 'Framing Terror: The Strategies Newspapers Use to Frame an Act as Terror or Crime', *Journalism & Mass Communication Quarterly* 93: 4 (2016), pp. 986–1,005; Erin Kearns, Allison Betus and Anthony Lemieux, 'Why Do Some Terrorist Attacks Receive More Media Attention than Others?', *Justice Quarterly*, 2017.

avowedly terroristic intent – have been portrayed as the acts of mad or bad individuals, or as freak incidents with no broader significance. Yet research has shown that the perpetrator is often linked to online and offline 'radical milieus' and movements.[18] This was particularly obvious in the wake of the attack conducted by Anders Breivik. On 22 July 2011, a bomb placed in a van opposite a government building killed eight people in the centre of Oslo, before Breivik travelled to the Island of Utøya, where he killed sixty-nine teenagers participating in a Labour Party youth gathering.[19] While his attacks had been carefully planned, and his ideology thoroughly defined and documented in a 1,500-page manifesto citing a number of prominent figures from the global conservative, far and extreme right, he was widely described as a 'lone wolf', despite having been part of Norway's powerful far-right Progress Party for a number of years.

Other examples of this lone-wolf individualisation include the case of Thomas Mair, who murdered UK Labour MP Jo Cox on 16 June 2016, at the height of the EU referendum campaign. The fact that Mair shouted 'Britain first! This is for Britain! Britain will always come first!' as he confronted, stabbed and shot Cox – a Remain campaigner and champion of refugees – seemed to confirm the link to the referendum, and particularly to Brexit rhetoric. He was also linked to the extreme right; 'Britain First' is also the name of an extreme-right group, and he was found to have a range of white-supremacist and neo-Nazi materials in his home. Yet Mair was described as a mentally unstable loner by UKIP and Leave.EU leader Nigel Farage ('one man with serious mental health issues'), by *Spiked*'s Brendan O'Neill ('warped killer') and by the *Daily Mail* (a 'loner' seeking counselling).[20] The extreme right itself has denied any links, partially to avoid sanction. Britain First distanced itself from Mair, their leader Paul Golding asking: 'Was he referring to an organisation?

---

18   Bart Schuurman, Lasse Lindekilde, Stefan Malthaner, Francis O'Connor, Paul Gill and Noémie Bouhana, 'End of the Lone Wolf: The Typology that Should Not Have Been', *Studies in Conflict and Terrorism* 42 (2018).

19   Sindre Bangstad, *Anders Breivik and the Rise of Islamophobia* (London: Zed, 2014).

20   Aaron Winter, 'Brexit and Trump: On Racism, the Far Right and Violence', *Institute for Policy Research (IPR) Blog*, 2 April 2017.

Was he referring to a slogan? Was he just shouting out in the middle of an EU debate: "Putting Britain first"? You know, I've heard this almost every day.'[21]

Terrorist attacks obviously represent the most extreme form of illiberal racism. They mark out extremists from acceptable white society, the legitimate democratic state (with its ability to legislate and legitimise violence) and the realm of liberal discourse that claims all speech is legitimate, but that violence crosses the limit of acceptability (unless it is state-sanctioned). One fascinating contradiction is that the speech behind extreme-right actions is often defended by the liberal and libertarian free-speech movement as the ultimate test of a society's liberal credentials. At the same time, despite this liberal veneer, when an individual of another racial or ethnic group, religion (in the case of Muslims) or ideology commits an act of terror, the group is viewed with collective suspicion and guilt, requiring anyone associated with it – no matter how tenuously, or how large and diverse the group may be – to take a stand individually and denounce the act, or else be accused of complicity. This is because, in the transformation from white supremacy to post-race, whiteness takes up the position of hegemonic norm – still calling the shots, but invisible. This is where racism, so deeply entrenched within society, emerges to protect the extreme right which it also legitimises.

The relationship between the far right, individualisation and racial privilege come together in the case of Timothy McVeigh, who bombed the Alfred P. Murrah Federal Building in Oklahoma City on 19 April 1995, killing 168 and injuring over 680 people. In the *Time* magazine issue on the bombing, the cover image was of McVeigh's mug shot, with the headline: 'The Face of Terror'. In the related article, Elizabeth Gleick argued that 'a sense of guilty introspection swept the country when the FBI released the sketches of the suspects, distinctly Caucasian John Does one and two.'[22] In his essay 'Can Whiteness Speak?', Mike Hill argued that, rather than inducing guilt and introspection, the image and headline were terrifying to *Time*'s

---

21   Ibid.

22   Mike Hill, 'Can Whiteness Speak? Institutional Anomies, Ontological Disasters, and Three Hollywood Films', in A. Newitz and M. Wray, eds, *White Trash: Race and Class in America* (New York: Routledge, 1997), p. 172.

implied white readers because they rendered whiteness distinct or particular, as opposed to universal, as it became directly implicated in the terror.[23] But this was wishful thinking. The hegemonic universalism that renders whiteness invisible and non-racialised, from its own perspective, is not challenged by the act of an individual (or even a suspicious pattern of individuals' behaviour who happens to be aligned with a movement), because the opposite of white universalism is not particularism, but instead individualism.[24] Even in the post-9/11 era, Muslims seemed to be the sole focus of the American media, politicians and security services, despite the fact that Eric Rudolph – an extreme-right activist who had bombed Centennial Park at the high-profile Atlanta Olympics in 1996, as well as abortion clinics – was still on the run and committing attacks.[25]

The Christchurch attack in March 2019 may have had an impact on this narrative. Brenton Tarrant wrote a manifesto, named after Renaud Camus' *The Great Replacement*, clearly outlining his ideology and his inspiration, including references to Trump and Breivik, as well as a number of famous far-right intellectuals. Tarrant also clearly captured the increasingly popular and mainstreamed white-victim narrative which has emboldened the extreme right internationally. This has led to more reflection on the part of some of the media, but it remains to be seen whether this trend will last.

REACTION, ADAPTATION AND DISCURSIVE RECONSTRUCTION

If the Second World War marked a shift in how racism and the far and extreme right were seen, so too did the social upheaval of the 1960s and 1970s. The extreme right would play the functional role of illiberal scarecrow for the liberal mainstream for the better part of the post-war period, providing a distraction from liberal racism. While some embraced this extremism, even though they had once been mainstream, others attempted to reshape their discourse and strategy to adapt to their

---

23   Ibid.

24   Aaron Winter, 'White Terror and the Racialization of Violence', *Open Democracy*, 8 December 2015.

25   Aaron Winter, 'Anti-Abortion Extremism and Violence in the United States', in G. Michael, ed. *Extremism in America* (Gainesville: University Press Florida, 2013), pp. 218–48.

new context in a more counter-hegemonic fashion. Through the case studies below, we attempt to trace a number of trajectories espoused by key actors and their impact on the political landscape.

American Reconstruction(s)

In the post-civil rights period, the Klan, which provides a point of reference for representations of the American extreme right, has very much played the role of functional bogeyman in the United States because of its combination of racism and violence. But what is often ignored is just how embedded in the mainstream the organisation and its members were. While the first era Klan was a southern, confederate organisation, the second era – formed in 1915 in the wake of D. W. Griffith's film *Birth of a Nation*, and frequently invoked in relation to Trump because of its anti-immigrant 'nativism' and his father Fred's arrest at a 1927 Memorial Day Klan rally in New York – became a national mainstream mass movement. At its peak, in 1925, it had up to five million members.[26] On 8 August that year, more than 50,000 members marched on Washington, DC,[27] and Texas Klansman Earl Mayfield was elected to the Senate. Congress also passed the Klan-supported anti-immigrant Johnson-Reed Act of 1924,[28] designed to keep out southern and eastern Europeans, particularly Italians and Jews, as well as Africans and those from the Middle East. It also barred Asian immigration.

But the era most frequently invoked in post-racial narratives and representations was the third, or civil rights–era Klan. This era occurred between 1954 and 1969, and centred on white-supremacist opposition to desegregation, civil rights and voting rights in the south. The hegemonic racial, religious and national identifications and commitments of the Klan can best be illustrated by the creed articulated in the *American Klansman* in 1952, which stated:

---

26   David Chalmers, *Hooded Americanism: The First Century of the Ku Klux Klan 1865–1965* (Garden City: Doubleday, 1965), p. 31.

27   Joshua Rothman, 'When Bigotry Paraded through the Streets', *Atlantic*, 4 December 2016.

28   Ibid.; Michael Cox and Martin Durham, 'The Politics of Anger: The Extreme Right in the United States', in Paul Hainsworth, ed., *The Politics of the Extreme Right: From the Margins to the Mainstream* (London: Pinter, 2000), pp. 290–1.

WE RECOGNIZE our relation to the Government of the United States of America, the Supremacy of its Constitution, the Union of States thereunder, and the Constitutional Laws thereof, and we shall be ever devoted to the sublime principles of a pure Americanism and valiant in the defense of its ideals and institutions. WE AVOW THE distinction between the races of mankind as same has been decreed by the creator, and shall ever be true in the faithful maintenance of White Supremacy and will strenuously oppose any compromise thereof in any and all things.[29]

Unlike the extremists they are seen as today, the Klan and its members were on the side of the political establishment and of law enforcement, defending and enforcing segregation and white supremacy. They exchanged support and protection, worked together, and had overlapping membership. When the buses of Freedom Riders arrived in Birmingham on 14 May 1961, Eugene 'Bull' Connor, city commissioner in charge of the Birmingham Police, provided no police protection, allowing the Klan to lie in wait and attack.

The murders, on 21 June 1964, of civil rights activists James Earl Chaney, Andrew Goodman and Michael Schwerner in Mississippi precipitated change. The perpetrators were members of the Klan and of law enforcement, including Neshoba county sheriff Lawrence Rainey and deputy sheriff Cecil Price. This provided the impetus for both the passing of the Civil Rights Act and additional federal action. In response, and under pressure from President Johnson and Attorney General Robert Kennedy, the FBI established the COINTELPRO (Counter Intelligence Program) 'White Hate Groups' Programme in 1964,[30] designed to 'expose, disrupt, misdirect, discredit, or otherwise neutralize' these organisations.[31] This recapitulated the use of COINTELPRO against alleged communists and civil rights activists since 1956, and the same approach would be repeated against the Black

---

29   Knights of the Ku Klux Klan, 'The Ku Klux Kreed', *American Klansman*, January 1952, p. 14.

30   Christopher Hewitt, *Understanding Terrorism in America: From the Klan to Al Qaeda* (London: Routledge, 2003), pp. 97–8; David Cunningham, *Klansville, USA The Rise and Fall of the Civil Rights-Era Ku Klux Klan* (Oxford: Oxford University Press, 2010), p. 197.

31   Cunningham, *Klansville*, p. 196.

Panthers and the New Left.[32] Yet violence against voting-rights activists in Selma, the recruitment of Klansmen by Dallas county sheriff James Gardner Clark to prevent voter drives in 1964–65, and the murder of Viola Liuzzo in 1965 led Johnson to call for hearings of the House Un-American Activities Committee (HUAC) into the activities of the Klan.[33] The hearings and resulting report, *The Present-Day Ku Klux Klan*, condemned the group as terrorists and un-American.[34]

The combined effects of the Civil Rights and Voting Rights Acts, COINTELPRO and the HUAC hearings, as well as popular opinion and changing times, forced the Klan into decline. They experienced a drop in membership from between 40,000 and 50,000 at their peak, between 1960 and 1967,[35] to fewer than 10,000 between 1967 and 1974. What is particularly significant here is that, while the Civil and Voting Rights Acts were designed to end aspects of institutional white supremacy and discrimination (social, political and economic), the destruction of the Klan in this way allowed it to become symbolic of the end of racism, akin to an exorcism of an evil within the nation, as identified in post-racial narratives. This allowed Southern civil society to be redeemed and reconstructed, even though it did not mark the end of the extreme right.

Many in the Klan saw this as evidence of both their persecution by the federal government and the final loss of white supremacy. In response, the organisation retreated into the political wilderness, and underwent a split. From the mid 1970s, David Duke pursued a mainstreaming strategy, largely following his predecessors' nonviolent electoral tactics, and eventually running for office. His campaigns included

---

32   Ibid.

33   Clive Webb, *Rabble Rousers: The American Far Right in the Civil Rights Era* (Athens: University of Georgia Press, 2010), p. 180.

34   United States Government, *Activities of Ku Klux Klan Organizations in the United States, Hearings before the Committee On Un-American Activities*, House of Representatives, Eighty-Ninth Congress, 19 October 1965–28 January 1966; United States Government, *The Present-Day Ku Klux Klan Movement*, Hearings before the Committee On Un-American Activities, House of Representatives, Ninetieth Congress, 11 Dec 1967. See also Aaron Winter, 'The Klan *Is* History: A Historical Perspective on the Revival of the Far-Right in "Post-Racial" America', in J. Morrison, A. Silke, J. Windle and A. Winter, eds, *Historical Perspectives on Organised Crime and Terrorism* (Abingdon: Routledge, 2018), pp. 109–32.

35   Cox and Durham, *The Politics of Anger*, p. 292.

a successful run for the Louisiana House of Representatives in 1989 and unsuccessful presidential primary campaigns in 1988 and 1992. He also established the National Association for the Advancement of White People, appropriating what he and other racists thought had 'worked' for the NAACP and black Americans in the civil rights era. This was also a response to their perceived loss of white power and need for advocacy, as if they were oppressed by a black (and Jewish) power structure. In the mainstream political sphere, Nixon, with his 'Southern Strategy', would find an opportunity in the existing white supremacy and racist white resentment of the South.[36]

But most of the Klan and the wider extreme right followed the more radical path articulated by Texas Klansman Louis Beam, Jr, in his call to arms: 'Where ballots fail, bullets will prevail.'[37] His position was a rejection of the Klan's mainstream tactics and objectives in favour of more violent and insurgent ones, which defined the organisation's fifth era, running from the late 1970s to the 1990s. In a sense, this was a mainstream extreme right that became more extreme in response to its lost status. It was also during this period that former Klansman and Christian Identity Pastor Robert Miles issued his call for whites, allegedly having lost America, to form their own nation. If the Klan's Kreed of the third era demonstrated its hegemonic identifications and commitments, Beam's statement in the mid-1980s, at the peak of the fifth era, would explain his rationale for the re-politicisation and increasing radicalisation of the extreme right. According to Beam,

> Political, economic, religious, and ethnic conditions in the United States have reached the point where patriots are faced with a choice of rebellion or departure. That this is indisputably the case, and further, that the sun has forever set on the American Republic of our Forefathers resulting in the necessity of such choice [sic] being made, is clear upon a collateral deduction that departure ... is a sound method of re-establishing a new constitutional republic.[38]

---

36   Sara Diamond, *Roads to Dominion: Right-Wing Movements and Political Power in the United States* (New York: Guilford, 1995).

37   James Ridgeway, *Blood In the Face: The Ku Klux Klan, Aryan Nations, Nazi Skinheads, and the Rise of a New White Culture* (New York: Thunder's Mouth Press, 1990), p. 146.

38   Louis Beam, Jr, 'Seditious Conspiracy', *Calling Our Nation* 58 (1987), p. 21.

The enemy was now the government just as much as racialised groups.[39] The extreme right itself also embraced new ideologies and forms, undergoing paramilitarisation and Nazification. This was witnessed in Beam's call to arms, and formalised when the majority of local or state Klan groups or klantons, including Duke's former Louisiana one, established supplementary armed paramilitary units. These included the Invisible Empire, established by Bill Wilkinson of the Louisiana Klan; the White Patriot Party, established by former green beret and American Nazi Party member Glenn Miller of the North Carolina Klan; and the Texas Emergency Reserve, established by Beam. The period also saw the formation of White Aryan Resistance (WAR), established by John and Tom Metzger of the California Klan, which embraced the neo-Nazi skinhead movement.

At the same time, between 1977 and 1981 new organisations developed, to some extent replacing the Klan and the John Birch Society. Unlike their predecessors, they adhered to new counter-hegemonic 'un-American' ideologies and identities. These organisations included the Christian identity groups Posse Comitatus, Aryan Nations and the Order, which rejected Judeo-Christianity, embraced fascism, and mobilised to defend white farmers in the Midwest and Pacific Northwest (as opposed to the traditional South) against the state during the Reagan-era farm crisis. Aryan Nations also established annual Unite the Right–style Aryan World Congresses at their Idaho compound. They would become the organisational engine of Miles's white-separatist plan the Northwest Territorial Imperative. In addition, the National Alliance emerged from the American Nazi Party and its off-shoot the Youth National Alliance in the 1970s.

These groups dominated the 1980s and early 1990s, but were overshadowed by anti-government militias inspired by the government sieges at Aryan Nations associate Randy Weaver's home in Ruby Ridge, Idaho (1992), and of the Branch Davidian Compound in Waco, Texas (1993). These sieges also led to the Rocky Mountain Rendezvous held by leaders of the Christian Patriot movement, and launched Beam's Leaderless Resistance strategy. The era peaked with

---

39   Michael Omi and Howard Winant, *Racial Formation in the United States: From the 1960s to the 1990s* (New York: Routledge, 1994), pp. 118–20.

the bombing of the Murrah Federal Building by McVeigh and Terry Nichols in April 1995. The building was home to an office of the Bureau of Alcohol, Tobacco and Firearms (ATF), which had led the raids on Ruby Ridge and Waco. In response to the bombing, the government held five Senate subcommittee hearings on the following issues in 1995 and 1997: *Combating Domestic Terrorism*;[40] *The Federal Raid on Ruby Ridge, ID.*;[41] *The Militia Movement in the United States*;[42] and *The Nature and Threat of Violent Anti-Government Groups in America*.[43] This last development brought the fifth era to the peak of its significance, and into the corridors of mainstream political power. It was also at this point that the extreme right entered into decline.

Racism remained present in this period, but was 'coded' through dog-whistle election campaigns, welfare reform and developments in criminal justice policy and enforcement. This did not, however, follow the path of the explicit, illiberal racism and coordinated state racism of Jim Crow, instead remaining within mainstream liberal (and centrist-conservative 'New Right') boundaries – although its targets and meaning were clear. Examples of this trend included Nixon's Southern Strategy, Reagan's racial-ised 'working-class' populism, culture war, rhetoric concerning 'welfare mothers', and opposition to school busing and affirmative action. According to Michael Omi and Howard Winant, Reagan, who had opposed the Civil Rights and Voting Rights Acts, sought to 'define and eliminate the "new racism" *against whites*' by

---

40   United States Federal Government, *Combating Domestic Terrorism*, Hearing before the Subcommittee on Crime, of the Committee on the Judiciary, House of Representatives, 104th Congress, First Session, 3 May 1995.

41   United States Federal Government, *The Federal Raid on Ruby Ridge, ID*, Hearings before the Subcommittee on Terrorism, Technology and Government Information, of the Committee on the Judiciary, United States Senate, 104th Congress, First Session, 15 June 1995.

42   United States Federal Government, *The Militia Movement in the United States*, Hearing before the Subcommittee on Terrorism, Technology and Government Information, of the Committee on the Judiciary, United States Senate, 104th Congress, First Session, pp. 6–8, 12, 14–15, 19–22, 26 September and 13, 18–19 October 1995.

43   United States Federal Government, *Nature and Threat of Violent Anti-Government Groups in America*, Hearing before the Subcommittee on Crime of the Committee on the Judiciary, House of Representatives, 104th Congress, First Session, 2 November 1995.

creating a 'color-blind' society. For Reagan's Civil Rights Commission chairman, it was supporters of civil rights who were the 'new racists', because they 'exhibit the classical behaviour system of racism. They treat blacks differently than whites because of their race'.[44] The coded racism would continue with George H. W. Bush's Willie Horton ad. (to which Trump's campaign is often compared); the war on drugs; the 'bell curve' IQ debates; Rudolph Giuliani's zero-tolerance anti-crime strategy in New York; voter suppression, and more explicitly, the promotion of the anti-liberal and anti-immigration 'America First' paleoconservatism of Pat Buchanan (an advisor to Nixon, Ford and Reagan).

While the US extreme right appears to have radicalised in the last quarter of the twentieth century, it would eventually intersect, via Donald Trump, Steve Bannon and the alt-right, with the more liberal and conservative mainstream.[45] The 'alt-right' as both term and movement, has become familiar in the wake of Trump's campaign and election, and has inserted both the far and extreme right back into mainstream public consciousness. The Southern Poverty Law Center (SPLC) defines it as 'a set of far-right ideologies, groups and individuals whose core belief is that "white identity" is under attack by multicultural forces using "political correctness" and "social justice" to undermine white people and "their" civilization'.[46] It is known for its intensive use of social media, including trolling; its deployment of online memes such as #whitegenocide and Pepe the Frog; its rejection of establishment conservatism; its edginess and orientation towards young people; its espousal of white identitarianism and white nationalism; and its combined mobilisation of fascism and liberal free-speech tropes.[47]

The term 'alt-right', based on 'alternative right', was coined in 2008 by Richard Spencer, a Trump supporter who had been the editor

---

44   Omi and Winant, *Racial Formation in the United States*, pp. 133–5 (emphasis in original).

45   For more detail, see Aaron Winter, 'Online Hate: From the Far-Right to the "Alt-Right", and from the Margins to the Mainstream', in E. Harmer and K. Lumsden, eds, *Online Othering: Exploring Violence and Discrimination on the Web* (London: Palgrave, 2019), pp. 39–63.

46   Southern Poverty Law Center, *Alt-Right*, n.d.

47   Ibid.

of the *American Conservative* and *Taki's Magazine*, executive director of Washington Summit Publishers, founder of the *Radix* journal, and head of the white-nationalist think tank National Policy Institute.[48] He launched the movement in 2010 with the 'Alternative Right' blog. Other high-profile proponents have included Greg Johnson of the Counter-Currents publishing house, Jared Taylor of *American Renaissance*, and Matthew Heimbach of the neo-Nazi Traditionalist Youth Network.[49]

Two websites, and their wider virtual communities, are central for the alt-right: the *Daily Stormer* and *The Right Stuff* (TRS).[50] The *Daily Stormer* is a neo-Nazi site founded in 2013 by Andrew Anglin, which replaced Total Fascism. It was named after the Nazi paper, *Der Stürmer*, and is known for its memes and troll army.[51] TRS is an online forum established by Mike 'Enoch' Peinovich. It began as a political blog in 2012, but became one of the largest alt-right media platforms, hosting a message board called the 504um, as well as numerous podcasts.[52]

Beyond its more official websites, the alt-right was also highly active on mainstream social media, until many companies were forced to take action and ban hateful extreme-right content and users.[53] For Anglin, 'the movement is, at this point, entirely leaderless. The people involved in contributing to and/or consuming the content are on different alt-right sites and forums, many are on Twitter, Reddit, 4chan etc.'.[54] The population of the alt-right is composed of relatively anonymous young men who were originally exposed to it through online message boards and discussion threads like 4chan and 8chan's /pol/. Mainstream internet platforms like Reddit, Facebook, Twitter and YouTube also played a key role early on in spreading its

---

48   SPLC, *Alt-Right*, n.d.

49   Ibid.

50   Hatewatch, 'McInnes, Molyneux, and 4chan: Investigating Pathways to the Alt-Right', 19 April 2018.

51   Hatewatch, 'Andrew Anglin Brags about "Indoctrinating" Children into Nazi Ideology', 18 January 2018.

52   Hatewatch, 'McInnes, Molyneux, and 4chan'.

53   George Hawley, *Making Sense of the Alt-Right* (New York: Columbia University Press, 2017).

54   Ibid., p. 70.

message, until their links to particular events made them a business liability as the mainstream racist and misogynist backlash grew. Another important component of this movement are the alt-lite and more mainstream enablers and influencers, such as the so-called Intellectual Dark Web (IDW), Rebel Media and Steve Bannon's own Breitbart News, which have been able to use liberalism to mainstream both white nationalism and misogyny. Central to this discursive reconstruction and mainstreaming was Bannon himself, who later became Trump's advisor. Bannon is a long-time advocate of the work of Alain de Benoist, who was central to the French reconstruction, and in 2013 delivered an influential lecture at the National Policy Institute, Spencer's think tank.

The counter-hegemonic struggle in France

The response to developments and challenges in the post-war era was different in Europe where a process of discursive reconstruction was necessary for the far right to ensure electoral credibility. While the process has been uneven and dependent on context, some trends have become common in the reshaping of extreme-right politics into far-right politics. The impetus towards discursive reconstruction really took shape in the 1980s, when groups of intellectuals devised ways for the extreme right to escape the position it had been forced into after the defeat of fascism in the Second World War. The archaic nature of extreme-right discourse, based on biological racism and fascist nostalgia, was underscored by the rise of progressive counter-movements in the 1960s based second-wave feminist, civil rights, anti-colonial and anti-racist ideas. As extreme-right support reached a nadir, and mainstream conservative parties on the right were forced to give way to a number of progressive measures, it became necessary for the more strategically minded actors on the right-wing fringe of politics to seek a way out of the margins without diluting their ideological beliefs. For this to be possible, the extreme right needed to engage in a process of discursive reconstruction which would provide it with a way into the mainstream, contrasting it with the more illiberal forms of right-wing politics. As the twentieth century drew to a close, far-right parties that adopted this more strategic approach became increasingly forceful in their discursive rejection of the extreme right – though links between them would remain alive, if concealed. While we focus here particularly on the far right, it is worth noting that a galaxy of small but influential extreme-right groups remain present in France, and are often linked more or less closely and officially to the Front National/ Rassemblement National (FN/RN).

In France, while the election of Marine Le Pen as president of the FN in 2011, where she replaced her father Jean-Marie, is often heralded as the crucial turning point in the fate of the party, the process of normalisation had in fact begun much earlier. This process is often referred to in the French media and academia as *dédiabolisa-tion*, which can be loosely translated as de-demonisation. This terminology tells us much about how the party, its ideas and its actors were perceived within elite discourse, but also about the population, who overwhelmingly understood the party as a threat to democracy. Jean-Marie Le Pen had been a central figure of the extreme right since the end of the Second World War: he became the youngest parliamentarian in the Fifth Republic when he joined the Poujadist movement in the 1950s, he was an ardent defender of Vichy regime leader and Nazi collaborator Marshal Pétain, and he was offered a part in the Algerian officers' coup in 1960.[55] By the end of the 1960s, however, Le Pen had partly lost faith, as the extreme right received only 200,000 votes in 1967, while the events of May 1968 demonstrated that the political momentum was on the left.

He returned to politics in 1972 to lead a new political venture. While the idea for the party originated from neo-fascist Ordre Nouveau, Le Pen was believed to be a more moderate figure than leaders of the movement to help unite the broad far right. Biological racism, Holocaust denial and support for Pétain had become taboo in post-war politics, and a traditional extreme-right platform was simply no longer viable electorally. It was not until the early 1980s that the fortunes of the FN turned, and it began to make a mark on the French political landscape. In doing so, it benefited from the fertile

55   Harvey G. Simmons, *The French National Front: The Extremist Challenge to Democracy* (Boulder: Westview, 1996), p. 44.

environment present in intellectual circles on the extreme right since the 1960s, and the development of strategies aiming to update the doctrine to the new post-racial context. The Nouvelle Droite (New Right), and particularly the Groupement de Recherche et d'Etudes pour la Civilisation Européenne (European Civilisation Study and Research Group – GRECE), were key actors, and had a significant and long-lasting impact in the process of discursive reconstruction, in France and beyond.[56] For Tamir Bar-On, the Nouvelle Droite 'is neither a political party nor a violent extra-parliamentary outfit. Rather the ND is a cultural "school of thought" ': 'The ND's "politically correct" discourse, which is allegedly "anti-racist", "anti-fascist", "anti-nationalist" (or pro-regionalist and pan-European), and "anti-anti-Semitic", is coded to suit the changing times.'[57]

Learning from their enemies, GRECE thinkers borrowed much from Italian Communist thinker Antonio Gramsci, and particularly his key notion of hegemony: cultural power should come before political power. To ensure this took place, the movement dedicated itself to creating a coherent worldview which could become accepted by the wider population. This meant that the most toxic elements of extreme-right ideology would have to be abandoned, or at least redrawn to fit within a discourse which would not be flatly rejected by the mainstream. To achieve these goals, GRECE worked on the creation of a counter-cultural narrative. For Harvey Simmons, GRECE believed that 'the ability to determine the "taken for granted" beliefs of the ordinary citizens was the ability to control society itself'.[58]

While initially a strong believer in racial inequalities and the racial superiority of European civilisation, GRECE eventually opted for 'differentialism', defined in opposition to 'egalitarianism' and 'universalism': it advocated for the radical separation of cultures on the basis that it was the only way to protect them and maintain their uniqueness. As a result, openly and unmistakably racist vocabulary

---

56   See Pierre-André Taguieff, *Sur la Nouvelle droite: Jalons d'une analyse critique* (Paris: Descartes et Cie, 1994); Tamir Bar-On, *Rethinking the French New Right: Alternatives to Modernity* (Abingdon: Routledge, 2013).

57   Bar-On, *Rethinking the French New Right*, pp. 10–32.

58   Simmons, *French National Front*, p. 44.

was replaced by a vocabulary based on difference, people and culture. In the mid 1970s, Alain de Benoist went further, position-ing himself strongly against 'all forms of racism'.[59] While his belief in race remained intact, he drew a false equivalence between the crud-est form of biological racism and anti-racism, opposing to both what he termed 'intelligent anti-racism'. For Pierre-André Taguieff, this was 'based on the *fact* of cultural difference, positioned as a *norm* (to be a good anti-racist, you must respect and protect all 'differences', inter-individual and inter-group)'.[60] His aim was there-fore to make a clear break with the most reviled articulations of racism, while couching his own racist theory in a language that would be less easy to attach to fascism or Nazism, but also opaque enough to appeal to a wider population that had learned to reject racism, as an outright taboo.

We can begin to discern here the foundations of the discourse of anti-white racism which has become prominent on the contemporary far right. By superficially rejecting any hierarchy of races, the new doctrine would discursively level an uneven playing field, ignoring entrenched power relationships built over centuries of exploitation and oppression. It claimed that colonisation was bad both then and now, creating another false equivalence between white colonialism and post-colonial immigration. De Benoist's condemnation of 'all racisms' echoed the 'White Lives Matter' movement, and many other elements of the contemporary far-right discourse on identity politics, including the idea of the self-hatred of the white elite and their culture of repentance. In de Benoist's words:

> I am for non-discrimination, for decolonisation, for the right of people to govern for themselves. But on one condition: that this rule suffers no exception. If one is for decolonisation, then one must be for reciprocal decolonisation, that is to say against all forms of colonisation: strategic, economic, cultural, artistic etc. One has the right to be for Black Power, but only if one is at the same time for White Power, Yellow Power and Red Power . . . We can see ideologues

---

59 Taguieff, *Sur la Nouvelle droite*, p. 194. Our translation.
60 Ibid., p. 195. Emphasis in the original, our translation.

demand respect for all races. Bar one: ours (which by the way is also theirs).[61]

While GRECE played a diffuse role on the discursive reconstruction of the FN, one of its offshoots played a more active one. Distancing itself from the paganism of de Benoist, the Club de l'Horloge was pro-Catholic, and had close links to the parliamentary right. It was also pro-capitalist and French nationalist, rather than Europeanist – factors that made it more palatable to the economic and nationalist approach of the FN in the 1980s. The inclusion of the 'Horlogers' made the FN acceptable to a more moderate electorate. Extreme-right measures and ideological tenets came to be hidden under a veneer of softer rhetoric; the concepts of invasion, conspiracy and violence remained omnipresent throughout the programme, but were camouflaged by apparently positive or at least unthreatening headings. Instead of advocating an outright neoliberal agenda, the FN stressed its belief in liberties, as opposed to the abstract Liberty derived from the Revolution and promoted by the left. For Bruno Mégret, Le Pen's number-two, these attempts at infiltrating moderate politics with extreme-right concepts were part of the 'vocabulary battle' against the left hegemony. While Mégret would fail to take over the FN, and eventually left it in a dramatic split in 1998, his impact on the party was deeply felt.

One of the key changes in the FN's strategy was the conscious use of populist discourse. This allowed Le Pen to move from the traditional extreme-right appeal firmly located in the lower middle classes to a broader targeting of the working class (*classes populaires*), which was highly symbolic despite limited success. While the term 'populist' had been used positively by prominent members of the party from the mid 1980s, Le Pen himself began to use it in 1991; he asserted that, if being a populist meant being a democrat, then he was a populist.[62] Increasingly, the party added to its social and economic programme, pushing for a *capitalisme populaire* (popular capitalism) – a clear

---

61   Alain de Benoist, 'Contre tous les racismes', *Eléments* 8-9 (November 1974 – February 1975), pp. 13–23. Our translation.

62   Taguieff, *Sur la Nouvelle droite*, pp. 249–50.

break from the times when Le Pen had seen himself as the French Reagan. This did not yet go as far as Marine Le Pen's protectionist welfare chauvinism, but the path was clear. Despite this conscious, albeit uneven discursive reconstruction, however, it is crucial to note that the FN's recent success had not been entirely due to Le Pen and his allies. Their mainstream political opponents played a major part in the process of mainstreaming (see Chapter 3). It was no accident that Le Pen managed his first breakthrough when Socialist president François Mitterrand attempted to split the right-wing vote in the early 1980s by giving the leader of the then-tiny FN some rare opportunities to voice his ideas on prime-time public television.[63]

In 2002, the FN was allowed to make a lasting impact on French politics and became an agenda setter. This was partly through its own actions, but more importantly because of the role it served as a decoy. With 4.8 million votes (16.9 per cent) in the presidential election, Le Pen beat Socialist Party candidate and favourite Lionel Jospin to reach the second round in a face-off against Gaullist candidate Jacques Chirac. The *bête immonde* ('filthy beast') had reached the gates of power in the French Republic built on the ruins of the fascist Vichy regime. A sense of horror was palpable across the media, from the left to the right of the spectrum, with words such as 'shock', 'catastrophe' and 'nightmare' splashed across front pages and throughout the news. The French, who had grown tired of choosing between more or less benevolent versions of capitalism since the Socialist Mitterrand's betrayal of left-wing ideals and his turn to austerity in 1982, were asked to vote for Chirac 'For the Republic's Sake', according to left-leaning *Libération*'s front page. *L'Express* encapsulated the union of the press against the FN, calling to vote for Chirac 'for France, for the Republic, for Democracy'. *Le Monde 2* concluded that it was not so much Chirac, but 'the Republic being re-elected'. The defeated candidates in the first round, from the Revolutionary Communist League to ultra-conservative Chasse, Pêche, Nature et Traditions (Hunting, Fishing, Nature and Traditions) pleaded with their voters to put a vote for Chirac in the second round. Only the Trotskyist Lutte

---

63   Emmanuel Faux, Thomas Legrand and Gilles Perez, *La main droite de Dieu: Enquête sur François Mitterrand et l'extrême droite* (Paris: Ed. du Seuil, 1994), p. 25.

Ouvrière (Workers Struggle) called for abstention. During the two-week period between the two rounds, tens of thousands of people demonstrated against Le Pen on a daily basis, reaching over a million on 1 May. On 5 May, left-wing voters went to the ballot box wearing gloves, or with pegs on their noses, to vote for what had been thought unthinkable two weeks previously: a right-wing candidate embroiled in a series of corruption scandals. Chirac was re-elected with 82.2 per cent of the vote. Popular magazine *Paris Match*'s front page praised the 'hope' triggered by 'republican enthusiasm . . . to say no to Le Pen': the 'wounded Republic' was ultimately victorious.

In the media and elite discourse, echoed in the street by ordinary people, the threat seemed all too real. But this understanding of the situation was based on little more than emotion. Careful analysis of the context demonstrated not only that it was virtually impossible for Le Pen to win, but that the real cause of his qualification for the second round lay elsewhere. First, Le Pen's performance in 2002 was far from exceptional, as demonstrated by Table 1.1.

	Number of votes	Per cent of vote	Per cent of registered vote	Position
1988	4,376,742	14.38	11.47	4
1995	4,571,138	15	11.42	4
2002	4,804,713	16.86	11.66	2

Table 1.1. Votes for Le Pen in French Presidential Elections.

In fact, the FN's lack of progress in growing its vote over a fourteen-year period is astounding, despite a high level of media coverage of both the party and its key issues. This very clear fact was entirely omitted in elite coverage in the aftermath of the election. The party's stagnation is particularly clear in terms of its share of the vote, with a modest increase of 500,000 at a time when the electorate was becoming larger. More importantly, if registered voters, including those who abstained, are taken into account, the FN was unable to appeal to more than 12 per cent of the electorate at the time. Just as stark was Le Pen's ability to reach the second round on the basis of a 16.8 per cent share of the vote – a result that would have put him fourth in the two previous elections. How can we explain Le Pen's ascent to the second round of the election, if not through rising support for far-right politics? The answer is to be found in the number of abstentions, the splintering of the vote by smaller parties, and the spread of post-democratic politics. The real news – and the real concern for French democracy in 2002 – was not so much that the FN reached the second round, but that the parties which had led France from the Second World War in their various iterations could no longer garner more than 12 per cent of registered voters each in the country's major electoral battle. While this trend was not new, as demonstrated in Figure 1.1, it reached a nadir in 2002, when the three main parties (centre, centre-left and centre-right) received between them a similar number of votes in the first round to the number of abstentions. The FN was thus not the alternative to the system; its electoral good fortune was a product of abstention, despair and disillusionment. The election of Chirac in the second round with over 82 per cent of the vote thus appeared all the more ridiculous.

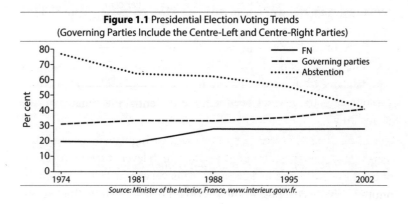

Figure 1.1 Presidential Election Voting Trends
(Governing Parties Include the Centre-Left and Centre-Right Parties)

Source: Minister of the Interior, France, www.interieur.gouv.fr.

In the post-2002 panic, Le Pen's discourse was now firmly anchored in populist attacks on the mainstream elite, while immigration had become an unavoidable subject of discussion at the elite level. This exaggerated focus on the FN's 'breakthrough', and the widespread ignorance of the failure of mainstream politics to satisfy the electorate, led to skewed attempts to address the situation on the part of mainstream parties of both left and right, which accepted that the FN was indeed speaking for 'the people'. This led to the 2007 election of Nicolas Sarkozy, who, having borrowed much of Le Pen's rhetoric, managed to deal a serious electoral blow to the FN.[64] However, when Marine Le Pen was asked whether her father's severe defeat marked the end of his political career, she responded: 'I don't think so. In any case, this is the victory of his ideas!'

In the twenty-first century, and even more so under the new leadership of Marine Le Pen, the party has continued to redefine its discourse, if not its ideology, in its ongoing effort to reclaim key concepts of the French national psyche.[65] This has proved particularly powerful as the FN has taken hold of the liberal racist narrative – a trend that became inevitable in French public discourse as mainstream parties failed to offer ways out of the various crises, both real and perceived, plaguing the country. Therefore, contrary to what is often claimed, the FN has not gone from strength to strength, but rather has benefited from its opponents' failures, and their opportunism when presented with convenient scapegoats. While the FN itself has remained something of a scapegoat, derided for its vague positioning between the extreme and far right, the illiberal and the liberal, the hijacking of its discourse by mainstream parties meant that the illiberal side of the FN has become less repulsive to many. As a result, its less palatable ideas have gained an increasing foothold in mainstream discourse, as the FN has been made into the only alternative to the status quo.

Political opportunism, memory and nostalgia in the UK

In the United Kingdom, the story is different again. The place occupied by the nation as the last remaining bulwark against Nazism and

---

64 Aurelien Mondon, *A Populist Hegemony? Mainstreaming the Extreme Right in France and Australia* (Farnham: Ashgate, 2013).

65 Sylvain Crépon, Alexandre Dézé and Nonna Mayer, eds, *Les faux-semblants du Front National* (Paris: Les Presses de Sciences Po., 2015); Cécile Alduy and Stéphane Wahnich, *Marine Le Pen prise aux mots: Décryptage du nouveau discours frontiste* (Paris: Seuil, 2015); Mondon, *A Populist Hegemony?*

fascism during the Second World War has given a particular twist to the way the extreme and far right have organised ever since. The national narrative constructed around this idea, with all its inevitable simplification and glorification, has made it more difficult for the far right to separate itself from the extreme right and draw upon nostalgia than it has been in France and the United States. This was made particularly clear when Nick Griffin of the British National Party (BNP) tried to use Spitfires in one of his campaign posters, and faced near-universal condemnation when he was automatically associated with the enemy of this national emblem of the fight against the Nazis. This is a similar tension to the more recent use of liberal free speech tropes to enable and mobilise fascist ideas and politics. This has meant that, rather than achieving a slow reconstruction, the UK far right has had to be more reactive and opportunistic in its approach.

While Oswald Mosley remained a haunting figure on the extreme right, his influence was limited. In a way that resembles the formation of the FN, the National Front (NF) was created in 1967 to bring together three groups who 'stood at different points on the spectrum between the fascist and the non-fascist far right'.[66] A year later, Tory maverick Enoch Powell gave his infamous 'Rivers of Blood' speech, which the NF supported, hoping to bring into their ranks Tory supporters feeling disappointed by the lack of reaction from their leadership. This represented a clear attempt to gain more mainstream support; but it would have necessitated cutting ties with the more radical elements within the party – something the FN achieved successfully, at least formally, when Le Pen broke free from the neo-fascist Ordre Nouveau. It was John Tyndall who, having returned from being expelled from the party, led it to its major breakthrough in the 1973 West Bromwich by-election, where it received 16 per cent of the vote. For David Renton, 'Tyndall understood that the Front needed to modernise if it was to appeal to supporters of the Monday Club and other Conservatives. He was equally determined that this process should not change the NF's basic character.'[67] This success

---

66 David Renton, *Never Again: Rock Against Racism and the Anti-Nazi League 1976–1982* (Abingdon: Routledge, 2018).

67 Renton, *Never Again*.

proved short-lived. Faced with increasingly coordinated and dedicated anti-fascist opposition, the party began its slow decline, and returned to more traditional extreme-right politics,[68] thus departing from the reconstruction strategy that was starting to bear fruit in France as the FN slowly evolved. The context beyond the far right was, of course, crucial, and resistance against the NF proved far better organised and more decisive than that against the FN.[69] Anti-immigration sentiment had also been hijacked by the Conservatives, whose flirtation with new racism would later be harnessed by Margaret Thatcher.[70]

The British National Party (BNP) was launched by John Tyndall in 1982 after he left the NF. He was persuaded to create a new organisation by an anti-fascist who had infiltrated the scene and hoped to divide the extreme right further. Building on the success of reconstructed far-right parties on the continent that had moved from biological racism to more cultural forms, some factions within the party pushed for more radical discursive reconstruction in the 1990s – a demand resisted by Tyndall. In 1999, Nick Griffin was elected leader of the party, and attempted to move it away from the fringes and build a more acceptable image. Whereas the FN had begun its discursive reconstruction in the 1980s, and its leadership soon adhered to the cause, albeit unwillingly, the BNP had to attempt the radical reshaping of the discourse of a party still haunted by Tyndall's intransigence. The context was fertile for such a move, as 9/11 allowed the party to move decisively from biological to cultural racism, focusing on Islam and Muslims as the new enemy. This led to some success in the 2000s, as the party gained a number of

---

68   Alan Sykes, *The Radical Right in Britain: Social Imperialism to the BNP* (Basingstoke/New York: Palgrave Macmillan, 2005).

69   Renton, *Never Again*.

70   Martin Barker, *The New Racism: Conservatives and the Ideology of the Tribe* (Frederick: Aletheia, 1981), distributed by University Publications of America. Stuart Hall would also develop his theory of 'authoritarian populism' in response to Thatcher. He defined it as 'an exceptional form of the capitalist state – which, unlike classical fascism, has retained most (though not all) of the formal representative institutions in place, and which at the same time has been able to construct around itself an active popular consent', including in the area of opposition to immigration and racism. See Stuart Hall, 'The Great Moving Right Show', *Marxism Today*, January 1979.

councillors, and eventually, in the 2009 European election, garnered almost a million votes. For John E. Richardson, the BNP had reached 'a level of electoral success that is unparalleled in the history of British fascism'.[71] Nonetheless, this remained a rather modest performance compared to how the fortunes of reconstructed far-right parties across Europe had developed; they had anchored themselves more decisively in the political landscape, while the BNP remained unable to rid itself of its legacy.[72]

In the early 2000s, a new party was on the rise that would allow for a more successful mainstreaming of far-right ideas in the British context: the UK Independence Party (UKIP). Aware of the importance of legacy in the British political sphere, UKIP refused to enter into an alliance with the BNP in the early 2000s.[73] UKIP's lack of ties to the traditional extreme right has allowed supporters of a more reconstructionist approach to claim that this marked the end of extreme-right politics altogether. As Brendan O'Neill argued in the *Spectator* in 2016: 'There is a great disparity between the handwringing over hate crime and what Britain is actually like. The open racism even I can remember in the 1980s has all but vanished . . . The likes of the BNP and EDL have withered due to lack of interest.'[74] In this context, it was no surprise that Nigel Farage was even able to claim that he had acted as a bulwark against the extreme right:

> I destroyed the British National Party – we had a far right party in this country who genuinely were anti-Jew, anti-Black, all of those things, and I came along, and said to their voters, if you're holding your nose and voting for this party as a protest, don't. Come and vote

71   John E. Richardson, 'Race and Racial Difference: The Surface and Depth of BNP Ideology', in Nigel Copsey and Graham Macklin, eds, *British National Party: Contemporary Perspectives* (Abingdon/New York: Routledge, 2011), p. 41; Daniel Trilling, *Bloody Nasty People: The Rise of Britain's Far Right* (London: Verso, 2012).

72   Nigel Copsey, *Contemporary British Fascism: The British National Party and the Quest for Legitimacy*, 2nd edn (Abingdon/New York: Routledge, 2008); Nigel Copsey and Graham Macklin, eds, *British National Party: Contemporary Perspectives* (Abingdon/New York: Routledge, 2011).

73   Copsey, *Contemporary British Fascism*, p. 154.

74   Brendan O'Neill, 'Britain's Real Hate Crime Scandal', *Spectator*, 6 August 2016.

for me – I'm not against anybody, I just want us to start putting British people first, and I, almost single-handedly, destroyed the far right in British politics.[75]

However, the rise of UKIP as a force to contend with on the far right in the UK was all but certain. Founded by academics in 1993, the party began as a single-issue Eurosceptic party. Unlike many successful far-right parties on the continent, or to previous attempts to reinvent the far right in the UK, UKIP began as a conservative force, built on conservative foundations, and was clearly unaligned with the BNP or NF at first. In fact, much in the history of UKIP is reminiscent of the formation of the Alternative für Deutschland (Alternative for Germany). The absence of links with the historic far right allowed the party to start from a less marginal place. The use and mainstreaming of far-right ideas thus proved far more successful, as UKIP was able to define itself against unreconstructed extreme-right parties and movements, including failed ones – and, in particular, against the BNP, which, despite Griffin's attempts at moving beyond illiberal racist politics, still struggled to shed its extreme-right character. UKIP also received funding from wealthy donors throughout its existence – something which proved vital, and would have been impossible had the party had clear ties with the extreme right. Unsurprisingly, it was in the European elections that the party had its first breakthrough; in 2004, it polled 16.1 per cent of the vote. It is worth remembering, of course, that these elections are often referred to as 'second-order elections', since they usually produce very low turnout, and voters tend to vote more radically than in national elections. The single-issue nature of the party was confirmed in the general election the following year, when UKIP's vote fell from over 2.6 million to just over 600,000 (a 2.2 per cent share). While some UKIP members hinted that an alliance with the BNP should be struck, their rising star, Farage, opposed any such strategy – a wise decision in hindsight. Farage became leader in 2006, soon after the Conservative Party had elected David Cameron and taken a liberal turn in tone.

---

75   Press Association, 'Nigel Farage: I Destroyed Far-Right in British Politics', *Irish Examiner*, 12 August 2016.

This allowed UKIP to broaden the scope of its politics towards more conservative issues, which seemed increasingly abandoned under the new Tory leadership.

Here, too, abstention has played a key role in the hyped rise of UKIP. Its apparently strong performance in the 2009 European election, where it finished second, provided the party with ample coverage. 'UKIP "Second in the Great Euro Race"', trumpeted the *Daily Mail*, claiming that the party was 'heading for a big win in the European elections . . . as disgruntled voters desert the political establishment'. On the left, the *Guardian* led with the headline: 'UKIP: Eurosceptics Claim Second Place Is Political Earthquake', as the party hoped 'to reap reward of anger against main parties'. For the *Independent*, it was clear that 'Eurosceptics exploit [the] unpopularity of the major parties'. Despite such headlines, taking UKIP's own narrative of its performance at face value, Farage's first election at the helm of the party proved somewhat disappointing. UKIP finished second, but its vote actually slumped by more than a 100,000 votes, while the BNP's share of the vote increased by over 120,000 votes to just under 1 million. It was the election of Cameron and the demise of the BNP that would prove extremely beneficial to UKIP, as it could capitalise on both by offering itself as a more conservative alternative to the Tories, but also as a viable receptacle for far-right supporters disappointed by the BNP. It was no surprise that Farage dog-whistled to these supporters during the campaign, praising the 'guts' of Enoch Powell, for example.

As Figures 1.2 and 1.3 show, at no point did the combined vote of UKIP and the BNP reach 10 per cent of the registered vote. At best, therefore, the British far right only ever came close to garnering the support of one out of ten voters on one occasion – hardly an earthquake, or the 'people's army' that Farage likes to tout. Just as striking is how stable turnout remained during these elections, making clear that the left-behind and disenfranchised remained so, despite much talk about UKIP targeting them. While UKIP's performance was not as impressive as is commonly assumed in elite discourse, it is worth noting that the party surged when Cameron made his 2013 promise to organise a referendum on the European Union should he be re-elected in 2015. This promise prompted much of the elite narrative to be driven by issues central for UKIP, but also for the far right generally. It was thus not surprising that, in this context, UKIP managed to gain some momentum – even though, until 2014, the party had only appealed to just over 5 per cent of the electorate, in extremely favourable electoral contexts based on their key issue. Of course, we do not mean to downplay UKIP's performance or its impact on British politics or on those at the sharp end of its politics, but only to point out that its portrayal as the alternative to the status quo and receptacle for discontent was exaggerated, in turn feeding into what had become a self-fulfilling prophecy.

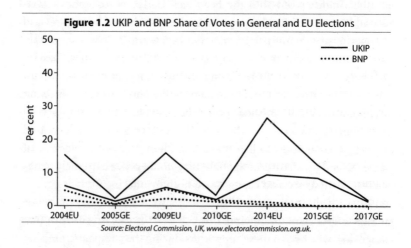

Figure 1.2 UKIP and BNP Share of Votes in General and EU Elections

Source: Electoral Commission, UK, www.electoralcommission.org.uk.

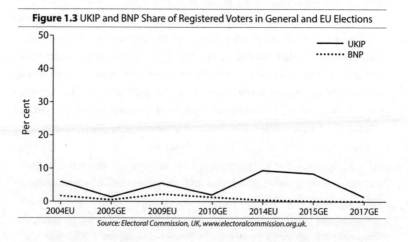

Figure 1.3 UKIP and BNP Share of Registered Voters in General and EU Elections

Source: Electoral Commission, UK, www.electoralcommission.org.uk.

Strikingly, UKIP followed an almost inverted trajectory to that of the FN. UKIP moved beyond traditional Euroscepticism, found in large swathes of the Conservative party, adding a more targeted fear of the other, in the form of Brussels as the elitist enemy and the immigrant as the coloniser. While its 2015 manifesto clearly shied away from traditional far-right discourse, the party's media strategy during the 2014 and 2015 campaigns made it clear that UKIP's issue with immigration was not just 'about space'.[76] In fact, numerous incidents during 2014 and 2015 highlighted that UKIP's discourse evoked that of the reconstructed far right across Europe, and at times even of the extreme right. Farage himself was often on the frontline, rendering UKIP's denunciations of rogue candidates unconvincing. During UKIP's 2014 spring conference, Farage declared that 'in scores of our cities and market towns, this country in a short space of time has frankly become unrecognisable', and that 'this is not the kind of community we want to leave to our children and grandchildren', demonstrating clearly the threat posed by an outsider to an imagined national identity.[77] Four days before the European elections, having already declared on LBC that he would be 'concerned' if a 'group of Romanian men' were to move next door to him,[78] Farage insisted that 'any normal and fair-minded person would have a perfect right to be concerned' in such circumstances.[79] This added to a series of other gaffes, culminating in racist outbursts from Godfrey Bloom, Kerry Smith and Rozanne Duncan, among others, as well as the departure of prominent supporters over UKIP's lurch to the far right. For its original founder, Alan Sked, the party had become 'a Frankenstein's monster'. Borrowing further from other European far-right parties, UKIP has also surfed the wave of Islamophobia, most notably when Farage attempted to capitalise on the tragic attack on *Charlie Hebdo* in

---

76   UKIP, *Believe in Britain: UKIP Manifesto 2015*, 2015, p. 11.

77   Andrew Sparrow, 'Nigel Farage: Parts of Britain Are "Like a Foreign Land"', *Guardian*, 28 February 2014.

78   LBC, *Nigel Farage v. James O'Brien*, London: LBC, 16 May 2014.

79   UKIP, 'UKIP Leader Stands by His Assertion that People Have a Right to Be Concerned if a Group of Romanians Move in Next Door', 18 May 2014.

France, declaring: 'We have got no-go zones across most of the big French cities.'

But UKIP, and Farage in particular, managed to use the less reconstructed far right and the illiberal extreme right to their advantage. UKIP's juxtaposition with the BNP in the early years of its rise allowed Farage to compare his party positively to one whose roots lay in the extreme right, and whose illiberal outbursts were far more damaging. With the liberal turn of the Tories, he was able to position himself between the reviled extreme right, denounced as racist, and the mainstream, increasingly portrayed as an out-of-touch elite as the main parties continued to converge and austerity began to bite. This position allowed him to deflect attacks such as those uttered by Cameron in 2006, when he described the party as 'a sort of a bunch of . . . fruitcakes and loonies and closet racists mostly'. As the UKIP threat grew stronger and its success was hyped, Farage was allowed to play a defining role in the EU referendum campaign, making his far-right agenda based on opposition to immigration a key part of the narrative. As demonstrated by Martin Moore and Gordon Ramsay's extensive survey of the media coverage of the referendum, while the economy was the most heavily covered issue, 'Coverage of immigration more than tripled over the course of the campaign, rising faster than any other political issue', and became 'the most prominent referendum issue, based on the number of times it led newspaper print front pages.' The impact of UKIP, which echoed the discourse of the right-wing tabloids, could be felt as 'coverage of the effects of immigration was overwhelmingly negative. Migrants were blamed for many of Britain's economic and social problems – most notably for putting unsustainable pressure on public services', and specific nationalities were singled out.[80]

It was in this context that the UK has witnessed the resurgence of the extreme right, particularly in the person of English Defence League (EDL) founder Stephen Yaxley-Lennon, also known as Tommy Robinson. As the climate became increasingly polarised

---

80   Martin Moore and Gordon Ramsay, *UK Media Coverage of the 2016 EU Referendum Campaign*, Centre for the Study of Media, Communication and Power, King's College London (2017), pp. 7, 8.

and far-right issues were mainstreamed, Robinson's utterances in the late 2010s were no longer as shocking to elite discourse as they had been a decade earlier, when he had delivered them from within the confines of the most extreme right. While the right, and Farage himself, tried to distance themselves from his rising popularity as he became involved with UKIP in 2018, the damage had been done. Before his conviction in 2019 which stopped his ascension, Robinson occupied a place he could have only dreamed of a mere year beforehand. Farage went on to form the Brexit Party, in preparation for the EU elections. UKIP played the extreme-right counterpart to his new far-right party and to its positions which have become increasingly anchored within the mainstream as demonstrated by the Conservatives' rightward move under Boris Johnson's leadership.

ILLIBERAL RACISM AS THE CONVENIENT ENEMY

The term 'illiberal racism' describes articulations of racism deemed to be in conflict with the post-war liberal order and consensus. They are associated with delegitimised ideas (biological racism, genocide, racist violence, segregation, and so on) claimed to have been defeated by the forces of liberalism during the war, and posited as a challenge to 'our' tolerant, egalitarian liberal societies. When they do appear, they are represented as remnants of the past and as individual aberrations, as opposed to part and parcel of contemporary mainstream society. Yet we have shown that, while the extreme right has been defined and positioned by the mainstream to push and reinforce particular narratives, it has also been an active force in its own right, either adapting or reacting to the post-war, post–civil rights eras.

Central to our argument is the claim that the concept of illiberal racism (and with it both the extreme right and far right) is not an autonomous, ahistorical form, but a contingent and functional one that allows liberal societies to represent themselves as post-racist. Moreover, we argue that this coinage, and the exclusion of its referent from the mainstream, limits our understanding of racism to caricatured and outdated modes, and thereby our ability to challenge and contest it where it occurs within our own structures and institutions. To be clear, we do not deny the threat of the extreme and far right, which is both real and extremely concerning, but simply insist that we must examine how it is constructed and deployed functionally, and the implications this has for the task of understanding and combating racism as part of a system. In the following chapter, we explore liberalism and the processes and discourses through which the illiberal, extreme and far right have been constructed as an effect or product of the very emergence of the liberal post-war hegemony, given its need for an illiberal or extremist foil.

CHAPTER TWO

Liberal Racism

LIBERALISM AND RACISM

Today, most people in the west would accept that they live in liberal democracies, regulated by elections, protected by the rule of law, with a system which provides us with security, equality of opportunity and some choice in our future – albeit all limited to some degree. Most would add caveats, but would not muster enough evidence of wrongdoing to negate the democratic quality we proudly attach to our political environment. Liberalism is espoused almost naturally, as the only ideology which could protect our individual rights, particularly when compared to fascism or Stalinist communism – two extreme forms that still seem to define the limits of our political imagination. In short, liberalism is hegemonic. Thus, we usually take for granted that liberalism is essentially a force for good, driving us towards progress and pushing our societies to overcome illiberal ills such as sexism and racism. Our liberal democracies tend, in their national narratives, to celebrate their proud record of abolishing slavery, and later defeating fascism and segregation. We also praise the struggle to give the right to vote to some men, then to all men, and finally to women – people of colour often being granted it with conditions, obstacles and obstructions. While the rights that liberalism is argued to have bestowed upon us are unevenly and unequally distributed, they offer us a degree of protection others do not have, and thus come to be accepted by the majority of individual interests and votes, which are seen as the basis of our democracy. If some should suffer along the way for us to retain these rights, then it is simply argued that democracy has spoken, and that our generosity must have its limits.

While this chapter focuses on liberalism, it is not a thorough overview of liberal traditions. It does not attempt to trace all relevant theories, strands and debates, but rather to examine and challenge liberal narratives about racism. We argue that, instead of lying at the basis of progress, liberalism did not emerge in opposition to what we commonly consider illiberal evils today, but instead participated in the sustenance of some, until they were wrestled away – often against its interests and wishes. We also argue that liberal ideals have been used to legitimise reactionary ideas today. This does not mean that liberalism has not improved the fate of many people, and it certainly provided room for emancipation unseen beforehand. Yet, much of the progress achieved in the past two hundred years was rarely a result of mainstream liberals' own volition, but rather against their will, when they were forced by external events or politics to adapt. This can be seen most obviously in the case of slavery, which was part and parcel of the early liberal outlook. While liberals pat themselves on the back for the individual liberty which underpinned the British constitution, and later that of the United States, this liberty was not extended to slaves. When the slaves demanded such liberty in San Domingo in the aftermath of the French Revolution, it became clear that this was not to be part of the liberal plan, with French revolutionaries eventually declaring abolition more for strategic reasons, to gain an edge on the British and Spanish empires, rather than on principle.[1] This was followed by two centuries of denial in which French colonialism was excused for the sake of its universal destiny and civilising mission. For Charles W. Mills, this was at the core of what he termed the 'Racial Contract':

> The particular contract to which I am referring, though based on the social contract tradition that has been central to Western political theory, is not a contract between everybody ('we the people'), but between just the people who count, the people who really are people ('we the white people').[2]

By the same token, the emancipation of women and the working class, and their entry into political agency, was also fought by liberals, like that of many other groups.

---

1   See C. L. R. James, *The Black Jacobins* (London: Penguin, 2001 [1938]); Charles Forsdick and Christian Høgsbjerg, *Toussaint Louverture: A Black Jacobin in the Age of Revolutions* (London: Pluto, 2017).

2   Charles W. Mills, *The Racial Contract* (New York: Cornell University Press, 1997), p. 3.

Yet it is common today in our liberal societies to praise our system for achieving the progress its own elite and leaders formerly prevented, delayed or denounced. We celebrate the abolition of slavery, the welfare state and women's right to vote as if these were wrestled from the hands of dictators whose interests lay in bygone ideologies. This is despite the obvious fact that it was the fight against liberal elites which led to these achievements, against liberals' most direct interests. Of course, one cannot ignore that some liberals did indeed fight for various forms of emancipation, and that it was the more conservative branches, often tied to the old order, whose persistent hold on power stood in the way of change. Nonetheless, many liberal thinkers and politicians continue to be celebrated today as progressive, despite the fact that many – American, British and French – were slave-owners, ruthless colonisers, entrenched elitists, racists and/or misogynists.

For Domenico Losurdo, what saved liberalism was its flexibility and ability to adapt to its opponents.[3] The combination of a clear historical link to exclusionary practices with the ability to adapt is exactly what makes the liberal articulation of racism so powerful when opposed to its illiberal counterpart. Indeed, from its inception, liberalism was based on a contradiction that persists to this day: while its central concern is the liberty of the individual, how can we explain that the liberty of some individuals has always come at the expense of others, be they slaves, the poor, women or foreigners? Despite its universalist pretensions, liberal hegemony has never managed to actualise its claim that its principles should indeed be applied equally to all. Ishay Landa pushes this insight further, arguing that the contradictions at the heart of liberalism were in fact central to the development of fascism:

> Fascism was not an outsider to the liberal, 'open society', but in fact an *intimate insider* to that society, which was not particularly open either. Far from being the antithesis of fascism, its absolute Other, the liberal order significantly contributed to fascism, informing many of its far reaching manifestations . . . Fascism was an organic

---

3 Domenico Losurdo, *Liberalism: A Counter-History* (London: Verso, 2011), p. 343.

product of developments largely (that is to say: not entirely) from within liberal society and ideology. It was an extreme attempt at solving the crisis of liberalism, breaking out of its aporia, and saving the bourgeoisie from itself.[4]

The UK is a particularly good example for our purposes, as it has often slipped between liberalism and illiberalism in racial terms. Historically, it has branded itself as victor over the slave trade and liberator of slaves through the Slave Trade Act 1807 and the Slavery Abolition Act of 1833, respectively. Barack Obama was even offered a copy of Shadow Foreign Secretary William Hague's biography of white British abolitionist William Wilberforce by David Cameron, during his pre-election campaign visit in 2008.[5] Yet, positioning Britain as an emancipatory vanguard ignores the fact that, while it supported abolition and 'emancipated' slaves in defence of its Empire during the American War of Independence (a white settler-colonial revolt against monarchy and taxes, not against colonialism),[6] it supported the French planters and slave-owners during the Haitian Revolution. It would later also side, for economic reasons, with the slave-holding Confederacy: north-west England's economy depended on cotton from the American south, which in turn was reliant on Britain for the tobacco trade.[7] It also ignores both resistance to decolonisation and the role and influence of those in the colonised world in both anti-colonial resistance globally and the spread of anti-colonial ideas and activism in Britain itself, as Priyamvada Gopal argues in *Insurgent Empire: Anticolonial Resistance and British Dissent*.[8] Yet a nostalgic longing for Empire and colonial times remains popular

---

4   Ishay Landa, *The Apprentice's Sorcerer: Liberal Tradition and Fascism* (Chicago: Haymarket, 2010), p. 9.

5   James Macintyre, 'Cameron's a Lightweight', *New Statesman*, 4 December 2008; See also Aaron Winter, 'Race, Empire and the British-American "Special Relationship" in the Obama Era', *Obama, US Politics and Transatlantic Relation: Change or Continuity?* ed. G. Scott-Smith (Oxford: Peter Lang, 2012), pp. 229–246.

6   Simon Schama, *Rough Crossings: Britain, the Slaves and the American Revolution* (London: Vintage, 2009), p. 14.

7   Amanda Foreman, *A World on Fire: An Epic History of Two Nations Divided* (London: Penguin, 2010).

8   Priyamvada Gopal, *Insurgent Empire: Anticolonial Resistance and British Dissent* (London: Verso, 2019).

among the elite, and was particularly prominent during the Brexit campaign. Former foreign secretary Liam Fox floated the idea of an 'Empire 2.0', while Fox's successor Boris Johnson attributed Obama's support for Remain to his Kenyan heritage and anti-colonial view of the British Empire.[9]

Interestingly, American racism even played a role in Britain's construction of itself as liberal. When US troops started to arrive in Britain in 1942, concerns were raised about the way they might impose their segregationist practices on black colonial subjects.[10] Following a meeting of the War Cabinet to discuss proposed limits on black troops coming to Britain, Anthony Eden's private secretary, Oliver Harvey, wrote: 'It is rather a scandal that the Americans should thus export their internal problem. We don't want to see lynching begin in England. I can't bear the typical Southern attitude towards the negroes. It is a great ulcer on the American civilization and makes nonsense of half their claims.'[11] The notes from this Cabinet meeting were circulated by the War Office in November 1942, and found their way into the article 'The Colour Problem as the American Sees It', in the 5 December issue of the army's journal, *Current Affairs*.[12] It noted: 'The colour problem is one of the most difficult of all internal American questions. We have nothing in any way remotely approaching it in our own home land.'[13] Colonial and domestic racism were thus unacknowledged, and already the problem of racism was pinned onto an other whose racist practices could be seen or represented as more obvious and illiberal, and could serve as a distraction. Ironically, following the war, America pressured Britain to abandon its Empire in the cause of winning the battle over Nazi racism and fascism, but took the opportunity to establish its own neo-colonial hegemony. In this context, black soldiers returned to Jim Crow America as the state increased pressure on the left and on Civil

---

9   Jon Stone, 'Boris Johnson Suggests "Part-Kenyan" Obama May Have "Ancestral Dislike" of UK', *Independent*, 22 April 2016.

10   Graham Smith, *When Jim Crow Met John Bull: Black American Soldiers in World War II Britain* (London: St. Martin's 1987), p. 40.

11   Ibid., p. 48.

12   Ibid., p. 79; unknown author 'The Colour Problem as the American Sees It', *Current Affairs*, December 1942, pp. 10–14.

13   Smith, *When Jim Crow Met John Bull*, p. 13.

Rights activists as liberal democracy turned illiberal during the Red Scare and McCarthyism.

Inconsistencies and contradictions of this kind, which underpin liberalism, rest on powerful mechanisms of displacement, denial or selective ignorance. The focus on particular narratives and myths in our public discourse feeds into constructions of national identity. Through the celebration of certain national events and the erasure of others, our societies have managed to ignore, downplay or deny many of the darkest aspects of the political system currently underpinning our societies. This is not just an issue of historiography: it has a real, direct impacts on our politics and societies, and has often informed and justified aspects of domestic and foreign policy.[14] After the evil of the Second World War, and even more so after the putative 'end of history' that followed the collapse of the Soviet Union, it has been widely accepted that only liberalism will allow for the development of peaceful, meritocratic and fair societies. For Francis Fukuyama, writing in 1989, the Cold War marked 'the end point of mankind's ideological evolution and the universalization of western liberal democracy as the final form of human government', adding that 'the triumph of the West, of the Western idea, is evident first of all in the total exhaustion of viable systematic alternatives to Western liberalism'.[15] While it has been widely debunked, and history has clearly not ended, the idea that liberalism defines our shared political horizon has retained its grip on our political imagination, and few consider exploring beyond its confines. In fact, when alternatives are presented in the mainstream political discourse, they are often demonised and represented as threats to democracy itself, as spectres of defeated evils, whether in the form of fascism or Stalinist communism. While communism has proved far less easy to revive in the post–Cold War era, whether in a mimetic or updated fashion, the former has become both a real possibility and a convenient scarecrow to brandish in order to reinforce the grip of liberal elites on the political imagination.

---

14   See, for example, Gholam Khiabany, 'Refugee Crisis, Imperialism, and Pitiless Wars on the Poor', *Media, Culture and Society* 38: 5 (2016), pp. 755–62.

15   Francis Fukuyama, 'The End of History', *The National Interest*, 16 (Summer 1989), pp. 3–18.

The internalised understanding of democracy as liberal democracy, combined with the ubiquity of capitalism as the only legitimate economic system, has been vital in reinforcing this narrative. We argue here that it is the strength and flexibility of liberal hegemony which has enabled the persistence of racism as a systemic phenomenon. This has been entrenched by the delimitation of illiberal racism as the only real racism, even though its origins are intricately woven within the liberal tradition.

To be clear, we are not saying that liberalism is innately and necessarily tied to racism (or other supposedly illiberal practices); obviously, many liberals have fought against exclusionary practices. Yet, we are trying to emphasise that we must challenge and move beyond the hegemonic idea that liberalism and racism (and, following Landa, fascism) are antithetical, and that liberalism is therefore necessarily the logical opponent to the far right, as is often argued in the mainstream media and parts of academia. Instead, we must understand the mechanisms at play within liberalism, how it is deployed, and the ways in which racism remains anchored to and travels through it today. Illiberal racism is in fact essential to the existence of, and tolerance for, liberal racism, acting as a diversion from more systemic and diffuse forms of racism that remain central to our liberal societies.

THE EMERGENCE AND POSITIONING OF
THE FAR AND EXTREME RIGHT

It is impossible to understand the contingent nature of the far and extreme right today without acknowledging the particular historical, political and cultural context in which they arose – namely, that of the ideological realignment that took place after the Second World War, and particularly after the 1960s. This led to four key developments we have already discussed: the defeat of Nazism and rise of liberal democracy; the reconstruction of racism as illiberal and extreme; the emergence of the concept of the 'radical' or 'extreme' right, as both a reconstruction of once-mainstream fascism and racism, and a repository for now unacceptable racism in liberal democracies; and the discursive reconstruction of the far and extreme right as they reacted and adapted to the new context.

What is significant about the various labels used – 'radical', 'ultra', 'far' or 'extreme' – is that they are defined in relation to a normative and hegemonic centre (both liberal and right), which is itself contingent on historical, political and social developments. This contingency is key, as it is what dictates what is defined as extreme or mainstream at any given time, as these can change in form and content depending on context. Racism may be mainstream in one context, but – through various historical and political processes, such as the defeat of Nazism or passing of the Civil Rights Act – become unacceptable, and thus be deemed 'radical' or 'extreme', constituted through such manifestations or displaced onto them. This applies to the concept of illiberal racism embodied by the extreme right, but also to our notion of mainstreaming (see Chapter 3). The emergence of the term 'radical right' represents this very contingency and function. The term was coined in the 1950s by neo-conservative Seymour Martin Lipset in the collection *The New American Right*, edited by Daniel Bell.[16] The term was used by Lipset to describe those movements, organisations and actors – including the Ku Klux Klan, the John Birch Society and McCarthyism – that desired 'far-reaching changes in American institutions', because they sought 'to eliminate from American political life those persons and institutions which threaten either its values, or its economic interests'.[17] Other characteristics included rejection of the existing order, including tolerance and establishment conservatism. According to Lipset, the reason such movements were a threat is that they rejected traditional democratic procedures, such as lobbying and the ballot box, in favour of agitation, and practices which 'threaten to undermine the social fabric of democratic politics'.[18] This conceptualisation was itself normative, and represented a defence of the hegemonic post-war liberal-democratic order, which was also racist and anti-communist, but abided by traditional democratic procedures.

For many neoconservatives and centrist liberals, the spectre of totalitarianism – specifically fascism and communism as represented

---

16   Seymour Martin Lipset, 'The Sources of the "Radical Right"', in Daniel Bell, ed, *The New American Right* (New York: Criterion, 1955), pp. 166–234.

17   Ibid., p. 166.

18   Ibid., p. 167.

by Nazism and the Soviet Union – played a role in both their opposition to extremism on the right and left, and their defence of the liberal-democratic order and 'centre' in the post-war era, and particularly during the Cold War. The role of fascism and communism in the construction and affirmation of the liberal centre can be seen in Arthur Schlesinger Jr's *The Vital Center*, published in 1949.[19] For Schlesinger, it was in the centre that mainstream political discourse existed and, for that discourse to function, he argued, society had to demarcate lines to determine and police what was and was not acceptable. The centre was a point of demarcation not between left and right, but between democracy and totalitarianism, with the latter being represented by communism and fascism, including the far right domestically.

According to Schlesinger, the experience of fascism and communism represented an occasion for re-education and awakening: 'The consequence of this historical re-education has been an unconditional rejection of totalitarianism and a reassertion of the ultimate integrity of the individual. This awakening constitutes the unique experience and fundamental faith of contemporary liberalism . . . This faith has been and will continue to be under attack from the far right and the far left.'[20]

In 1970, Lipset and Earl Raab published *The Politics of Unreason: Right-Wing Extremism in America, 1790–1970*.[21] Following on from the former's work on the radical right in the 1950s, and responding to Richard Hofstadter's work on the 'paranoid style',[22] this book represented an attempt to psychopathologise and delegitimise the 'extremes' as lacking the reason and rationality of the political discourse of the mainstream democratic system, its procedures and values, and thus illegitimate. These were not merely scholarly definitions. According to Sara Diamond, the typology was not neutral:

---

19   Arthur M. Schlesinger, Jr., *The Vital Center: Politics of Freedom* (Boston: Houghton Mifflin, 1949).

20   Ibid.

21   Seymour Martin Lipset and Earl Raab, *The Politics of Unreason: Right Wing Extremism in America, 1790–1970* (New York: Harper & Row, 1970).

22   Richard J. Hofstadter, 'The Paranoid Style in American Politics', *Harper's Magazine*, November 1964.

"'Radical" and "extremist" are pejorative terms. They reveal their origination's sympathy for the political status quo but elucidate little else. The "radical-extremist" frame limits the honest study of those few who fit the description. It implies that movements so designated operate outside normal political processes and ought not to be taken seriously, which is generally not the case.'[23]

Furthermore, such movements can be directly linked to the very processes by which the mainstream state cracked down on so-called radicals on both right and left from the 1950s to the 1970s, in a manner that demonised, delegitimised and repressed dissent, affirming the rational centre and liberal democracy. According to Chip Berlet, such frameworks and labels (and the analysis which accompanies them) represent 'counter-subversion' and 'pluralist-extremist' models[24] – or what Diamond terms the 'radical-extremist frame'.[25] For Berlet, the counter-subversion model originates in state intelligence circles, particularly the FBI's Counter-Intelligence Program (COINTELPRO), formed in 1956, to undermine the left and civil rights movement, and later taking on the Klan, the Black Panthers and the revolutionary left. It applies the label to oppositional or counter-hegemonic political activists in order to delegitimise them, representing them as dangerous subversives, thereby justifying state surveillance, censorship and suppression.[26] This model, informed by radical-right theorists, not only serves to marginalise, pathologise and repress such activists and movements, but also asserts the primacy and hegemony of the centre or status quo, negating any overlap between them – particularly with respect to the racism and anti-communism that also exist in the mainstream.

---

23   Sara Diamond, *Roads to Dominion: Right-Wing Movements and Political Power in the United States* (New York: Guilford, 1995), p. 5.

24   Chip Berlet, 'Three Models for Analyzing Conspiracist Mass Movements of the Right', in Eric Ward, ed., *Conspiracies: Real Grievances, Paranoia, and Mass Movements* (Seattle: Peanut Butter, 1996), pp. 48–9.

25   Diamond, *Roads to Dominion*, p. 5.

26   Berlet, 'Three Models', p. 48.

LIBERAL RACISM

The contingent construction of the hegemonic centre opposed to all forms of totalitarianism, and to the racism exhibited on the extreme right, has enabled the celebration of racial progress, and ignorance or even denial of the forms of racism which persist and have deep roots in liberalism. As Albert Memmi wrote: 'There is a strange enigma associated with the problem of racism. No one, or almost no one, wishes to see themselves as racist; still, racism persists, real and tenacious.'[27]

Racism is the other. While there is wide acknowledgement that racism persists, its denunciation is usually limited to what we call illiberal racism. Racism is reduced to exception and happenstance: extreme and individual manifestations represent the last echoes and ripples of a bygone era in what is assumed to be post-racial societies. It is no surprise, therefore, that most mainstream social analysis, and the majority of Americans, view racism as 'individual-level animosity or hatred towards people of colour', associated primarily with its most explicit and historical manifestations.[28] For Eduardo Bonilla-Silva:

> Whites have developed powerful explanations – which have ultimately become justifications – for contemporary racial inequality that exculpate them from any responsibility for the status of people of color ... Whereas Jim Crow racism explained blacks' social standing as the result of their biological and moral inferiority, color-blind racism avoids such fragile arguments. Instead, whites rationalize minorities' contemporary status as the product of market dynamics, naturally occurring phenomena, and blacks' imputed cultural limitations.[29]

---

27 Albert Memmi, *Racism* (Minneapolis: University of Minnesota Press, 1999).

28 Eduardo Bonilla-Silva with Victor E. Ray, 'Getting Over the Obama Hope Hangover: The New Racism in "Post-Racial" America', in Karim Murji and John Solomos, eds, *Theories of Race and Ethnicity: Contemporary Debates and Perspectives* (Cambridge: Cambridge University Press, 2015), p. 59.

29 Eduardo Bonilla-Silva, *Racism without Racists: Color-blind Racism and the Persistence of Racial Inequality in the United States* (New York: Rowman & Littlefield, 2006), p. 2.

Bonilla-Silva has highlighted four frames of reference within which to understand colour-blind racism, how it operates, and the ways in which it takes hold: abstract liberalism, naturalisation, cultural racism and minimisation of racism.[30] Abstract liberalism is an abstract approach to explaining racial matters based on the belief that all people are now equal in terms of rights and opportunities.[31] This allows us to celebrate racial progress as a liberal achievement: through examples of individual achievement deemed representative or universalised, white people can righteously claim that barriers have been lifted and the onus is now on the (liberal) individual to make their own life, thus ignoring the many structural and systemic discriminations still in place. For Tim Wise, Obama's election did not signify the post-racial death of racism, but the usurpation of 'Racism 1.0', the 'old-fashioned bigotry . . . that, in its most extreme moments has precipitated racist murder, lynching, and terror' by 'Racism 2.0' – 'a form that allows for and even celebrates the achievements of individual persons of color'.[32] Naturalisation refers to racial phenomena being explained by allegedly natural causes: segregation is natural, and people of the same 'race' naturally gravitate towards each other. Cultural racism shifts the blame for the inferior standing of minorities onto their supposed cultural predisposition (laziness, and so on). Bonilla-Silva's colour-blind racism is similar to what others have called new or 'cultural' racism.[33] Finally, Bonilla-Silva's fourth frame, the minimisation of racism, suggests that once there was racism, but that it is no longer structural, and that we must now move on. For Charles Gallagher, 'the core belief that undergirds colour-blind egalitarianism is the conviction that white privilege is a prerogative of the past'.[34] He argues that the claim of colour-blindness thus makes it

---

30   Ibid. On colour-blind racism and the transformation of racism in the post–Civil Rights era, see also Michael Omi and Howard Winant, *Racial Formation in the United States: From the 1960s to the 1990s* (New York: Routledge, 1994).

31   Bonilla-Silva, *Racism without Racists*, pp. 28-9.

32   Tim Wise, *Between Barack and a Hard Place: Racism and White Denial in the Age of Obama* (San Francisco: City Lights, 2009), p. 26.

33   See Etienne Balibar and Immanuel Wallerstein, *Race, nation, classe; les identités ambiguës* (Paris: la Découverte, 1997).

34   Charles Gallagher, 'Color-blind Egalitarianism as the New Racial Norm', in Karim Murji and John Solomos, eds, *Theories of Race and Ethnicity: Contemporary Debates and Perspectives* (Cambridge: Cambridge University Press, 2015), p. 42.

impossible to acknowledge that society is still organised in ways that benefit whites or enable white privilege. Similar mechanisms have been at play in Europe and much of the west, where the widely acclaimed meritocratic nature of liberalism and liberal democracies has been internalised despite all evidence pointing to the uneven playing field in terms of race, gender and other intersecting identities.

These four frames of reference not only depend on the comfortable, and sometimes wilful, ability to deny systemic racist practices, but also normalise whiteness, returning it to a position of universality and invisibility. As Alana Lentin and Gavan Titley note, in the post-racial state, 'racelessness is now equated with racial neutrality, which in turn is interpreted as whiteness'.[35] The violent hegemony of whiteness and the terror it conjures for many is thus concealed. As bell hooks points out, 'Black people still feel the terror, still associate it with whiteness, but are rarely able to articulate the varied ways we are terrorized because it is easy to silence by accusations of reverse racism or by suggesting that black folks who talk about the ways we are terrorized by whites are merely evoking victimization to demand special treatment'.[36] This concealment of terror is further entrenched by the non-white being constantly reminded that the source of terror is in fact in their midst, and that suspicion is warranted, while whites are exempted from communal guilt when a 'lone wolf' strikes.

For Reni Eddo-Lodge, the problem is that whiteness is not seen as other 'colours': 'neutral is white'.[37] This obscures the simple and well-evidenced fact that being born white comes with a number of privileges. This does not mean that white people cannot suffer from various ills, from poverty or even face discrimination, but it will not be because of their whiteness and being white will place them in a more favourable situation than people of colour structurally. It does not mean that they have not worked hard to get where they are, but that they did not suffer from the barriers placed in the way of others, simply because of their 'race' (or

---

35   Alana Lentin and Gavan Titley, *The Crises of Multiculturalism: Racism in a Neoliberal Age* (London: Zed, 2011), p. 81.

36   bell hooks, *Killing Rage, Ending Racism* (London: Penguin, 1995), p. 47.

37   Reni Eddo-Lodge, *Why I'm No Longer Talking to White People about Race* (London: Bloomsbury, 2017), p. 85.

gender, or any other identity category that departs from the dominant and 'norm').

The invisibility of privilege can also be seen in the racialisation of the working class, which deflects issues clearly based on class towards a divisive race struggle benefiting the elite oppressor. This is particularly relevant for our purposes in relation to liberal racism. We are taught early on to believe that there is indeed no such thing as innate privilege, that it was abolished by enlightenment ideals, more or less peacefully, more or less quickly, and that we are all born free and equal.[38] Certainly, there remain illiberal racists whom we denounce as a society, but they are the other. Yet it is clear that the odds are not even. As Peggy McIntosh noted in 1988, 'whites are carefully taught not to recognize white privilege, as males are taught not to recognize male privilege'.[39] As Zeus Leonardo argues, while most privileged people may be oblivious to the fact, they nonetheless participate daily in the reproduction of the oppressive system they benefit from.[40]

Bonilla-Silva argues that 'color-blind racism has rearticulated elements of traditional liberalism (work ethic, reward by merit, equal opportunity, individualism, etc.) for racially illiberal goals'.[41] However, we believe that this goes further, and that other, supposedly core liberal values, outlined below, have in fact served a very liberal agenda, rather than an illiberal one – one that was also central to the fight against the values now used to justify the stigmatisation and exclusion of the new other. The LGBTQ+ community, workers and women were for a long time denied equal rights, the granting of which was believed to threaten the good liberal order. Yet they are now co-opted opportunistically as if they had always been part of the liberal compact, even though their equal rights often remain precarious or unfulfilled. This narrative, of course, wilfully ignores the fact that these communities had to fight liberalism to emancipate

38   For a thorough discussion of privilege in the twenty-first-century UK and US, see Kalwant Bhopal, *White Privilege: The Myth of a Postracial Society* (Bristol: Policy, 2018).

39   Peggy McIntosh, 'White Privilege: Unpacking the Invisible Knapsack', *Peace and Freedom Magazine*, July/August 1989, pp. 10–12.

40   Zeus Leonardo, 'The Color of Supremacy: Beyond the Discourse of White Privilege', *Educational Philosophy and Theory* 36: 2 (2004), pp. 137–52.

41   Bonilla-Silva, *Racism without Racists*, p. 7.

themselves in the first place. As Lentin and Titley argue, 'Racism persists because there has been no serious effort made to challenge the interconnections between the idea of race and the institutions and structures of the modern nation-state. Race has been semantically conquered, but it remains deeply ingrained in the political imaginaries, structures and practices of 'the West'.[42]

The post-racial becomes subject to what Titley refers to as 'debatability' – that is, the 'incessant, recursive attention as to what counts as racism and who gets to define it'.[43] For Lentin, it is linked specifically to the function of 'frozen racism': 'racism thus becomes debatable, not because the racisms of the past are called into question, but precisely because by fixing "real" racism solely in historical events, the continuities between racisms past and present are made undecideable'.[44] For Bonilla-Silva, this debatability often occurs through 'sincere fictions' of colour-blindness (underpinned by and filtered through one or more of the four frames), which act as powerful tools of denial of deep systemic inequalities in terms of work, wealth, education, life expectancy and pretty much any other area of social life. If the problem is acknowledged, the blame is shifted squarely onto the shoulders of the victims of what is clear systemic discrimination. One of Bonilla-Silva's 'sincere fictions' is that most whites today 'believe that if blacks and other minorities would just stop thinking about the past, work hard, and complain less (particularly about racial discrimination)', then we could all get along.[45] We see this in the frequent appropriation by conservative and libertarian commentators of Martin Luther King Jr.'s line: 'I have a dream that my four little children will one day live in a nation where they will not be judged by the color of their skin but by the content of their character.' This turns King's claim on its head, placing the blame for racism on black people, as they apparently refuse to let go of the past, identity politics, racialised thinking, and even hatred of white

---

42   Lentin and Titley, *Crises of Multiculturalism*, p. 49.

43   Gavan Titley, *Racism and Media* (London: Sage, 2019).

44   Lentin, 'Racism in public or public racism', p. 3.

45   Bonilla-Silva, *Racism without Racists*, p. 1. Bonilla-Silva writes about the United States, but we argue that his argument could be extended to the European context, and to France and the UK in particular.

people. This can also be seen in the 'All Lives Matter' response to Black Lives Matter, as if the latter excludes others as opposed to highlighting a racist disparity in police killings, which appear to matter less than flawed liberal notions of inclusion and universalism.

While whiteness is presented as universal, neutral and benevolent, this appearance can be tested by accusations of racial inequality and racism. What is ironic here, but powerful in its effect, is that whiteness structures the west, but that the post-racial allows for denial, and even a claim of lost privilege. Thus, whiteness simultaneously serves as both neutral arbiter of racism and target of offence and attack that must be defended, yet never as the source or structure of racism and/or power. In that sense, whiteness cannot be acknowledged or recognised unless it is articulated as powerless and victimised. For Miri Song, what the post-racial does is create a false logic, or even culture, of 'racial equivalence': 'A key manifestation of this culture of racial equivalence is the growing number of allegations of "reverse racism" against ethnic minority people and race conscious policies.'[46] We see this in both mainstream liberal back-lash discourses and far- and extreme-right white-nationalist and identitar-ian white-victim discourses. The responses to Black Lives Matter are again illustrative of this point: All Lives Matter is the liberal, post-racial, colour-blind response; White Lives Matter is the extreme-right one. Another response is Blue Lives Matter – encapsulating the state's response, and giving its name to the US Blue Lives Matter Act of 2016, which extended the definition of hate crimes to include offences against police officers.[47]

Despite claims that the United States is a post-racial society, that the UK is a multicultural society, and France does not see race because of the universalist nature of the Republic, evidence shows that racism remains deeply embedded and ongoing. According to Stanford's Center on Poverty and Inequality *State of the Union* report for 2017, 'profound racial and ethnic inequalities' still remain in terms of employment, health and housing in the United States.[48] The report

---

46   Miri Song, 'Challenging a Culture of Racial Equivalence', *British Journal of Sociology* 65: 1 (2014), pp. 107–29.

47   United States Congress, *All Bill Information for H.R.4760 – Blue Lives Matter Act of 2016*, 2016.

48   David B. Grusky, Charles Varner and Marybeth Mattingly, eds, *State of the Union 2017*, Stanford Center on Poverty and Inequality, 2017.

was issued following Trump's campaign and election, which claimed – and was often taken at its word – to represent the white working-class 'left behind', and mobilised broader white resentment, victimisation narratives and claims of reverse-racism. The Stanford report shows that one in four black people, one in four Native Americans and one in five Hispanic people were classified as poor. By contrast, only one in ten whites and one in ten Asians were poor, while median earnings for black males were 32 per cent lower than for whites; the earning gap between white and Hispanic men had grown from 29 to 42 per cent between 1970 and 2010. The employment rate for black men had been between 11 and 15 percentage points lower than that for whites since January 2000. Black and Hispanic people were also more likely to live in poorer neighbourhoods than white people with working-class incomes.[49] This was in addition to the high level of racial profiling and killings of black people by the police, as well as mass incarceration, in response to which Black Lives Matter had mobilised.

According to a review by the British Equality and Human Rights Commission, which looked at employment, housing, pay and criminal justice, there is a 'very worrying combination of a post-Brexit rise in hate crime and long-term systemic unfairness and race inequality', which it described as 'entrenched'.[50] The review was published in August 2016, at the height of the Brexit campaign, with its rhetoric about the white working class and 'native' (read: white) British people being marginalised and victimised by immigration, multiculturalism and political correctness. According to the report, 35.7 per cent of members of ethnic minorities were more likely to live in poverty, compared with 17.2 per cent of whites, while Pakistani, Bangladeshi and black adults were more likely to live in 'substandard' accommodation than whites. Unemployment rates were higher for ethnic minorities, at 12.9 per cent, compared with 6.3 per cent for whites; black workers with degrees earned 23.1 per cent less on average than whites. In terms of criminal justice, rates of prosecution

---

49   Braden Goyette and Alissa Scheller, '15 Charts that Prove We're Far from Post-Racial', *Huffington Post: Black Voices*, 7 February 2016.

50   Equality and Human Rights Commission, *Healing a Divided Britain: The Need for a Comprehensive Race Equality Strategy*, 2016.

and sentencing were three times as high for black than for white people.[51] Moreover, according to the Runnymede Trust/CLASS *Minority Report: Race and Class in Post-Brexit Britain*, socioeconomic inequality and related problems (poverty, lack of social mobility, low wages, poor housing, limited institutional representation), represented as problems of the white working class left behind in the context of Brexit, cut across racial groups, with racial and ethnic minorities suffering the brunt of austerity politics[52] – which, according to Leah Bassel and Akwugo Emejulu's research on Britain and France, have a disproportionate effect on women of colour.[53]

Systemic racism and discrimination are more difficult to gauge in France because of the lack of official statistics on race and ethnicity, among other markers. Yet, a number of reports have demonstrated similar trends to those found in the United States and the UK.[54] This tendency has been further entrenched by a turn to a reactionary and militant understanding of *laïcité* ('secularism'), which has strongly undermined the freedom of Muslim communities and other racialised minorities, but also by the impact of recent terrorist attacks and the normalisation of the state of emergency.

THE HIJACKING OF EMANCIPATORY
STRUGGLES FOR REACTIONARY ENDS

While targets of illiberal racism are defined by the construction and assertion of their non-belonging to a particular racialised group (be it a race, nationality or ethnic grouping), targets of liberal racism are

---

51   Ibid.

52   Omar Khan and Faiza Shaheen, *Minority Report: Race and Class in Post-Brexit Britain*, Runnymede Trust/CLASS, 2017. See also Runnymede Trust, *The 2015 Budget Effects on Black and Minority Ethnic People*, Runnymede Trust, 2015.

53   Leah Bassel and Akwugo Emejulu, *Minority Women and Austerity: Survival and Resistance in France and Britain* (Bristol: Policy, 2017); Bassel and Emejulu, 'Whose Crisis Counts? Minority Women, Austerity and Activism in France and Britain', in J. Kantola and E. Lombardo, eds, *Gender and the Economic Crisis in Europe: Politics, Institutions and Intersectionality* (London: Palgrave, 2017).

54   See, for example, Commission Nationale Consultative des Droits de l'Homme (CNCDH), 'Rapport 2017 sur la lutte contre le racisme, l'antisémitisme et la xénophobie' (Paris: CNDCH, 2018); Open Society, 'Equality Betrayed: The Impact of Ethnic Profiling in France', *Open Society*, September 2013.

defined, at least discursively, in terms of their non-belonging to 'our' liberal societies and their rules based on human rights and the legacy of the Enlightenment. Such a constructed separation is built on foundations just as shaky as those that underpin illiberal racism, but the key difference is that they are hegemonic in our societies – that is, accepted uncritically by most. Liberal racism is currently mostly aimed at the Muslim other(ed), although it is easy to see how it might soon target others. Building on a vast body of literature, we understand the term 'Islamophobia' not literally to mean fear, but as a form of racism.[55] It is

> a construct, and the Muslim signifier [is] one which does not come from the individual Muslim in a subjective manner, but is defined by the onlooker in a position of power and imposed onto people through various types of generalization, misperception and stigmatization, such as the so-called secular and anti-terrorist laws, but also through the media coverage of Islam.[56]

As highlighted by David Theo Goldberg, 'Islam is taken in the dominant European imaginary to represent a collection of lacks: of freedom; of a disposition of scientific inquiry; of civility and manners; of love of life; of human worth; of equal respect for women and gay people.'[57] Of course, this kind of racism is not entirely new or original. As Enzo Traverso notes, 'European nationalisms are structured today

---

55   See, for example, Nasar Meer and Tariq Modood, 'Refutations of Racism in the "Muslim Question"', *Patterns of Prejudice* 43: 3–4 (2009), pp. 332–51; Chris Allen, 'Islamophobia: From K.I.S.S. to R.I.P', in S. Sayyid and A. Vakil, eds, *Thinking Through Islamophobia: Global Perspectives* (London: Hurst, 2010), pp. 51–64; Raymond Taras, 'Islamophobia Never Stands Still: Race, Religion, and Culture', *Ethnic and Racial Studies* 36: 3 (2013), pp. 417–33; Pnina Werbner, 'Folk Devils and Racist Imaginaries in a Global Prism: Islamophobia and Anti-Semitism in the Twenty-First Century', *Ethnic and Racial Studies* 36: 3 (2013), pp. 450–67; Sayyid and Vakil, *Thinking Through Islamophobia*.

56   Aurelien Mondon and Aaron Winter, 'Articulations of Islamophobia: From the Extreme to the Mainstream?', *Ethnic and Racial Studies Review* V. 40, #13. For more detail on the role of the media in the construction of Islamophobia, see Arun Kundnani, *The Muslims are Coming: Islamophobia, Extremism and the Domestic War on Terror* (London: Verso, 2014); Julian Petley and Robin Richardson, *Pointing the Finger: Islam and Muslims in the British Media* (Oxford: One World, 2011).

57   David Theo Goldberg, 'Racial Europeanization', *Ethnic and Racial Studies* 29: 2 (2006), p. 345.

through Islamophobia, as they were by antisemitism in the first half of the twentieth century.'[58] This has occurred for a number of reasons, but most notably because the liberal racism we see today is predicated on the overcoming of illiberal racism associated with Nazism and fascism, for which anti-Semitism is a model and signifier. This has resulted in the weaponisation of philosemitism (often articulated as pro-Israel Zionism) against Muslims because of assumptions about their politics and prejudices, rather than reflecting sincere opposition to anti-Semitism and racism.

One of the ways liberal racism has set itself apart from illiberal racism is in its apparent support for movements which would usually be opposed by the latter. Two of the most prominent causes which have been hijacked for reactionary ends to promote liberal racism have been women's and LGBTQ+ rights. Apparent defence of these communities has allowed liberal racists to set themselves apart from illiberal racists, since these groups are often targets of the more extreme right. We argue that this approach has been adopted mostly out of opportunism, as the liberal racist defenders of women's and LGBTQ+ rights are only ever vocal when the threat to them comes from certain enemies. Since clear breaches of human and equal rights are perpetrated by the governments of certain countries that claim to rule on the basis of Islam, it has been easy for liberal racists to generalise the behaviour of certain states, or the conservatism of some communities, to the entire Muslim community, despite its diversity, and to anyone associated with it, however loosely. At the same time, liberal racists have been quick to paint the 'Judeo-Christian' west with a broad progressive brush, as if the rule of law and western civilisation had created an egalitarian haven for otherwise underprivileged communities. When challenged on this, and in particular on the poor record in the west regarding equal rights, it is therefore not surprising that the liberal racist will resort to simplistic responses such as: 'Why don't you go and live in Saudi Arabia?', as if it were not possible to stand against all oppressive practices indiscriminately. Such responses also rely on the assumption that there is a typical Muslim, and that Muslim men are usually sexist and controlling, while women are

---

58   Enzo Traverso, *Les nouveaux visages du fascismes* (Paris: Textuel, 2017), p. 85.

subservient and in need of our help. This is clearly reminiscent of the traditional racist myths of Orientalism.[59]

The contradictions of such a stance have been well covered by others. While it is not our aim to add to this wealth of literature, we believe that it is important to outline certain issues that are closely associated with the argument we develop in this book. Two concepts have been particularly useful to understand the rise of such trends: homonationalism, developed as a concept in the work of Jasbir Puar, and femonationalism, in the work of Sara Farris.[60] For Puar, 9/11 and its aftermath marked a turn in the way in which homosexuality was used in American politics:

> Even as patriotism immediately after September 11 was inextricably tied to a reinvigoration of heterosexual norms for Americans, progressive sexuality was championed as a hallmark of US modernity. For despite the reentrenchment of heteronormativity, the United States was also portrayed as 'feminist' in relation to the Taliban's treatment of Afghani women (a concern that had been previously of no interest to US foreign policy) and gay-safe in comparison to the Middle East.

It is indeed ironic that this position was adopted under the conservative presidency of George W. Bush – who, in his 1994 campaign for governor of Texas, had defended the Texas sodomy law, which made sexual activity between same-sex adults illegal, as a 'symbolic gesture of traditional values'. He went on, during his presidency, to oppose same-sex marriage, and it took until 2003 for sodomy laws still in place in fourteen states to be invalidated by the Supreme Court.

A similar concept was later developed by Sara Farris regarding the use of women's right in the French, Dutch and Italian cases. For Farris, femonationalism describes, 'on the one hand, the attempt of Western European right-wing parties and neoliberals to advance a xenophobic and racist politics through the touting of gender equality

---

59   Edward W. Said, *Orientalism* (London: Penguin, 2003 [1978]).

60   Sara Farris, *In the Name of Women's Rights: The Rise of Femonationalism* (London: Duke University Press, 2017); Jasbir Puar, *Terrorist Assemblages: Homonationalism in Queer Times* (London: Duke University Press, 2007).

while, on the other hand, it captures the involvement of various well-known and quite visible feminists and femocrats in the current framing of Islam as a quintessentially misogynistic religion and culture.[61]

This liberal framing, in terms of freedom and gender, has become commonplace in the United States since Bush stated in his 9/11 address, prior to the establishment of the Department of Homeland Security and passage of the Patriot Act: 'They hate our freedoms: our freedom of religion, our freedom of speech, our freedom to vote and assemble and disagree with each other.' These words became a mantra of the American-led war on terror. It is easy to imagine, though, that this attitude might soon extend to other minorities, or present a slippery slope leading to the legitimisation of illiberal racism, or the blurring of boundary between them. Despite the usefulness of the concepts of homonationalism and femonationalism, we have chosen the term 'liberal Islamophobia' in our own analysis of this phenomenon, as the former place the emphasis on gender and sexuality (and consequently on feminist and LGBTQ+ activism and rights), as opposed to the racism in whose service they are weaponised. Moreover, it does not always serve or emanate from the nation or nationalism, and more often than not is simply an articulation of racism. It is also worth noting that the history of racism – including its illiberal forms and articulations, such as that of the Ku Klux Klan – has often been bound up with claims to be protecting and avenging the 'virtue' of white women against black men.

For Christine Delphy, the racialisation of Muslims in the name of women's rights has led to a deeply damaging split among feminists between anti-sexism and anti-racism, as many felt they had to side either with women oppressed by Islam or with Muslims oppressed by western states.[62] Delphy argues that this is a false dilemma, and that the opposition between anti-sexism and anti-racism can only work if

---

61   Farris, *In the Name of Women's Rights*, p. 4. See also Irene Zempi and Neil Chakraborti, *Islamophobia, Victimisation and the Veil* (London: Palgrave Macmillan, 2014); Naaz Rashid, *Veiled Threats: Representing the Muslim Woman in Public Policy Discourses* (Bristol: Policy Press, 2016); Narzanin Massoumi, *Muslim Women, Social Movements and the 'War on Terror'* (London: Palgrave Macmillan, 2015).

62   Christine Delphy, 'Antisexisme ou antiracisme? Un faux dilemme', *Nouvelles Questions Féministes* 25: 1 (2006), pp. 59–83. See also Christine Delphy, *Separate and Dominate: Feminism and Racism after the War on Terror* (London: Verso, 2015).

one assumes that the victims of racism are only men, but also that women only suffer sexism from men within their own family or community. In turn, this generates a hierarchy in the struggle, as women 'less oppressed' must defer to those 'more oppressed' or oppressed in an 'extraordinary manner'. The opposition is also based on the idea that Muslim women lack any form of agency, and can only be conceived as victims, necessitating that the colonising subject grant them some form of freedom – albeit one that comes at the cost of the removal of certain liberties and forms of agency (such as the right to practise religion in any way they see fit, or simply to wear particular garments). This is not to say that there is no sexism in Muslim communities, or that it should not be criticised, but merely that sexism is hardly confined to Muslim communities, or innate to them, and that combating it exclusively in those communities is both racist and hypocritical.

The French case is particularly enlightening here because of the laws against the hijab and burqa passed in recent years and the reaction to same-sex marriage legislation.[63] The 2004 law banning 'conspicuous' religious symbols in schools was the logical conclusion of the racialisation of Muslims in France, whose agency and subjectivity could no longer be tolerated as they came to be naturalised as the enemy of *laïcité*.[64] The liberal-racist agenda behind the law was particularly clear, as the hijab was very much a non-issue at the time, since 'the number of headscarf-related disputes, according to the French Ministry of Education, fell from 300 in 1994 to 150 in 2003 [with] 146 of these incidents quickly resolved through compromise'.[65] While the revered and yet widely misinterpreted

---

63 On the 'burkini affair', see also Aurelien Mondon, 'Defending the Indefensible: France, the Burkini Affair and the Further Mainstreaming of Racism', opendemocracy.net, 1 September 2016.

64 As various scholars have noted, the creation of an 'imaginary Islam' can be traced back to the 1970s. See, for example, Thomas Deltombe, *L'islam imaginaire: La construction médiatique de l'islamophobie en France, 1975–2005* (Paris: La Découverte, 2005); Abdellali Hajjat & Marwan Mohammed, *Islamophobie. Comment les élites françaises construisent le 'problème musulman'* (Paris: La Découverte, 2016); Jean Beaman, *Citizen Outsider: Children of North African Immigrants in France* (Berkeley, CA: University of California Press, 2017).

65 Pierre Tévanian, *Le Voile Médiatique. Un Faux Débat: 'L'affaire Du Foulard Islamique'* (Paris: Editions Raisons d'Agir, 2005). Our translation.

1905 law aimed to protect the right of French citizens both to have and *not* to observe a religion, its meaning became increasingly geared towards the protection of a mythical French universalism against a stereotyped and orientalised vision of Islam. Muslim communities, and anyone associated with Islam, were thus assumed to be worthy of suspicion, while never given the opportunity to express concerns or agency, which came increasingly to be seen as further evidence of guilt.[66] It is not surprising that when, the 2010 law against the burqa was passed in France, the office of Eric Besson, a former Socialist politician turned minister of immigration and national identity for the Sarkozy government, commented that the law was necessary for 'life in society and civilisation to be explained' to those guilty of wearing the garment.

Yet, beyond the inconsistencies highlighted by many,[67] it was the demonstrations against the law authorising same-sex marriage which fully revealed the extent of French secular hypocrisy.[68] In 2013, over 300,000 demonstrators took to the Paris streets to protest against new legislation on same-sex marriage. Led by organisations with clear religious links and intent, the aims of the demonstrations were exclusivist and a clear interference with politics, in a direct infringement of the 1905 law. Beyond its visible presence in the streets, this radical understanding of society based on a religious vision of the family infiltrated the National Assembly, gaining the support of prominent figures, in contrast with women and girls wearing the hijab or burqa, who were argued to pose a threat to the survival of the secular Republic. Yet, while many public figures opposed the demonstrations, it was never suggested that these

---

66   Pierre Tévanian, Ismahane Chouder and Malika Latreche, *Les filles voilées parlent* (Paris: La Fabrique Edition, 2008).

67   See, for example, Joan Wallach Scott, *The Politics of the Veil* (Princeton, NJ: Princeton University Press, 2010); Mayanthi Fernando, *The Republic Unsettled: Muslim French and Contradiction of Secularism* (London: Duke University Press, 2014); Laurent Lévy, *'La gauche', les noirs et les arabes* (Paris: La Fabrique, 2010); Pierre Tévanian, *La République du mépris: Les métamorphoses du racisme dans la France des années Sarkozy* (Paris: La Découverte, 2007); Pierre Tévanian, *Le Voile Médiatique. Un Faux Débat: 'L'affaire Du Foulard Islamique'* (Paris: Editions Raisons d'Agir, 2005).

68   For more detail, see Aurelien Mondon, 'The French Secular Hypocrisy: The Extreme Right, the Republic and the Battle for Hegemony', *Patterns of Prejudice* 49: 3 (2015), pp. 392–413.

demonstrations represented a danger to the Republic and to secularism. Nor was the extreme behaviour of some protesters generalised to the entire Catholic population in France. Only when LGBTQ+ communities were allegedly threatened by the Muslim spectre would the liberal racist come out to defend their rights.

FREE SPEECH AS A REACTIONARY TOOL

The use of free speech to push liberal-racist agendas has also become prominent in the post-9/11 world, and in particular after the 2015 attack against French magazine *Charlie Hebdo*.[69] The niche left-wing magazine had gained notoriety when it published the Mohammed cartoons which had first appeared, in 2005, in Danish conservative newspaper *Jyllands-Posten*.[70] Fleming Rose, the editor of the newspaper, now a senior fellow at the libertarian-right Cato Institute, claimed that the aim of the cartoons was to test 'the boundaries of censorship in a time of war'.[71] For Ferruh Yilmaz, the moral panic whipped up by the Danish newspaper amounted to a self-fulfilling prophecy: Jyllands-Posten was 'extremely successful in (a) creating an intense debate that can easily be described as a "moral panic" about Islam's compatibility with "western" values, (b) making freedom of speech the central question in the debate, and (c) mobilising sides on the basis of Muslim and western "identities", regardless of what their own identifications and arguments are otherwise'.[72] After the horrendous 2015 attacks, *Charlie Hebdo* came to be uncritically acclaimed as a beacon of free speech against Muslims and Islam. The impossibility of free speech in deeply unequal societies where the ability to shape public discourse is concentrated in very few hands has been widely

---

69   For further detail, see Gavan Titley, Des Freedman, Gholam Khiabany and Aurelien Mondon, eds, *After Charlie Hebdo: Terror, Racism and Free Speech* (London: Zed, 2017).

70   Jytte Klausen, *The Cartoons that Shook the World* (New Haven/London: Yale University Press, 2009); Aurelien Mondon and Aaron Winter, 'Charlie Hebdo, Republican Secularism and Islamophobia', in Titley et al., *After Charlie Hebdo*.

71   Adria Battaglia, 'A Fighting Creed: The Free Speech Narrative in the Danish Cartoon Controversy', *Free Speech Yearbook* 43: 1 (2006), pp. 20–34.

72   Ferruh Yilmaz, 'The Politics of the Danish Cartoon Affair: Hegemonic Intervention by the Extreme Right', *Communication Studies* 62: 1 (2011), pp. 5–22.

ignored. Instead, the discussion has centred on the necessity to uphold some form of absolute freedom of speech against one particular threat. The hypocrisy and double standards here are clear, as those who felt unfairly targeted had no right of response: criticising *Charlie Hebdo* in the aftermath of the attack became akin to blasphemy in France, as discussed below.

Yet, the racist rationale behind the publication of the cartoons, and more importantly behind the support *Charlie Hebdo* received – from the left in particular – was clear. The publication and defence of the cartoons had little to do with freedom of speech; it was yet another attack on Islam and anyone even remotely associated with the religion. *Charlie Hebdo*'s supporters claimed that the magazine was an equal-opportunity offender, but failed to acknowledge the relative power (or powerlessness) of various targets, and that the potential impact on Muslim communities had come at a time of growing Islamophobia. It is this context, that enhanced the power and popularity of the images, and provided a ready-made framing and response for the discourse counterposing Islam with western liberal values and freedom of speech.

The use of free speech to push a reactionary agenda is not new. In fact, it emerged during the culture wars in the 1960s and 1970s. As the civil rights, anti-colonial, anti-racist, feminist and environmental movements began to grow, their combative stance against patriarchy and white supremacy was quickly challenged by those in power on the grounds of freedom of expression. The tactic proved particularly useful for the right in general, creating false equivalences between equal-rights issues and their reactionary counterparts. Free speech has often been linked to the idea of debate as core to democratic society, allowing right-wing actors to legitimise ideas which are minoritarian or have been widely debunked. It is therefore common to hear free-speech crusaders demand debates on topics such as whether the Holocaust really took place, or whether climate change is indeed a reality. They will, of course, claim that they do not necessarily believe the reviled and discarded alternatives, but that bad ideas should be challenged and defeated in the 'marketplace of ideas', rather than 'censored'. This has become so internalised as a core tenet of our (reactionary) democracies that countless articles and speeches have used a quote mistakenly attributed to French enlightenment philosopher Voltaire to defend terrible ideas, or the idea that terrible ideas should be able to be voiced, no matter what: 'I disapprove of what you say, but I will defend to the death your right to say it.' Free speech is thus one of those concepts which has increasingly come to be taken for granted as something both tangible and positive. While the latter might be true in a society where free speech indeed existed, its absence quite simply makes the claim moot. Indeed, while we often hear people (usually white reactionary men) lament the demise of free speech, they very rarely define it in concrete and legal terms, acknowledge the limitations of the concept and its clear absence from our societies historically, nor acknowledge the uneven distribution which they never really suffer from, as demonstrated by their very ability to raise the issue.

Even if free speech simply meant the possibility to say anything at any time, there are limits to free speech in many of our societies. Some countries, for example, have passed 'memorial laws' enforcing a certain view of some particular historical events. In France, for example, Holocaust denial is punished by law. A number of countries have also implemented various pieces of legislation to outlaw hate speech or incitement to racial hatred. With regard to such laws, the United States stands at an extreme in relation to freedom of speech, as defended by the First Amendment of the Constitution. Nonetheless, the debate over free speech and its disappearance rages as much there as it does in Europe. However, it is new forms of censorship which liberal racists have used to position themselves as victims of the censorious left and 'social justice warriors' (SJWs). This kind of self-defence position is best summarised by the term 'snowflake', usually used by right-wing pundits to characterise young people on university campuses as 'woke' SJWs, over-sensitive, easily offended or 'triggered' and unable to engage with contentious ideas and debates. To protect their weakness, these snowflakes resort to no-platforming, part of what the liberal, libertarian and conservative reactionaries refer to as 'cancel culture', and the creation of safe spaces. In this schema, racism, in a perfect post-racial construction, is reduced to mere offensiveness, with nothing real at stake for those referred to or targeted. Ironically, those using this derogatory term not only deny their own privilege, but also often fail to see that they are the real snowflakes, unable to accept that their ideas are simply not welcome or supported, rather than censored. This would be laughable if these people did not have direct and broad access to public discourse through the media, for example. In the current context, it is deeply concerning and dangerous.

The reactionary use of free speech has been absorbed into the mainstream through a number of avenues. Often, and quite hypocritically, the defence of reactionary forms of free speech have been at the expense of the free speech of others. In France, children as young as eight were sent to the police station from school for not being supportive enough of the #JeSuisCharlie commemorations: not being pro-Charlie free speech was an unwelcome free-speech position. In the UK, the last two Conservative universities ministers, Jo Johnson and Sam Gyimah, have focused much of their attention on the issue.[73] Johnson's Office for Students was tasked with cracking down on no-platforming, demanding that students become 'resilient and learn to deal with controversial opinions'. Gyimah followed suit, promising tough measures in a climate he described as 'chilling' – something he supported with two incidents he had witnessed personally. He was later suspected of having invented them, as no evidence for either could be found. In 2018, the centre-right think tank Policy Exchange organised a discussion on whether there was 'an ideological monoculture at British universities', as if this was a key concern in contemporary Britain.[74] In the discussion, Eric Kaufmann argued that there was a 'dark underbelly of far-left academics styling themselves antifascists allied with radical students', and that it was a 'pernicious movement that we somehow need to control'. He went on to ask, apparently without irony: 'How do we police the virtue police?'

It is therefore not surprising that, when some academics decided to launch a peer-reviewed journal which would publish articles anonymously, reactionary free-speech crusaders threw in their

---

73 For more detail, see Evan Smith, *No Platform: A History of Universities, Anti-Fascism and the Limits of Free Speech* (London: Routledge, 2020).

74 Policy Exchange, 'Is There an Ideological Monoculture at British Universities, and Does It Matter?', 2018.

support.[75] They claimed that criticism and scrutiny amounted to bullying and a threat to their careers – a surprising claim considering that such individuals are usually in secure, senior positions. This is a typical line of argument, whereby the free-speech crusader demands free speech only to push reactionary ideas, crying for help and a safe space when someone criticises their ideas, or demands some form of equal treatment – usually someone with far less access to public platforms. Once again, the irony escapes the reactionary, whose aim is not to create a solid argument or defend an even playing field where speech was indeed free and equal, but rather to troll and push reactionary ideas into the spotlight, whatever the cost.

LEGITIMISERS

The increased acceptance and visibility of liberal racism, particularly through its use against Muslim communities and those perceived to be Muslim, has led to a radicalisation of reactionary discourses, but also to their further legitimisation by mainstream actors. Under the auspices of traditional and classical liberal values and concepts, most notably free speech, we have witnessed a backlash predicated on a supposed post-racial equivalence that views criticisms of power and privilege, in the form of anti-racism and identity politics, as opposed to the Enlightenment and to universal values, and even anti-white racism (in the form of 'reverse racism'). Related to this, while women's rights have been deployed in the cause of liberal Islamophobia, the reactionary backlash which makes a liberal case against identity politics and intersectionality is often anti-feminist (particularly where Muslims are not a factor). This overlaps with white nationalism and the extreme right's racism and misogyny, demonstrating that the borders between the liberal and illiberal are fuzzy, and that both ultimately operate within the same reactionary paradigm.

This new stage in the culture wars has brought back into public discourse a number of ideas which many thought had been discarded for good. Yet, it is their status and use of the liberal-racist apparatus

---

75 See Anoosh Chakelian, 'Do Academics Need Pseudonyms to Protect their Freedom?', *New Statesman*, 14 November 2018.

which has allowed reactionary figures to bring into the mainstream ideas traditionally found on the far right. These actors have often built a following away from their traditional milieu in academia or journalism by pandering to far-right movements and supporters, framing themselves as the voice of the 'left behind'. While it is their elitist credentials and background which have often allowed them access to the many mainstream platforms necessary to spreading their ideas, they usually claim that they are on the side of the voiceless. As Marina Hyde pointedly noted, 'Like the rest of the gang, [Jordan] Peterson apparently imagines himself "locked out" of the mainstream media, despite having sold 2m books and being interviewed every 10 minutes by actual international media outlets. I can't help feeling that Jordan is "locked out" of the mainstream media in the same way that Justin Bieber is "locked out" of pop music.'[76]

The 'gang' Hyde refers to is the growing cohort of academics, pundits and pseudo-intellectuals who have found a lucrative business in their self-portrayal as politically incorrect thought leaders. They can be found within the IDW in the United States, the growing libertarian right – and libertarian far right – in the UK and traditional reactionary intellectual circles in France. They position themselves against what they claim to be a politically correct, 'woke', left-wing, social-justice establishment that promotes feminism, LGBTQ+ rights, anti-racism, multiculturalism, identity politics and cultural relativism, and often see themselves as defenders of the enlightenment, universalism, rationality, equality of opportunity (as opposed to outcome) and the achievements and worth of western civilisation. This 'business model' has grown tremendously in recent years. It has brought together a number of academics, politicians and pundits who appear to have given up on seeking respect from their peers, turning instead to the far right who give them cheap admiration in exchange for status legitimisation. Away from scrutiny, they have received support from the broad far right, which has been only too happy to support people with respectable backgrounds and

---

76   Marina Hyde, 'Pity Jordan Peterson. Can a Giant Lobster Analogy Ever Replace a Sense of Humour?', *Guardian*, 1 November 2018.

positions. Far from being marginalised, they have also been supported by extremely poor publishing and journalistic practices, and by the complacency of many of their colleagues, who, while they generally oppose their ideas and practices, have feared their role as gatekeepers and shied away from public condemnation. They have thus been given powerful platforms to spread their widely discredited and unethical ideas, while those who are critical can usually only express their concerns on much smaller platforms, as discussed further in the case studies below.

Nonetheless, we are told by these self-appointed free-speech crusaders that they stand alone in their fight against the 'thought police' plaguing academia and the media. Political correctness has gone mad and 'Cultural Marxism' is everywhere![77] Of course, far from being courageous or representative of the views of a conveniently silent majority (see Chapter 4), their agenda is not only harmful but also cowardly, inasmuch as it targets minority communities already suffering from various forms of discriminations. To project shadows beyond their lucrative publishing deals, they have benefited from terrible media practices which have given them countless platforms to push their views. This has emboldened them and some have become increasingly bold in their approach, their racism occupying an ever fuzzier space between the liberal and the illiberal.

The following case studies are in no way exhaustive, but represent a selection from within the broader trends that form the basis for our argument. Our aim is to provide a clear idea of how reactionary trends can develop, and how mainstream actors with often prestigious positions and access to broad platforms can act as a bridge between the far right and the mainstream, and facilitate the transfer of ideas between liberal and illiberal racisms. Whether they themselves hold far right views or legitimise them consciously or not is irrelevant; in fact, as is described below, they often come from varied backgrounds. What matters to us here is how their discourse has played a key role in the denial and perpetuation of racism. What we are trying to highlight is that it has taken only a small number of

---

77 Samuel Moyn, 'The Alt-Right's Favorite Meme Is 100 Years Old', *New York Times*, 13 November 2018.

savvy public figures to fill the space opened up by poor elite practices in the current (neo)liberal landscape. These loud voices have managed to occupy much of the public space by positioning themselves as rebels, while pushing extremely reactionary and conservative positions predicated on the superiority of the white man. This pitch, with its ability to generate highly marketable polemical confrontation, has proved appealing to media platforms on both the left and the right. As the left has so far failed to counter these strategies decisively, the reactionary right has been allowed to shape much of the agenda, supported in this enterprise by those whose interests are threatened by egalitarian movements, who also happen to control much of the media landscape.

Freedom of Speech, Racism and Culture Wars in the United States

The liberal principle of free speech occupies a central position in the identity, mythology and political discourse of the United States. The First Amendment states: 'Congress shall make no law respecting an establishment of religion, or prohibiting the free exercise thereof; or abridging the freedom of speech, or of the press; or the right of the people peaceably to assemble, and to petition the Government for a redress of grievance.' These words were central to left-wing student activism in the 1960s in challenging government repression of dissent. More recently, however, a growing number of self-identifying 'classic liberals', libertarians and conservatives have used the principle of free speech to defend their reactionary ideas and attack their opponents. Notably, 'liberals' used to refer to the American left (either incorrectly or because they were not really left). Yet the return of terms such as Marxist, socialist and even communist has led reactionaries to appropriate the term. This is particularly striking in a loose coalition of online commentators and public 'intellectuals' known as the IDW, a term coined by Eric Weinstein and publicised by Bari Weiss in the *New York Times* in 2018.[78] These include increasingly prominent commentators, authors, YouTube vloggers and

---

78   Bari Weiss, 'Meet the Renegades of the Intellectual Dark Web', *New York Times*, 8 May 2018.

podcasters, such as Sam Harris, Ben Shapiro, Dave Rubin, Joe Rogan, Ayaan Hirsi Ali, Douglas Murray, Steven Pinker, Christina Hoff Sommers, Claire Lehmann, Carl Benjamin (a.k.a. Sargon of Akkad – a candidate for UKIP in the 2019 EU elections) and Maajid Nawaz of Quilliam, who coined the term 'regressive left'; academics including Jordan Peterson, Jonathan Haidt, Eric and Bret Weinstein.[79] Like his brother Eric, biology Professor Bret Weinstein, who identifies as left-wing and progressive, played an important role in the IDW and wider intellectual backlash. In 2017, he opposed a change to the Day of Absence at Evergreen State College in Washington. Traditionally, this day, named after the play *Day of Absence* by Douglas Turner Ward, saw black and other racialised students staying home in a type of walkout or strike. The change in 2017 would mean that instead, white staff and students would stay off campus. Weinstein's opposition to this led to student protests against him and the wider issue of racism on campus, demands that he be fired, and a confrontation. Weinstein and his wife Heather Heying, also a faculty member at Evergreen, launched a lawsuit against the college and eventually resigned.[80] His case became an IDW cause célèbre and he made the rounds on various podcasts, including those of Sam Harris and Joe Rogan, discussing his experience, free speech, identity politics and the state of the left. In addition to their individual podcasts and online platforms, IDW and wider reactionary intellectuals use other platforms, including *Quillette,* which is also present and active in the UK, Canada and Australia as well. *Quillette* was founded by Lehmann, amongst others, who is editor along with Toby Young of *The Spectator.* According to *Quillette*'s website: '*Quillette* is a platform for free thought. We respect ideas, even dangerous ones. We also believe that free expression and the free exchange of ideas help human societies flourish and progress. *Quillette* aims to provide a platform for this exchange'.

Much of this reactionary discourse blames the left, and particularly on university campuses and their role in creating generations of

---

79   Ibid. See also Winter, 'Online Hate'.
80   Scott Jaschik, 'Who Defines What Is Racist?', *Inside Higher Ed,* 30 May 2017; Scott Jaschik, 'Evergreen Calls Off "Day of Absence"', *Inside Higher Ed,* 22 February 2018.

'snowflakes'. This claim was highlighted by the Evergreen case and central to *The Coddling of the American Mind*, written by liberal Jonathan Haidt and his co-author Greg Lukianoff.[81] The book attacks the alleged illiberalism of left-wing university culture and education, and validated the notion that student politics regarding racism, sexism, homophobia and transphobia are a product of weakness, fear and offence. It argues that this is a product of cultural decline, rather than an analysis reflecting a real engagement with politics and experience. The same year saw the publication of liberal Mark Lilla's *The Once and Future Liberal: After Identity Politics*, which criticised identity politics as divisive, calling it 'a pseudo-politics of self-regard and increasingly narrow and exclusionary self-definition that is now cultivated in our colleges and universities'.[82] These texts are part of a broader attack on higher education which has witnessed campaigns such as the Foundation for Individual Rights in Education (FIRE), with its Campus Rights initiative and Campus Reform and Professor Watchlist. Various academics have attempted to prove the conspiracy, and to delegitimise so-called identity politics and social-justice scholarship. A notable example of this was the 'Grievance Studies' (a.k.a. 'Sokal Squared') hoax, in which American and British academics James Lindsay, Peter Boghossian and Helen Pluckrose wrote fake papers and submitted them to academic journals focusing on gender and sexuality, as well as fat and race studies.[83] Boghossian and Lindsay published *How to Have Impossible Conversations: A Very Practical Guide* in 2019,[84] and the former has appeared and collaborated with Stefan Molyneux, who trades in race science and 'race realism'.[85] Molyneux has also appeared on the more mainstream *Rubin Report* and *Joe Rogan Experience*.

---

81   Greg Lukianoff and Jonathan Haidt, *The Coddling of the American Mind: How Good Intentions and Bad Ideas Are Setting Up a Generation for Failure* (New York: Penguin, 2018).

82   Mark Lilla, *The Once and Future Liberal: After Identity Politics* (New York: HarperCollins, 2017).

83   Daniel Engber, 'What the "Grievance Studies" Hoax Actually Reveals', slate.com, 5 October 2018.

84   Peter Boghossian and James Lindsay, *How to Have Impossible Conversations: A Very Practical Guide* (Cambridge: Da Capo, 2019).

85   Zack Beauchamp, 'The controversy around hoax studies in critical theory, explained', *Vox*, 15 October 2018; Southern Poverty Law Center, 'Stefan Molyneux', *Southern Poverty Law Center*.

It is in the context of the culture war within higher education that Peterson, a professor of psychology at the University of Toronto, came to prominence and infamy in 2016, when he opposed the legal obligation to use preferred pronouns for transgender people. He challenged Bill C16, an amendment to the Canadian Human Rights Act and Criminal Code designed to protect transgender people from hate propaganda and discrimination by federally regulated institutions.[86] While Peterson is decidedly illiberal in respect to gender, sexuality and race, his liberalism asserts itself in his objection to these legislative changes in terms of his right to free speech. He sees these as part of a wider force of social justice, identity politics and so-called 'post-modern Neo-Marxist cult ideology'.[87] He argues this trend represents an attack on western civilisation, which, in its opposition to identity politics, can be read as code for white European:

> And so since the 1970s, under the guise of postmodernism, we've seen the rapid expansion of identity politics throughout the universities, it's come to dominate all of the humanities – which are dead as far as I can tell – and a huge proportion of the social sciences ... We've been publicly funding extremely radical, postmodern leftist thinkers who are hellbent on demolishing the fundamental substructure of Western civilization.[88]

In terms of race, Peterson opposes the concepts of structural racism and white privilege, advocating instead 'majority privilege' and 'culture' as natural and positive.

> Is that white privilege, or is that, like majority privilege? ... and if it's majority privilege, isn't that just part of living within your culture? ... Why would you bother building the damn thing if it didn't accrue

---

86 Parliament of Canada, Bill C-16, First Session, Forty-second Parliament, House of Commons, 16 May 2016.

87 Benjamin Doxtdator, 'Why Does Jordan Peterson Resonate with White Supremacists?' longviewoneducation.org, 14 April 2018.

88 Joshua Philipp, 'Jordan Peterson Exposes the Postmodernist Agenda', *Epoch Times*, 21 June 2017.

benefits to you? Well, you might say one of the consequences is that it accrues fewer benefits to those who aren't in the culture. Yeah, but you can't immediately associate that with race.[89]

In the end, for Peterson, what is racist is the accusation of racism directed at him: 'being called out on their white privilege, identified with a particular racial group and then made to suffer the consequences of the existence of that racial group and its hypothetical crimes, and that sort of thing has to come to a stop . . . [It's] racist in its extreme.'[90]

The most well-recognised 'liberal' within this trend is Sam Harris, a popular science and philosophy writer, new atheist and co-author, with Maajid Nawaz, of *Islam and the Future of Tolerance: A Dialogue*. For Harris, the left is too quick to take offence and when it comes to 'discussing' race: 'There's a culture of censorship and identity politics and a kind of addiction to being outraged – and a resort to outrage in place of reasoned argument, especially among young people – that is making it impossible to have productive conversations on important topics.'[91] Instead of offering evidence to support his claims, however, he assumes his own allegations to validate themselves, like many in the IDW: 'The fact that I've been worried about speaking about these issues in public was also bothering me. In fact, the implications of speaking about race in particular caused me to cancel a book contract I had last year.'[92]

Nothing better exemplifies the liberal and conservative discourses about racism being in the past, and the individualisation of both racism and responsibility, as well as black people being blamed for their failure to 'get over it', than this contribution from former Breitbart contributor, *Daily Wire* editor and podcaster Ben Shapiro:

So I want to go briefly through a couple of the intersectional hierarchy groups, people who feel that they are victims in American

89   David Marcus, 'What Jordan Peterson Gets Wrong – and Right – About White Privilege', *Federalist*, 31 January 2018.

90   Aaron Bandler, 'EXCLUSIVE: Q&A with Prof. Jordan Peterson on Genderless Pronouns and the Left's "PC Game"', *Daily Wire*, 4 November 2016.

91   Sam Harris, 'Racism and Violence in America: Podcast Transcript', samharris. org, 30 August 2016.

92   Ibid.

society and explain why you are not, in fact, a victim; why you need to take control of your own life and become an adult . . . How about the idea that if you're black in America there's a white supremacist hierarchy that is keeping you down? . . . Of course. Slavery, Jim Crow. Awful, evil treatment at the hands of awful, evil people . . . We all get that. But that's not what we're talking about. Now we're talking about now . . . You cannot fix past injustices with current injustices. The only way to fix past injustices is with individual freedom. That's it.[93]

Shapiro is the author of the 2004 book *Brainwashed: How Universities Indoctrinate America's Youth*, which helped lay the groundwork not only for his media career, but also for the current backlash – particularly in its focus on universities. This was followed by, among others, the book *Bullies: How the Left's Culture of Fear and Intimidation Silences Americans* (2013), and his celebration and defence of the west, *The Right Side of History: How Reason and Moral Purpose Made the West Great* (2019).[94] While Shapiro is an avowed conservative, Dave Rubin, presenter of *The Rubin Report*, had originally given the movement its progressive legitimacy as a reformed left-progressive who had seen the light. One of the difficulties with using the term 'liberalism' is that, in the US, 'liberal' has historically been used by the right to describe those allegedly on the left. In some cases, it has also been used by liberals who thought they were on the left to describe themselves. In the context of the backlash we are exploring here, it is a term used both by the right and by liberals (Lilla, Rubin and John Gray) to attack the left for having allegedly abandoned the liberalism they regard as having defined it in favour of an illiberal turn (particularly on free speech). In the case of Rubin, his politics were initially centrist as opposed to left-wing.

---

93   Ben Shapiro, 'Ben Shapiro: Teaching Minorities They Are Perpetual Victims is False, Backward, and Hurts Them', realclearpolitics.com, 16 September 2017.

94   Ben Shapiro, *Brainwashed: How Universities Indoctrinate America's Youth* (Nashville: Thomas Nelson, 2004); Ben Shapiro, *Bullies: How the Left's Culture of Fear and Intimidation Silences Americans* (New York: Threshold, 2013); Ben Shapiro, *The Right Side of History: How Reason and Moral Purpose Made the West Great* (New York: Broadside, 2019).

In reference to trigger warnings and no-platforming, with a nod to colour-blind politics, Rubin announced:

> I can no longer call myself a progressive . . . I don't really call myself a Democrat either. I'm a classical liberal, a free thinker, and as much as I don't like to admit it, defending my liberal values has suddenly become a conservative position . . . So, if you think people should be able to say what they think without being punished for it; that people should be judged by their behavior, not their skin color; and that people should be able to live the way that they want to live, without government interference, then there's not much left on the left for you.[95]

The IDW overlaps with alt-lite figures such as Yiannopoulos, Steve Bannon and Breitbart generally, with Rebel Media (now Rebel News) Canadians Stefan Molyneux, Lauren Southern and Gavin McInness of The Proud Boys, and with the illiberal alt-right more broadly. Yiannopoulos made his name trolling videogame reviewers who challenged the sexism and racism in games and gamer culture during the 'Gamergate' controversy of 2014. He eventually branched out as an anti-feminist, anti-trans, anti-Muslim free-speech activist, deploying these positions, as well as his gay identity and black boyfriend, as signifiers for liberalism. In 2017, he launched his 'Dangerous Faggot' tour across US universities, including the highly symbolic Berkeley campus, which resulted in counter-protests and violence that he attributed to the left.

While many of these figures claim to be 'classical liberals', they usually gravitate around libertarian, conservative and even the far right. The situation is different with Bill Maher, host of HBO's *Real Time*, who has been a key figure in the legitimisation of racism among liberals in the wider population, particularly in the form of Islamophobia. Both he and Harris are proponents of what has been called the 'new liberal Islamophobia' in the media.[96] In fact, a 2014

---

95   Aaron Bandler, 'Rubin: Why I Left the Left', *Daily Wire*, 11 February 2017.

96   Sonali Kolhatkar, 'The Rise of the New, Liberal Islamophobia', *Common Dreams*, 10 October 2014.

debate between Sam Harris and Ben Affleck on *Real Time*, where Affleck accused the other two of Islamophobia was an important turning point that informed the emergence and mobilisation of the IDW and the wider reactionary backlash.

According to Maher, 'Islam is the only religion that acts like the mafia that will fucking kill you if you say the wrong thing . . . If vast numbers of Muslims across the world believe – and they do – that humans deserve to die for merely holding a different idea or drawing a cartoon or writing a book or eloping with the wrong person, not only does the Muslim world have something in common with Isis. It has too much in common with Isis.'[97]

Maher has been extremely successful at separating anti-Muslim sentiment from the right, instead focusing his critique of Islam on issues of free speech, women's and LGBTQ+ rights, although often it would be limited to lesbian or gay rights. In response to accusations of Islamophobia following the Harris and Affleck debate, Maher proclaimed in his defence, 'We're liberals! We're liberals. We're not crazy tea-baggers'.[98] In addition to making Islamophobia acceptable to liberals and alienating the right, despite their Islamophobia, Maher has also attacked liberals for their lack of opposition to Islam:

> It amazes me how here in America we go nuts over the tiniest violations of these values while gross atrocities are ignored across the world. To count yourself as a liberal, you have to stand up for liberal principles: Free speech, separation of church and state, freedom to practice any religion *or* no religion without the threat of violence. Respect for minorities including homosexuals, equality for women.[99]

In the wake of Trumpism, *Salon*'s Jeffrey Tayler called for people to 'follow Bill Maher's lead, not Donald Trump: There's a way to critique ideology behind religion without resorting to hate', ignoring the fact that

---

97   Raya Jalabi, 'A history of the Bill Maher's 'not bigoted' remarks on Islam', *Guardian*, 7 October 2014.

98   Ibid.

99   Ian Schwartz, 'Maher Rips Liberals over Islam: "If We're Giving No Quarter to Intolerance, Shouldn't We Start with Honor Killers?"', realclearpolitics.com, 27 September 2014.

both targeted the same group, that the liberal version made Islamophobia acceptable, and that Maher would play host to Yiannopoulos and Bannon.[100] It is worth noting that in 2019, Trump's own son Donald Jr. would try to get in on the action with the publication of *Triggered: How the Left Thrives on Hate and Wants to Silence Us*.[101]

While those associated with the IDW sees themselves as an intellectual vanguard – most notably, Peterson on gender, Haidt on free speech, Harris on Islam – a separate trend has helped to provide sociological validation for the white nationalism of the Trump era. Two prominent figures who have lent credibility to these ideas are J. D. Vance and Arlie Russell Hochschild. Vance argues that, in order to understand Trump's electoral success, one must look at the economic and cultural crisis of the white working class and underclass in rural America.[102] For her part, Hochschild foregrounds issues of race, gender and sexuality: 'To white, native-born, heterosexual men . . . [Trump] offered a solution to the dilemma they had long faced as the "left-behinds" of the 1960s and 1970s celebration of other identities.'[103] As Gurminder Bhambra has observed, 'methodological whiteness' has distorted social-scientific analysis of Brexit and the Trump phenomenon: 'The politics of both campaigns was also echoed in those social scientific analyses that sought to focus on the "legitimate" claims of the "left behind" or those who had come to see themselves as "strangers in their own land", as Hochschild phrases it, both racialised as white.'[104] This, we argue, represents an acceptance and legitimisation of the narrative and political claim of loss, disenfranchisement and victimisation, but also of entitlement. In turn, it legitimises the white nationalism and racism underpinning

---

100   Dean Obeidallah, 'Bill Maher's Shameful Mainstreaming of Yiannopoulos' Hate', CNN, 20 February 2017.

101   Donald Trump Jr, *Triggered: How the Left Thrives on Hate and Wants to Silence Us* (New York: Center Street Books, 2019).

102   J. D. Vance, *Hillbilly Elegy: A Memoir of a Family and Culture in Crisis* (London: Harper, 2017).

103   Arlie R. Hochschild, *Strangers in Their Own Land: Anger and Mourning on the American Right* (New York: New Press, 2016).

104   Gurminder Bhambra, 'Brexit, Trump, and 'Methodological Whiteness': On the Misrecognition of Race and Class', *British Journal of Sociology: Special Issue – The Trump/Brexit Moment: Causes and Consequences* 68: S1 (2017), pp. S214–S232.

and flowing from it. This trend in academia is not new. As Mike Hill suggested in 2004,

> Recent scholarship on race has increasingly turned to the historical pressures now besetting the fiction Americans still insist on calling the white race. In doing so, it has marked the same attention to whiteness that made it possible for [American Renaissance's] men to echo, if not exactly endorse, the reckless claim that whiteness in the United States is effectively leaving the country.[105]

France's reactionary intellectual class

France has a long history of reactionary thinkers. From Arthur de Gobineau to Charles Maurras and Edouard Drumont, French intellectuals played a key role in shaping and legitimising racist theories, many taking an active part in the political arena, whether through their writing or organisations. While this tradition of reactionary intellectualism has often been eclipsed by the equally strong history of radical and revolutionary intellectuals, who seem to have prevailed in the public imagination, it has been argued that May 1968 had a dramatic impact on the status of the French intellectual. Despite often being seen as marking a left-wing moment, the aftermath of this movement and the slow demise of the communist hypothesis in its Soviet form led to the end of the prominent role enjoyed by engaged intellectuals on the left. This did not signal the end of intellectuals altogether; the French media continues to give them a prominent place, many being household names. Yet it did facilitate the rise of a new group: the *nouveaux philosophes*. In 1977, Gilles Deleuze highlighted a trend among these right-wing intellectuals which has only worsened since then:

> They had introduced in France literary or philosophical marketing . . . we must talk about a book and make people talk about it, more than the book itself talks or says anything. Up to a point, the aim is that the

---

105   Mike Hill, *After Whiteness: Unmaking an American Majority* (New York: New York University Press, 2004), p. 9.

multitude of newspaper articles, interviews, conferences and radio and TV appearances replace the book which might as well not even exist.[106]

The changing role of the media, with its growing focus on quick gratification and entertainment, has provided opportunistic actors with platforms to spread simplistic and polemical ideas. While a number of left-wing thinkers remain prominent in France, they have been outdone by right-wing pundits.[107] These self-described 'taboo-breakers' are everywhere – on television, in newspapers, on social media; yet they often claim to be subject to the diktat of the left and of political correctness. At times, their strategies match those of the nineteenth century: while anti-Semitic tropes have taken a back seat, Islamophobia – deployed against Muslims and anyone deemed to be their allies – have become the new enemy within.[108] Unlike during the nineteenth century, though, the new scapegoats are no longer able to rely on powerful allies or strong left-wing movements to counter the tide moving against them, despite claims on the right that a cultural hegemony persists that is led by *islamo-gauchistes* ('Islamo-leftists') who supposedly censor any dissenting voices. As former left-wing philosopher Michel Onfray declared on a very popular show on public television in 2015, without a hint of irony: 'Islam is a topic that we cannot talk about.'

Exactly thirty years previously, the right-wing *Figaro* magazine asked on its front page: 'Will We Still Be French in Thirty Years?' – a

---

106   Gilles Deleuze, 'Entretien sur les nouveaux philosophes', *Minuit* 24 (1977). Our translation.

107   See, for example, Sébastien Fontenelle, Mona Chollet, Olivier Cyran and Laurence De Cock, *Les éditocrates 2* (Paris: La Découverte, 2018); Sébastien Fontenelle, Mona Chollet, Olivier Cyran and Mathias Reymond, *Les éditocrates: Ou comment parler de (presque) tout en racontant (vraiment) n'importe quoi* (Paris: La Découverte, 2009); Pascal Boniface, *Les intellectuels faussaires: Le triomphe médiatique des experts en mensonge* (Paris: JC Gawsevitch, 2011); Sébastien Fontenelle, *Les briseurs de tabous: Intellectuels et journalistes 'anticonformistes' au service de l'ordre dominant* (Paris: La Découverte, 2009); Pascal Durand and Sarah Sindaco, eds, *Le discours 'néo-réactionnaire'* (Paris: CNRS Editions, 2015); William Blanc, Aurore Chéry and Christophe Naudin, *Les historiens de garde* (Paris: Libertalia, 2016).

108   For an excellent overview, see Gérard Noiriel, *Le Venin dans la plume* (Paris: La Découverte). See also, Julien Cassagne, 'On ne peut rien dire sur l'islam!' *OrientXXI* 27 (December 2018).

veiled Marianne hinting at the creeping Islamisation of the Republic. Since then, countless special issues of magazines, opinion pieces, television and radio shows and books published by mainstream publishers have saturated public discourse to warn us that; we can no longer talk about Islam! In contrast, the diverse Muslim communities in France have hardly any access to this public discourse, but somehow pose a unified threat to reactionary pundits. The impact of such public intellectuals is far-reaching. As early as 1989, a letter written by a number of prominent public figures ignited the controversy over the veil, which has since led to the ostracisation of many Muslim women from society and the removal of their agency in the name of forced emancipation. After a high school head-teacher refused entry to three students wearing a hijab, prominent mainstream philosophers Régis Debray, Alain Finkielkraut and Elisabeth Badinter, among others, declared in a mainstream magazine:

> To tolerate the Islamic veil is not to welcome a free being (a young girl in this case), but to open the door to those who have decided, once and for all and without discussion, to make her bow her head. Instead of offering this young girl a space of freedom, you tell her that there is no difference between school and the house of her father. By automatically authorising the Islamic veil, the symbol of female submission, you give free rein to fathers and brothers – that is, the patriarchy, the toughest on Earth. In the end, it is no longer respect for gender equality or free will that is the law in France.[109]

While we do not dispute that the hijab may indeed be used as a tool of patriarchy, and that, for example, we would indeed oppose laws in a country like Saudi Arabia that enforce its wearing, we argue that this letter and its repercussions serve as an example of liberal racism, rather than reflecting a real concern for girls and women. As we already noted, this was very much a non-issue at the time, as most cases were resolved through dialogue and compromise. Furthermore,

---

109   Elisabeth Badinter, Régis Debray, Alain Finkielkraut, Elisabeth de Fontenay and Catherine Kintzler, 'Profs, ne capitulons pas!' *Le Nouvel Observateur*, 2–8 November 1989. Our translation.

this concerned only a small minority of women, some of whom had clearly decided of their own free will to wear the hijab.[110] Yet listening to women was not the aim of the reactionary secularists. In 2003, Badinter declared that the feminist struggle was 'addressed to the women of the first generation of new arrivals, or to the young girls of Maghrebi origin. It is for them it must be led. Frankly, for a long time, in native French society [de souche], whether within Judaism or Catholicism, we cannot say that there is oppression of women.'[111] Sexism in France was thus to be found in the other. As liberticidal laws against Muslim garments were passed, reactionary discourse became increasingly potent. It could now wear the garb of once-progressive ideals which were central to the national narrative.

More recently, one of the most prominent legitimisers of liberal racism has been Eric Zemmour. Starting as a journalist for the right-wing Le Figaro, he later turned to writing and political punditry, providing a reactionary voice in countless mainstream media outlets, from political shows to infotainment. Benefiting from Zemmour's 'shocking' ideas and unapologetic style, producers have provided him with platforms that few commentators could access. Eventually, some publicly declared that they regretted having given so much air-time to him and his ideas; but this was too little, too late. Zemmour's reactionary positions were hardly concealed and in fact developed openly in a number of books. In 2006, he published Le Premier Sexe, a response to Simone de Beauvoir's Le Deuxième Sexe, in which he developed a masculinist argument that has become commonplace today on the far right. For Zemmour, feminism and homosexuality have emasculated the west, which has since been overtaken by a virile other: the Muslim man. We can see here that, while Islam acts as the liberal-racist decoy, the ideological basis of the book is distinctly illiberal. It is despite such racist and sexist arguments that Zemmour has gained increased prominence in recent years.

In late 2014, he published The French Suicide, a 500-page book which tracks the slow demise of France in a fashion reminiscent of traditional far-right theories and strategies, suggesting the need for

---

110   Tévanian, La République du Mépris.
111   Cited in Tévanian, La République du Mépris. Our translation.

rebirth.[112] May 1968 is blamed for having destroyed authority and led to self-hatred. While it was well received by the right-wing press, the book was criticised for pushing an agenda close to that of the Front National, which did not prevent hundreds of thousands of copies of the book to be sold. Academics were quick to point out the many mistakes it contained. Its most telling reactionary component was probably its chapter about Robert Paxton – the American historian who played a major part in the early 1970s in proving beyond doubt that the Vichy government had collaborated willingly and ideologically with Nazi Germany. This was a defining moment in French history and historiography. It forced the French to take a more honest look at their country's role in the Second World War, and dealt a decisive blow to the idea that evil was confined to a particular place and time: Nazi Germany. Reviving widely discarded theories casting General de Gaulle as the sword to Marshal Pétain's shield, Zemmour argued that the Vichy regime had protected the French Jewish population. A similar argument has commonly been deployed in France by the right, in particular with regard to colonialism and the so-called 'culture of repentance', which prevents 'us' from moving forward. Unsurprisingly, part of Zemmour's book purveyed shoddy demographic statistics, exaggerating or misreading data on immigration and its growth.[113] In 2018, Zemmour was found guilty of inciting religious hatred, having declared on television while launching a new book that Muslim people in France should 'choose between Islam and France', among other common Islamophobic tropes. In his view and that of his supporters, Zemmour had merely been using his freedom of speech. At the 2019 European elections, he was offered the opportunity to lead the Rassemblement National (formerly Front National) list – though he declined, feeling that he had more power outside party politics. Zemmour was again found guilty in September 2019 of incitation to religious hatred and offered a spot on a prominent new show on CNews a month later, only for this one to no longer be broadcast live after two weeks of 'faux-pas'

---

112   Eric Zemmour, *Le Suicide Français* (Paris: Albin Michel, 2014).
113   Benoît Bréville, 'Immigration, un débat biaisé' *Le Monde Diplomatique*, November 2018.

(*dérapages*) on topics as diverse as Vichy, Bashar al-Assad and Zemmour's belief that homosexuals should 'sleep with the other sex' if they want children.[114]

In this context, the borders have become increasingly fuzzy between liberal and illiberal racism. Extreme-right intellectuals such as Renaud Camus have since gained access to more mainstream platforms – most notably in the wake of the Christchurch attack, whose perpetrator, Brenton Tarrant, made use of Camus' 'Great Replacement Theory' in the title of his manifesto.

The French case demonstrates that the most vociferous reactionary intellectuals not only complain constantly of being silenced by the hegemonic left, but can also benefit from countless media outlets – whether as a product of ratings opportunism or ideological complicity.[115] Of course, one could argue that we have the media we deserve – that its contents reflect what the public thinks or wants. Yet in our view this is a convenient excuse for those overseeing public discourse to escape their responsibility for the spread of reactionary ideas.

The fuzzy borders between free speech and racism in the UK

In recent years, the UK has also seen the rise of a number of liberal, libertarian and conservative actors and organisations pushing reactionary agendas on the pretext of defending free speech and opposing political correctness. While most also complain of censorship and left-wing cultural hegemony – even invoking the idea of a 'thought police' – they have, as in France and the United States, been afforded powerful platforms by the media, both public and private. This has become particularly pronounced since the terrorist attacks of 7 July 2005, and even more so in the wake of the 2016 Brexit referendum. Islam, immigration and multiculturalism are now easy targets. As in the United States, university campuses have also been increasingly targeted by organisations such as *Spiked!* and its 'Free Speech Now!', 'Free Speech

---

114   LeMonde.fr, 'CNews: L'émission d'Eric Zemmour ne sera plus en direct', *Le Monde*. 29 October. Our translation.

115   Blanc, Chéry and Naudin, *Les historiens de garde*, pp. 133–7.

University Rankings' and 'Down with Campus Censorship' campaigns, and by the Academy of Ideas and its 'Battle of Ideas' conferences and 'Debating Matters' competition for students.[116] On both sides of the Atlantic, racism is consciously quarantined in the past, while anti-racism is not only no longer needed, but actually reactionary, since there is no such thing as racism in our societies. In some cases, racists (as well as transphobes) are defended and championed as necessary to ensure a commitment to classical liberalism and democracy: their platforming becomes a test of the claim that we live in liberal democracies. *Spiked!*, a libertarian website allegedly partly funded by the Koch brothers, has claimed 'Hate speech is free speech', and called for 'Free speech for all – even neo-Nazis'. While this is usually posited as a libertarian stance, we argue that it is reactionary: in our current context it is almost always far and extreme right ideas which are used to test the limits of free speech, while more progressive causes suffering from a lack of coverage or voice are constantly and conveniently ignored, or even attacked.[117]

One of the first mainstream voices to blur the borders between the liberal and illiberal was journalist David Goodhart. In 2004, he was already arguing that multiculturalism had made the UK 'too diverse'.[118] Ten years later, Goodhart was arguing that it was urgent to move on from political correctness – something he articulated in the *Political Quarterly*, a prominent academic publication, clearly demonstrating the censoriousness of academia towards right-wing perspectives. Political correctness had gone mad: 'Racist views in Britain are less common and less acceptable than ever before, yet the word racism pervades the national conversation.'[119] Making use of an increasingly common strategy deployed by mainstream pundits, intellectuals and academics attempting to push reactionary agendas, Goodhart claimed that he was simply speaking for the silent majority:

---

116   For a thorough analysis, see Smith, *No Platform*.

117   For an in-depth analysis of the evolution of this particular section of the contemporary libertarian right in the UK, see Bob From Brockley, 'The RCP's long march from anti-imperialist outsiders to the doors of Downing Street', *BobFromBrockley*, 27 July 2019.

118   David Goodhart, 'Too Diverse?' *Prospect*, 20 February 2004.

119   David Goodhart, 'Racism: Less is More', *Political Quarterly*. 85: 3 (2014), pp. 251–8.

'To describe as racist what many ordinary citizens regard as reasonable anxieties about rapid change is simply wrong, and a cause of great resentment.' The denunciation of racism was creating more racism, and it was thus time to stop and take these anxieties seriously – that is, to concede to them without reservation. It is worth citing Goodhart's article at length here, as it provides a vivid example of the way illiberal racism serves to justify its liberal counterpart:

> So what exactly is 'proper' racism? It is irrational hostility based on race, usually accompanied by a belief in the superiority or inferiority of certain races. Today, the most common form of racism is based around the idea of stereotyping: as I have argued, we all operate with more or less conscious stereotypes much of the time, but a racist stereotype is a distinctive type premised on the assumption of fixed, and usually negative, racial characteristics.
>
> Racism and racist stereotyping, as described above, is either literally illegal or at least illegitimate in British society, unacceptable to Nigel Farage as well as anti-racist activists. Racial equality is part of the common sense of British society, which is not to say it has been achieved.
>
> In trying to compensate for our racist past we have ruled out a proper spectrum in our thinking about prejudice. We need words to describe mild forms of prejudice and stereotyping – words that do not, like racism, conjure up images of slavery, the Holocaust or black men being beaten up in police vans.[120]

This preceded the release of *The Road to Somewhere* (2017), which purported to explain 'the populist revolt and the future of politics'. For Goodhart, mass immigration threatened social solidarity for the 'Somewheres' – those with roots in local communities, in opposition to the rootless, socially liberal, middle-class, cosmopolitan 'Anywheres'.[121] Of course, such ideas are far from original, having been peddled by nationalist and far-right theorists for many years. In

---

120   Ibid. p.255
121   David Goodhart, *The Road to Somewhere: The Populist Revolt and the Future of Politics* (London: Hurst, 2017).

fact, they are not only reminiscent of Enoch Powell, but also of theories developed in the late nineteenth century on 'the soil and the dead', which played a key part in the development of racist theories. As we discuss in Chapter 4, assumptions made on the basis of 'Somewheres' and 'Anywheres' are based on a skewed reading of data, and on nostalgic simplifications that pit the forgotten provincial 'left behind' against affluent, liberal city-dwellers. Suffice to say here, as Joe Kennedy notes in his book *Authentocrats*, 'That poor people live in cities, that many provincial working-class people are left-wing (and, vitally, not white) and that more than a few people in supposedly left-behind constituencies are materially well-off is neither here nor there to them.'[122] In Kennedy's view, these lines have been pushed not only by right-wing pundits, but also by the media, even on the left, whose own pundits demand that liberals get their heads out of the sand and acknowledge racist demands blamed on 'the people'.

Following in Goodhart's footsteps, a number of academics and pundits have begun to tap into such reactionary postures. These academics have secured countless media appearances by simply taking positions contrary to those of most academics and experts, whether on Brexit, free speech, immigration, or even climate change. A striking example of this was the organisation of a debate titled 'Is Rising Ethnic Diversity a Threat to the West?' The question was posited as necessary in addressing the rise of the far right, as opposed to reproducing its language and terms of reference, thus giving it more air-time. The concept of 'the West' seemed to be accepted uncritically – assumed to be ethnically homogenous, and specifically white. The title also suggested that ethnic diversity was rising in a concerning manner, and framed as a 'threat'. This automatically placed some of the most vulnerable minorities under a spotlight that affirmed racist fears, potentially legitimising and emboldening those who nursed them.[123]

The debate was sponsored jointly by *UnHerd* and the Academy of Ideas, often criticised for testing the limits of free speech with

122   Joe Kennedy, *Authentocrats* (London: Penguin Random House, 2018), p. 83.

123   For further detail, see Academics for Meaningful Debate, 'Framing Ethnic Diversity as a "Threat" Will Normalise Far-Right Hate, Say Academics', opendemocracy.net, 12 October 2018.

predominantly right-wing ideas as test cases. Claire Fox, founder of the Academy of Ideas, a former member of the Revolutionary Communist Party and successful candidate for Nigel Farage's Brexit Party in the 2019 EU elections, is a regular panellist on BBC Radio 4's *Moral Maze* and the author of *I STILL Find That Offensive!* The latter is an attack on no-platforming, safe spaces, trigger warnings and what she calls 'Generation Snowflake', reducing protests against speakers to oversensitivity.[124] The other four speakers have similar profiles, in that they speak from positions of power and have all been embroiled in the legitimisation of liberal-racist ideas in the past.[125] Matthew Goodwin and Eric Kaufmann both hold prestigious professorships in political science, at the University of Kent and Birkbeck, University of London, respectively. While they have not reached the celebrity status as free-speech martyrs enjoyed by their North American counterparts, it was telling when Kaufmann light-heartedly joked on Twitter whether they would 'become the next incarnation of the Sam Harris/ Jordan Peterson roadshow'. It was no surprise that this debate took place as both were releasing books with prominent publishers: Goodwin and Roger Eatwell's *National Populism* (Allen Lane) and Kaufmann's *Whiteshift: Populism, Immigration and the Future of White Majorities* (Pelican) came out on the same day, both at bargain prices and with wide distribution. The books pushed similar narratives, entrenching the idea of reactionary democracy in pseudoscientific academic prose: the rise of the far right is a democratic rebellion emerging from the left-behind, and it is only natural that 'white natives' feel threatened by change. As we demonstrate in the following chapters, these books not only hype the phenomenon and demonise the working class through racist assumptions, but participate in the legitimisation of the ideas central to the far right, thus playing a key part in potentially increasing its reach. Providing legitimacy through their status to politics which have for long been marginalised, these books are couched in 'objective', 'scientific' terms, pitting the professors against the 'many writers who claim to be

---

124   Claire Fox, *I STILL Find That Offensive!* (London: Biteback, 2018).
125   Mehdi Hasan, 'Who Needs Tommy Robinson and the EDL, when Islamophobia Has Gone Mainstream?', *New Statesman*, 10 October 2013; Poppy Black, 'Yes, Trevor Phillips: You Can Be Black and a Racist Too', *Guardian*, 27 February 2017.

impartial [but who] also find it hard to avoid being influenced by their own sympathy for liberal and left-wing politics'.[126]

In an article promoting his book, Kaufmann argued in *The NewStatesman* that pandering to latent racist tendencies within white populations was essential to prevent an illiberal turn:

> When whites can't express their sense of ethnic loss, they turn to the seemingly more 'respectable' alternatives of demonising Muslims, criticising immigrants who live in minority neighbourhoods, or voting for Brexit (a result of diverting concerns over ethnic change into hatred of the acceptably 'white' EU). Few things have contributed more to today's populist blowback than the demographic blind spot in Western political thought.[127]

A similar argument is made by liberal philosopher John Gray, who links the rise of populists and the far right to the alleged lack of 'majority control' over their key issue of immigration. He argues that the far right 'will continue its advance across Europe for as long as key policies such as immigration remain removed from majority control'.[128] This is also a critique of classical liberalism and its limitations at the current 'populist' juncture that simultaneously assumes the majority are racist, accepts the far right's declared rationale for its mobilisation, blackmails parties and governments to act under threat of insurgency, and calls for the mainstreaming of racism and the far right. It is also worth noting that Kaufmann's central claim in *Whiteshift*, about white population decline and whites being overtaken demographically, treads closely to typically far right concepts such as the 'Great Replacement'.

National Populism's central claims are along similar lines and based on selective use of data and sources, which ignores much of

---

126   Roger Eatwell and Matthew Goodwin, *National Populism: The Revolt Against Liberal Democracy* (London: Pelican, 2018), p. xiv.

127   Eric Kaufmann, 'White Majorities Feel Threatened in an Age of Mass Migration – and Calling Them Racist Won't Help', *New Statesman*, 17 October 2018.

128   John Gray, 'Deluded Liberals Can't Keep Clinging to a Dead Idea', *UnHerd*, 3 October 2018.

the literature on the topic which would refute its core argument.[129] In the book, racism is limited to the most illiberal acts – something that has been criticised by experts in the field. The creation of new terms by the authors in a field famous for its thorough typological and terminological argumentation further demonstrates a clear ideological attempt to change the narrative. This legitimises these movements through euphemisation ('national populism' instead of radical right, far right, racism, and so on), but also exaggerates their weight.[130] For example, the authors coin the term 'hyper ethnic change' to describe what the 'West' is currently going through, basing their claims on selective demographic surveys and an ignorance of any counterpoint to their ideological claims.[131] This is similar to something that Kaufmann had already advanced in a report for Policy Exchange entitled 'Racial Self-Interest Is Not Racism'.[132] The title itself should have set alarm bells ringing in what is usually considered a centre-right think tank; but in the current climate they apparently regarded this leading tagline as appropriate. Building on Goodhart's work, Kaufmann argues that it is crucial to 'avoid using charges of racism to side-line discussions of ethno-demographic interests' in relation to issues such as opposition to immigration. While this leaves space for the denunciation of the most egregious forms of racism (illiberal articulations), it creates suspicion regarding those less obvious ones, creating ready-made excuses and victimisation narratives to conceal more liberal ones. However, here again, we can see that the borders are fuzzy and can move rapidly: when Noah Carl was dismissed from St Edmund's College at the University of Cambridge following serious concerns raised

---

129   For early reviews by experts in the field, see Daniel Trilling, 'I'm not racist, but . . ', *London Review of Books*, 18 April 2019; David Renton, 'Roger Eatwell and Matthew Goodwin's Race Problem', *LivesRunning*, 1 November 2018; and Martin Shaw, 'Going Native: Populist Academics Normalise the Anti-Immigrant Right', politics.co.uk, 31 October 2018.

130   For more on the process of euphemisation, see Katy Brown, Aurelien Mondon and Aaron Winter, '"Populist" can be a weasel word for "racist"', *Open Democracy*, 16 October 2019.

131   Sabrina Tavernise, 'Why the Announcement of a Looming White Minority Makes Demographers Nervous', *New York Times*, 22 November 2018.

132   Eric Kaufmann, '"Racial Self-Interest" Is Not Racism', *Policy Exchange*, 3 March 2017.

regarding his research on race and intelligence as well as his attendance to the London Conference on Intelligence, which was accused to platform eugenics, both Kaufmann and Goodwin came to his defence, denouncing 'mob' rule and attacks on free speech.[133]

These are only a few examples of actors who have use their status and access to public platforms to apply a veneer of legitimacy to far-right ideas, whether for ideological or opportunistic reasons, consciously or not.

CONCLUSION: FUZZY BORDERS

Liberal racism is based on the premise that it is not racism. In this narrative, racism has been conquered – thanks to liberalism – or is framed as illiberal, pathological and individual. However, as demonstrated throughout this chapter, the borders between illiberal and liberal racism are fuzzy, and the mask often slips. As we have seen, liberalism is no stranger to racism, whether historically or systemically, but there are also many instances in which illiberalism has been mainstreamed by liberal individuals and organisations. We argue that this takes place through a three-step process: 1. The promotion and platforming of racist, illiberal, extreme ideas and actors (even as just a test case), and the creation of false equivalences between racist and anti-racist positions; 2. The emboldening of the far right; 3. The legitimisation and mainstreaming of far-right ideas and of far right itself. We see this blurring in the French context in the form of liberal 'femonationalism' being used to justify the bans on the hijab and burka, and the perverse reaction to the *Charlie Hebdo* attack giving rise to both liberal racism and increased illiberal securitisation. In the United States, liberal Islamophobia has legitimised a Muslim travel ban, hate crimes and far-right violence. For example, Milo Yiannopoulos's 'free speech' activism, characterised by Islamophobia, and his platform at Breitbart allowed him to move

---

133 Nicola Woolcock, 'Academics defend racism row scholar Noah Carl', *The Times*, 2 May 2019.

between the mainstream media, the IDW, alt-lite and alt-right, but also provided him with a variety of prominent international platforms and invitations. The convergence also became clear when Bill Maher hosted Yiannopoulos on *Real Time* on 17 February 2017. The two bonded, despite their different opinions on Trump, over their shared Islamophobia. In the interview, Yiannopoulos complimented Maher, saying, 'You're sound on Islam, unlike most people on your show', to which Maher responded, 'Yes, that's true.'[134] Another example is that of Charles Murray, co-author of *The Bell Curve*, who has been championed by the IDW and alt-lite as a fellow victim or martyr of political correctness and SJWs. His supporters argued that this was confirmed when his speech at Middlebury College in May 2017 was violently protested and shut down by students.[135] The attempt to resuscitate Murray's career and reputation is also linked to an attempt to revive illiberal race and gender science and positivism, as exemplified by the London Conference on Intelligence, secretly held at University College London, and attended by Toby Young and Noah Carl amongst others.[136] This is usually done in order to naturalise inequalities in opposition to Marxism, social constructionism, feminism, critical race theory and 'postmodernism' and so-called SJWs.[137] This trend is represented and advocated particularly by Jordan Peterson, a psychologist, and Sam Harris, a neuroscientist who hosted Murray on his podcast. It exposes the illiberalism underpinning their shared liberal pretence. In the UK, we saw former Prime Minister David Cameron's 'muscular liberalism' leading the attack on multiculturalism,[138] and his government launch the illiberal 'Go Home Vans' targeting immigrants. This occurred under the watch of Home Secretary Theresa May, who as PM, called for the

---

134   Obeidallah, 'Bill Maher's Shameful Mainstreaming of Yiannopoulos' Hate'.

135   Stephanie Saul, 'Dozens of Middlebury Students Are Disciplined for Charles Murray Protest', *New York Times*, 24 May 2017; Ezra Klein, 'Sam Harris, Charles Murray, and the Allure of Race Science', vox.com, 27 March 2018.

136   Kevin Rawlinson and Richard Adams, 'UCL to investigate eugenics conference secretly held on campus', *Guardian*, 11 January 2018.

137   See Saini, 'Why Race Science Is On the Rise Again' and Saini, *Superior*.

138   David Cameron, 'State Multiculturalism Has Failed, Says David Cameron', BBC News, 5 February 2011.

creation of an illiberal 'hostile environment' for immigrants and refugees, something we discuss further in Chapter 3.[139]

In this chapter, we have demonstrated that racism can be articulated in various ways, and that it can sometimes recruit clearly liberal, or even progressive discourses. Yet we argue that these are two sides of the same coin, rather than opposed or acting independently. It is only because illiberal racism can be denounced and easily recognised by the mainstream that the mainstream can justify its own articulation of racism: How can we be racist when we denounce the *real* racists? This limitation of racism to illiberal acts and discourses has been extremely prevalent in mainstream elite discourse, and has precipitated a misunderstanding of the ways in which racism continues to reign systemically, and of the ways in which it can be adapted discursively.

We argue that this ignorance has in turn facilitated the return of illiberal racist discourses, and fuelled more obvious racist acts, such as the Christchurch attack, whose perpetrator had clearly been influenced by both liberal and illiberal racist discourses, as demonstrated by his manifesto. Since the mainstream has failed to tackle the racism in its midst, it has been possible for the reconstructed far right, with the help of its opportunistic mainstream elite allies, to harness liberal racism to push an increasingly radical agenda. It is thus not surprising that the mask often slips, and that liberal racism can quickly turn illiberal. Indeed, actors themselves sometimes appear to be caught unaware, as during the so-called debate on rising ethnic diversity as a threat to the west. While it was very quickly recognised amongst colleagues as demonstrated in the public letter signed by over 200 experts that the terms of the debate echoed racist assumptions, whether consciously or not, it was telling that it took such public pressure for the title to be changed.[140] Goodwin and Kaufmann later

---

139 For more on the Go Home Vans, and British anti-immigration policies and state racism in this context, see Hannah Jones, Yasmin Gunaratnam, Gargi Bhattacharyya, William Davies, Sukhwant Dhaliwal, Kirsten Forkert, Emma Jackson and Roiyah Saltus, *Go Home? The Politics of Immigration Controversies* (Manchester: Manchester University Press, 2017); Nira Yuval-Davis, Georgie Wemyss and Kathryn Cassidy, *Bordering* (Cambridge: Polity, 2019); Maya Goodfellow, *Hostile Environment: How Immigrants Became Scapegoats* (London: Verso, 2019).

140 Academics for Meaningful Debate, 'Framing Ethnic Diversity as a "Threat" Will Normalise Far-Right Hate, Say Academics'.

complained while they 'are all for robust debate', more than 200 experts in the field voicing concerns amounted to a 'brand of anti-intellectualism'. This response was published in *Quillette* and generated a number of extremely violent comments against signatories to the OpenDemocracy letter.[141]

It is to this process of mainstreaming that we will now turn, as we illustrate more precisely how racism navigates between the extreme and the mainstream.

---

141   Matthew Goodwin and Eric Kaufmann, 'What Happened When We Tried to Debate Immigration', *Quillette*, 8 December 2018.

CHAPTER THREE

Mainstreaming the Far Right or Radicalising the Mainstream?

A NEW NORMAL? THE MAINSTREAM'S FLUID POSITION

So far, we have looked at the way racism and the extreme and far right have evolved in the late twentieth and early twenty-first century. We outlined the interaction between the liberal and illiberal articulations of racism, and how they have acted as mutually enabling, if not as two sides of the same coin: apparently opposed, yet indivisible. This may be best illustrated in the ways in which the post-war hegemony of liberal democracy has delimited the illiberal extreme right as the evil remnants of the old racist order, in opposition to the contemporary post-racial context. This has led to the marginalisation of racism and the extreme right in their more traditional forms, but also to the evolution of the discourse on the far right, with racism now hidden behind liberal themes such as free speech and gender and LGBTQ+ rights. In the end, we argue, this has paved the way for the eventual mainstreaming of racism and the far right, but also for the radicalisation of the mainstream itself. In this chapter, our aim is to outline the process which has allowed racism to (re)gain legitimacy, and eventually (re)enter the mainstream. We do not argue that racism ever disappeared, or even that it was relegated to the margins of society, but only that its most obvious forms had been marginalised and whitewashed within public discourse. It had become absent from our imaginary, except in its extreme forms – used to reassure us that we are indeed post-racial.

THE MAINSTREAM AND MAINSTREAMING

Many books and articles have focused on the ways the discourse of parties and movements once considered toxic has evolved or been adapted: 'From the margins to the mainstream' has become a popular refrain since the late 1990s and early 2000s.[1] These texts recognise how such parties have embraced more acceptable forms of scapegoating and exclusion. However, such analyses not only often maintain the traditional hegemonic logic that these elements represent a threat to liberal democracy, but also internalise a limiting framework in defence of the status quo – for example, it is fascinating to see how the term 'racism' has become almost absent from studies of the far right in political science. While studies in the field have proliferated tremendously, the mainstream reaction to the resurgence of racist politics has received less attention. We argue that enquiry on this point is essential to understanding how far what is considered mainstream may have moved over time. This raises the issue of the hegemonic status and contingent nature of the concept of 'mainstream', as well as whether the distinction between the mainstream and far right that so much of the post-war and especially post-1960s narrative has depended upon remains valid and necessary. While the concepts of 'mainstream' and 'mainstreaming' have become commonplace, they have seldom been defined by experts on the topic. For example, in the introduction to the edited collection *The Politics of the Extreme Right: From the Margins to the Mainstream*, Paul Hainsworth provides an excellent definition of the 'extreme right', as well as a clear outline of its resurgence after a period of defeat and decline in the post-war period, with a particular focus on electoral support.[2] The concept and process of mainstreaming remains far less well developed, however.

Defining the mainstream is itself a challenge, because of its contingency (as a descriptive and normative term), and its status as a functional floating signifier: it may refer to elements of society and politics (the government, media, parties, policies or discourses) or simply reflect the subjective positioning of experts. While most of us will feel we have a clear idea of what is mainstream, and position ourselves (and

---

1   See, for example, Paul Hainsworth, *The Politics of the Extreme Right: From the Margins to the Mainstream* (London: Continuum, 2000); and, more recently, Tjitske Akkerman, Sarah L. de Lange and Matthijs Rooduijn, eds, *Radical Right-Wing Populist Parties in Western Europe: Into the Mainstream?* (London: Routledge: 2016).

2   Hainsworth, *Politics of the Extreme Right*; Aaron Winter, 'The Politics of the Extreme Right: From the Margins and the Mainstream', *Journal of Ethnic and Migration Studies* 4: 28 (2002).

others) according to how we see ourselves (or others) in relation to it – whether to accept or contest it, belong to it or rebel against it – it is much harder to actually pin down precisely what and where it is. In this chapter, we unpack its use and function, and attempt to (however contingently) define it for the purpose of our argument.

When we think about politics and democracy today, our attention is often limited to elections. We would describe this process as institutional or electoral politics. This is opposed to more discursive forms of politics, in which ideas, concepts and ideologies more broadly get challenged, recomposed, destroyed or mainstreamed. Of course, the two do not work in isolation from one another, but are deeply intertwined. However, it is necessary to understand each in its own terms. Electoral politics is easier to describe, and would broadly relate to the rules and norms of liberal (capitalist) democracy. Its parameters are broadly based on the primacy of elections (though electoral systems differ from one case to another), the rule of law, and the protection of private property. While each of these elements may be defended or infringed more or less frequently and easily, they reflect the basic rules of politics in western societies, and are widely accepted as norms. What counts as politically acceptable, what challenges and changes are possible within the bounds of this contingent normality and the terms and processes through which they can be legitimately pursued – all of these are thus generally limited by this hegemonic framework. It is therefore not surprising that much of the scholarly work about the mainstreaming of the far right in Europe in the 1990s and 2000s, when its resurgence began, was based on mainstreaming through elections, in which far-right parties were the focus and the threat.

Yet focusing solely on parties and electoral politics risks underestimating certain phenomena, while exaggerating others. For example, a focus on electoral results may lead to the exaggeration or misinterpretation of the power of far-right parties. In 2014, the strong performance of far-right parties in the EU elections in France, the UK and Denmark obscured the fact that far-right parties in other countries performed unevenly, thus negating the idea of a 'populist rise' across Europe. The coverage also mostly ignored the huge rates of abstention, typical of such second-order elections. Attending to the difference between the number of votes cast and the number of registered voters draws an entirely different picture (Figs 3.1, 3.2). This difference is particularly striking among working-class voters, of whom up to two-thirds can abstain in these elections.

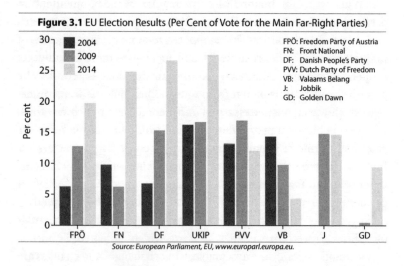

Figure 3.1 EU Election Results (Per Cent of Vote for the Main Far-Right Parties)

Source: European Parliament, EU, www.europarl.europa.eu.

Figure 3.2 EU Election Results (Per Cent of Registered Voters for the Main Far-Right Parties)

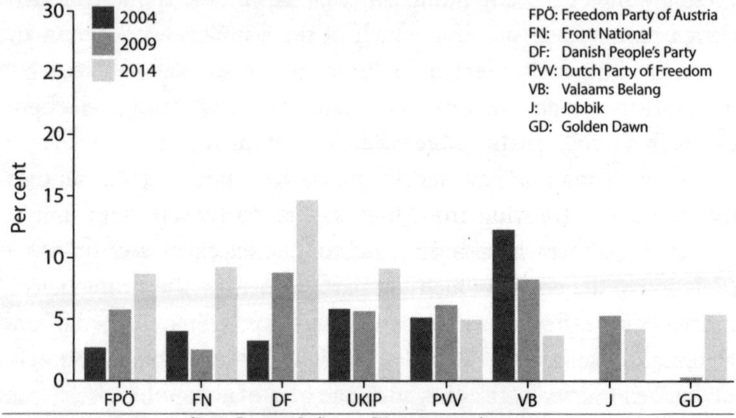

Source: European Parliament, EU, www.europarl.europa.eu.

Uncritical electoral analysis may also lead to a complacent attitude when these parties recede in the polls despite their ideas continuing to be mainstreamed, as was the case in France in 2007. As discussed in Chapter 1, when the Front National (FN) collapsed in 2007, Marine Le Pen saw it as a victory for her ideas, which had been swallowed up by the mainstream – and by the Sarkozy candidacy in particular. UKIP faced a similar fate after the Brexit victory. Nigel Farage, who was sidelined by the Tory government when seeking a role as ambassador or Brexit negotiator, was only too happy to say, as he stood down from the party leadership: 'The Ukippers will have been the turkeys who voted for Christmas.' In the United States, while the alt-right has remained electorally irrelevant, the prominence their discourse achieved through Trump's candidacy and election has been dramatic. White-nationalist figures such as Richard Spencer and Jason Kessler gained mainstream media platforms, including on liberal NPR, in the latter's case. Unlike in our other cases, Trump has not only sent them positive signals with his rhetoric and policies, but refused to condemn them when they have been associated with intimidation and violence.

While there is little work on the impact of the far right on the mainstream itself, and the construction of both the extreme and far right has historically been dependent on the concept of the mainstream (and vice versa), the mainstreaming of the far right has attracted increasing attention from researchers. This is partly because, despite their disruptive, rebellious and insurgent rhetoric and posturing – and in some cases 'unacceptable' racist and xenophobic ideologies and politics – many of these parties nonetheless accept the terms of the mainstream liberal-democratic system in the process of their reconstruction (moving from the extreme to the far right, in our framework). There have been a number of excellent and thorough analyses on the way in which far-right parties and movements have evolved discursively, and how this has at times been mistaken for ideological evolution away from racism and towards more palatable, albeit blurry forms of politics, such as populism.[3]

---

3 Analysis of the normalisation of the Front National has been particularly well developed because of the longevity of the party. For one of the most influential accounts, see

Too often, however, this mainstreaming has been studied as a one-way process in which the far right moves closer to the mainstream, whether ideologically, institutionally or discursively. This has been particularly true within political science, where psephology has become the most popular benchmark for research, and has thus limited the field of politics to discussion of elections and opinion surveys. For example, in a worthwhile attempt to create some clarity around the term, Tjitske Akkerman, Sarah de Lange and Matthijs Rooduijn focus on mainstreaming as 'a process in which radical parties change to become more like mainstream parties'. Their approach focused exclusively on electoral politics, and thus defined the mainstream and far right based on the composition and platforms of political parties, with 'radical right-wing populist parties [being] at once radical parties, niche parties and anti-establishment parties'.[4] Their analysis of mainstreaming is thus centred on the actions taken by the far-right parties themselves in an active attempt to move away from their radical positions and niche appeal. Yet the authors also clearly acknowledge that, while parties are 'actors that set goals and make strategic choices . . . their array of choices is defined by external and internal factors'. Other studies have relied on opinion surveys to demonstrate how public opinion has led the change, and how support for far-right parties highlights a latent social demand which has been (re)activated and should thus be addressed by mainstream politicians. Some analysis based on opinion surveys has taken the shape of the flawed 'left-behind' argument, which we discuss further in this chapter. This has had a dramatic impact on the process of mainstreaming, as it has legitimised key far-right concerns and turned them into popular, democratic demands. Consciously or otherwise, these conclusions ignore the power of elite discourse to set the agenda, placing the blame squarely on 'the people', or on far-right parties, rather than on flawed leadership and a dysfunctional system.

Sylvain Crépon, Alexandre Dézé and Nonna Mayer, eds, *Les faux-semblants du Front National* (Paris: Presses de Sciences Po, 2015). For a more general approach, see Brigitte Mral, Majid Khosravinik and Ruth Wodak, eds, *Right-Wing Populism in Europe: Politics and Discourse* (London: Bloomsbury Academic, 2013).

4   Akkerman, de Lange and Rooduijn, *Radical Right-Wing Populist Parties in Western Europe*, p. 10.

However, before turning to issues regarding our current demo-cratic predicament, we should remember that mainstreaming is indeed very much a two-way process, and that it cannot take place with the far right as its sole agent. No matter how hard a far-right party tries to reform itself, if the broader political system is not open to welcoming it and its ideas, it is bound to remain at the margins. The breakthrough of far-right politics has thus required the actions of mainstream actors such as politicians, of course, but also of the media and academics, to legitimise, if not its cause, then at least its presence in the political debate. Therefore, like Akkerman and his colleagues, we see the main-streaming of far-right parties as a dual process in which internal and external factors are both necessary. This was highlighted by Aristotle Kallis, in one of the most convincing attempts to explain the process of mainstreaming. For Kallis, demand and supply factors are essential in grasping the way ideas travel from acceptable to unacceptable, and vice-versa.[5] Ideas that begin as simply unacceptable can become acceptable, or even 'common sense', through the process of main-streaming. For this to happen, a number of elements are essential, and the context needs to be conducive. This can take place through a bottom-up process in which a critical mass can alter established beliefs and change the landscape more or less radically, bringing social groups (and demands associated with particular groups) into the mainstream and rendering their newly acquired rights as something natural or normal. This same effect can take place through a top-down process, in which the agenda is set by the elite.

A sense of crisis and urgency is essential for ideas to make their way into the mainstream, as they require a derogation from prevailing norms. For the far right, this is almost always related to perceived pressure created by an other – whether this takes the form of internal elements, including citizens who happen to be Muslims, Jews, or 'second- or third-generation immigrants'; or external ones, such as refugees, asylum seekers and immigrants. As Kallis notes, our current predicament is reminiscent of the mainstreaming of extreme-right ideas in the 1920s and 1930s, when certain groups were othered amid

---

5   Aristotle Kallis, 'Far-right "Contagion" or a Failing "Mainstream"? How Dangerous Ideas Cross Borders and Blur Boundaries', *Democracy and Security* 9: 3 (2013).

a deep economic crisis so as to deflect from systemic failures. Claims of self-defence were therefore deployed, initially to legitimise the discussion of othering, and then, once these discussions had been mainstreamed, to implement policies to enact it:

> The derogation of mainstream norms is then presented as an undesirable but necessary shift of both language and praxis (or of language and then praxis), without directly attacking the normative validity of the fundamental principles of non-discrimination and respect for minorities . . . this particular kind of 'license to hate' has a powerful altering effect on the individual and collective states of cognitive dissonance.[6]

A particular focus on discourse is thus central to the process – a focus that moves away from electoral politics qua politics, towards a more holistic approach, albeit one which is harder to quantify, and thus less appealing to traditional and mainstream political science, punditry and the media in general. Yet the mainstreaming of far-right ideas is just as important as the mainstreaming of far-right parties themselves, if not more so. To understand the way in which these ideas evolve, and how their position can change depending on context, a few key elements must be outlined. While they may seem obvious, they are too often taken for granted in our public discourse, preventing us from challenging what lies at the root of our current predicament.

The mainstreaming of the far right is not new. The measure for mainstreaming has often been predicated on the spectre of Nazism. In the post war period, with Nazism's crimes widely exposed and universally denounced, the extreme right and its ideas became irremediably linked and thus unacceptable in mainstream society and politics. It has since become common sense that we would not let this happen again. However, even before the Nazis, we had already witnessed the mainstreaming of once reviled extreme right politics. As discussed in Chapter 2, in 1915, the Ku Klux Klan, though destroyed by the post-Civil War Enforcement Act or Ku Klux Klan Act of 1871, managed to

---

6   Ibid., pp. 233–4.

re-emerge and over the next ten years played a central role in the mainstream anti-immigrant nativist period. This included the passing of the aforementioned Klan-supported 1924 Johnson-Reed Act, before the Klan was marginalised in the wake of revelations about crime and violence. This occurred again with the Klan's revival and mainstreaming in the third era in the 1950s and 60s. In this era, they defended racist laws and institutions and occupied positions in mainstream civil society, law enforcement and politics before being pursued and defeated by the FBI-COINTELRPO and HUAC. For U.S. Attorney General Nicholas Katzenbach, there was a 'unique difficulty' in 'gathering information on fundamentally lawless activities which have the sanction of local law enforcement agencies, political officials and a substantial segment of the white population.'[7] This mainstream pushing of the Klan to the margins would also inform David Duke's 'mainstreaming' electoral strategy in the 1970s to 1990s. In France, back in 1984, when the FN was hardly on the radar, French Socialist prime minister Laurent Fabius declared that 'the FN [was] asking the right questions, but offering the wrong answers', while Chirac, future president and saviour of the Republic against Le Pen in 2002, complained in a public meeting about 'the noise' and 'the smell' of African families in 1991. In 1978, Margaret Thatcher, then in opposition, declared on television that 'people are really rather afraid that this country might be swamped by people with a different culture', something Daniel Trilling saw as birth of a myth in British politics: 'that Margaret Thatcher stole the far right's thunder by addressing the tricky subject of immigration.'[8] Flirting with anti-immigration or openly racist rhetoric is not entirely new and mainstream politicians have done so for decades, despite these politics and ideas being marginalised and debunked countless times.

The mainstream is constructed, contingent and fluid. It is also dependent on what we contrast with it as 'extreme', which is also constructed, contingent and fluid. These are not ontologically nor

---

7   Ibid., p. 88.
8   Daniel Trilling, 'Thatcher: The PM Who Brought Racism in from the Cold', Verso Blog, 10 April 2013, at versobooks.com.

historically fixed phenomena, and the widespread tendency to see them as such is both uncritical and ahistorical. What is mainstream or extreme at one point in time does not have to remain so. The mainstream is itself a normative, hegemonic concept which imbues a particular ideological configuration or system with authority to operate as a given, or to naturalise itself as the best option – essential to the government or regulation of society, politics and the economy. Mainstream parties play a particularly important role in our democracies, where elections have often come to be equated with politics. As a result, whatever deviates from the parameters of the mainstream, even if it was once mainstream or would one day become mainstream, can be designated 'extreme'. The repositioning of the Klan corresponded to the liberal construction of the extreme and radical right that was explored in the work of Seymour Martin Lipset and Earl Raab, such as in *The Politics of Unreason*, and still informs designations and assumptions about the opposition between the 'extreme' and 'mainstream' today. Ideologies such as racism, sexism and homophobia, once acceptable in the mainstream, can thus be rejected by virtue of their association with the past and the extreme. Yet such tendencies, together with the structures or institutions which underpin them, do not disappear entirely; they may adapt to their new context, and a backlash and revival can always occur.

The mainstream is not essentially good or progressive. Mainstream politics, and parties in particular, are often considered reasonable, pragmatic and moderate, despite their record often demonstrating otherwise. As we have demonstrated, however, what are today considered the most extreme historical forms of racism – or those now defined as such in post-racial narratives – were indeed accepted and defended by the mainstream at some stage. The mainstream can be resistant to more radical structural and institutional change, which is essential in decisively countering racism. It typically responds to radical challenges with an appeal to its own hegemonic political procedures and democratic mandate, while giving a nod to the eventual advance of progress. This applies to its attempts to neuter not only reactionary and racist movements, through which it claims its anti-racist, progressive credentials, but also progressive and radical ones that seek to resist and overturn racist and other unjust systems and structures. The mainstream moves both ways, depending on circumstances.

This is also true, perhaps more broadly, on the level of mainstream political parties. Mainstream parties can move towards more progressive politics, just as they can move towards reaction, when under real or perceived pressure from far-right parties or public opinion, for example. We must then do away with the idea that the mainstream and centre in politics (which often intersect and affirm one another) reflect a range of positions that are broadly realistic, pragmatic and sensible, as is too often heard in conversation with mainstream elites whose privileged status depends on the defence of the status quo and the negation of any alternatives, be they radically left or right, as evil, impractical, authoritarian, idealistic, and so on. It is worth noting though, that while the mainstream and centre can be normative concepts and positions used to reign in more extreme or radical positions, something mainstream may not necessarily be centre, but the centre can move to the right as certain politics become more mainstream, as we saw with Reagan in the 1980s. At the current juncture in our cases, the far right is both causing the liberal moderate 'centre' to be reasserted and the mainstream to move further right. Therefore, to escape the crises we currently face, and whose roots are systemic – relating not only to racism, but also to the environment, poverty and inequality – we must think boldly, recalling the simple, obvious statement that the current stage of politics is historically contingent. It is what it is, but does not have to be so. This is particularly clear with regard to the ways in which the idea of the post-racial has been constructed by the mainstream, functioning as a distraction from the racism embedded in and exacerbated by social, political and economic structures, institutions and political parties.

Progress is not unidirectional or inevitable. The narrative typically evoked in defence of liberal democracy, particularly in the post-war period, is that of progress, including in its post-racial version. This narrative sees history and society moving forward in a constant (albeit slow), unidirectional trajectory towards greater freedom and equality of opportunity (based on systemic capitalist inequalities which remain unaddressed), eventually overcoming injustices such as colonialism, gender inequality, and so on. Yet this narrative rarely acknowledges the struggles of anti-racist, feminist and anti-imperialist movements against the resistance of 'liberal democracies', which have historically been an essential part of any positive change which has taken place in our societies. As history has shown time and again, rights have rarely been bestowed; they have had to be seized. This comfortable dogma also fails to address the persistence of racism, sexism and homophobia, or the possibility of a backlash by reactionary forces, some of which are mainstreamed through liberal discourses and central to its core mechanisms of control. The most notable case is that of the 'post-racial' already discussed, according to which the supposed overcoming of racism has been predicated on individual achievements by persons of colour. This represents racism in terms associated with the bad old days of the Nazis or the Klan, and serves to legitimise liberal racism and Islamophobia in particular. This can be witnessed in attacks on Islam and Muslims in the name of liberal values, rather than on grounds of race – such as then British Foreign Secretary Boris Johnson's attack on the burqa, or in the banning of religious symbols across Europe targeted directly at Islam. It is also notable in the Trumpian backlash that promised to 'Make America Great Again'.

Far-right parties also move both ways. On the one hand, they can become more mainstream by their own choices and actions, usually through a discursive shift towards less overtly racist and authoritarian politics, as well as an expansion of their programmes away from opposition to immigration as a single issue. This can give the impression that these parties have actually moved to the left, as they develop the socio-economic side of their programmes. Yet this would ignore the fact that these parties' defence of the welfare state and of workers is predicated on the exclusion of the other and scapegoating of migrant and racialised workers in particular. These so-called social policies are also often accompanied by an explicit expression of faith in the capitalist system and perks for the traditional elite, as well as the lower-middle class, traditional supporters of the far right, usually through tax cuts, deregulation, the curbing of unions, and other reactionary, right-wing proposals. Yet far-right parties can also be disentangled from the mainstream and rendered 'extreme' as the mainstream itself evolves. One can think here of the inter-war fascist leagues, and of the Klan in the US. Even UKIP, as it turned towards more openly racist politics, while the mainstream itself was growing more accepting of racist discourse, reflects this tendency.

On the other hand, their position can also be influenced by the actions (or inaction) of other parties and political actors, including the media. By providing media platforms or borrowing ideas during campaigns, elite actors have legitimised the far right. This has reached new heights as academics have started to provide a veneer of scientific rigour to their ideas. Perhaps surprisingly, other approaches have scarcely produced better results; for example, the *cordon sanitaire* placed around far-right parties towards the end of the twentieth century in many European countries, preventing mainstream parties from making alliances with them, has in fact often led to their legitimisation as real alternatives. This was exacerbated when this wall of separation started to crumble, as mainstream politicians failed to respond to the growing disillusionment, borrowing increasingly from far-right rhetoric and politics to distract the public from that failure.

Party politics and discourse can move together but they do not have to, or not at the same time. Parties can move left or right, faster or slower than public discourse does, putting them at odds with the mainstream political discussion, and thus alienating or marginalising them. This can be both positive and negative. At certain moments, figures within various parties have driven faster progress than public opinion seemed to support. On the other hand, we have also witnessed the refusal of elites to adopt progressive positions. To understand this mechanism in all its complexity, various levels of analysis must be undertaken. Does elite discourse – circulated by the media, academics, experts and politicians – reflect wider public discourse at the local or individual level? If these operate separately, then who is influencing who, and by what means? Do parties follow public opinion, or lead it? The way in which the far right is perceived can also influence the mainstream, based on a skewed account of its level of support – so much so that the mainstream may appropriate its ideas as a means of slowing a loss of votes. The momentum towards an EU referendum in the UK, for example, was accelerated by the constructed and hyped-up threat of UKIP, which sent both the Labour and Conservative parties into panic mode, as discussed in the following sections of this chapter.

Having set out the essential characteristics of the process of mainstreaming, we can now move on to define more precisely how it works. Figure 3.3 attempts to provide a clear, comprehensive model of how mainstreaming takes place. Anything less than this would not offer a precise enough picture, and would in fact create a real risk of misunderstanding the far right and its appeal and in turn facilitate its further mainstreaming.

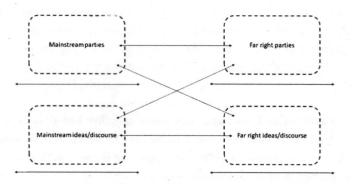

Figure 3.3. The Mainstreaming Process.

The arrows in Figure 3.3 highlight the importance of seeing both the mainstream and the far-right parties' positions as fluid; failing to acknowledge this would lead to a dangerous misunderstanding of the forces in play. For example, if it is assumed that only the far right moves, then the role played by the mainstream in facilitating the acceptance of certain ideas through co-option would be obscured. The figure thus highlights several points:

- Pull and push factors are essential on both sides. They depend on political opportunities, but also on the way in which parties themselves behave and respond to change. Mainstream parties can decide to tap into far-right support at the expense of their other voters, thereby mainstreaming certain ideas while taking votes away from far-right parties. Far-right parties may decide to radicalise their discourse to move away from the 'establishment', alienating the more moderate parts of their base, but reinforcing their appeal to disgruntled voters or their more ideological supporters.
- The borders around the mainstream and the far right are not fixed or impermeable. The dotted lines around each element in Fig. 3.3 highlight the necessity of considering each of them as porous. This means there is no such thing as mainstream parties in and of themselves – they are bound to change and evolve depending on context, adopting or rejecting ideas. The mainstreaming process is exactly that: the way ideas once considered extreme switch status through a process that involves both the mainstream and the extreme.
- This means that ideas and party politics can move independently, and even in opposite directions. Far-right ideas can be mainstreamed while far-right parties lose ground, and vice-versa:
  - Mainstream parties' failures, real or perceived, can be used by far-right parties to legitimise their own positions. Increases in unemployment or poverty, for example, are used to blame immigrants and the multicultural approach of the establishment. This process has been central to the politics of reconstructed far-right parties, which have taken advantage of low public trust in politicians following years of austerity and the increasingly similar politics proposed on both ends of the mainstream spectrum.
  - Similarly, the far right's links, real or perceived, to illiberal racism can be used to delegitimise them. Until the stigmatising terms 'far right', 'extreme right', 'radical right' and 'racist' came increasingly, and problematically, to be replaced by the term 'populist', these parties were marginalised through their association with fascism. To this day, many of the most

successful far-right parties in Europe have been those that have managed to navigate the line between their fascist and/or racist roots and a more nuanced discourse based on liberal articulations of racism – or else wait for the mainstreaming of racism through its liberal articulations before emerging.

- While the far right can adopt new strategies and cut ties with the elements of its programme and rhetoric that are viewed as more extreme, it can also passively benefit from the fact that mainstream parties borrow ideas from its toolkit, as well as from their failures to address new crises, real or perceived.

One element we have deliberately omitted from Figure 3.3 is the role of public opinion, and the demand which may result from it. The mainstreaming of the far right has been driven by elite discourse (see Chapter 4). This is successfully navigated by the reconstructed far right to gain undeserved prominence in the media and politics, given the level of popular support it enjoys even in the most favourable circumstances.

MAINSTREAMING IN PRACTICE

The line between what is liberally acceptable and what is not is thus in constant flux, and always contingent. It is generally assumed that much of the political discourse in liberal democracy has been based on what is good for the majority or the mainstream, while frequent warnings are issued about the threat posed by radical politics, whether from left or right. Yet this prevailing, commonsensical understanding of politics has failed, often wilfully, to engage with the more complex, constantly evolving nature of ideology. What is considered mainstream or moderate today was radical or reactionary only yesterday, and may once again be so tomorrow. The resurgence of reconstructed far-right parties and politics in the late twentieth and early twenty-first century has helped blur these lines further, changing the level of acceptability of certain discourses. While it is commonly assumed that political change takes time, recent events have demonstrated otherwise. For example, in Australia, Robert Manne pointedly noted about a racist letter published by political newcomer and future far-right leader Pauline Hanson, 'that by the political standards in early 1996, it was dynamite . . . by the political standards of 1998 such a letter would occasion hardly a stir'.[9] While the Australian case is not central to this book, it remains an interesting example, as we have argued elsewhere that it has been at the forefront of the mainstreaming of far-right politics, particularly through its treatment of asylum seekers.[10] After the short-lived success of Pauline Hanson's amateurish One Nation party, conservative Liberal prime minister John Howard declared after his election in 1996 that 'the pendulum [had] swung too far'. He managed to succeed in turning the clock back, returning to a parochial vision of the Australian nation based on stringent immigration and asylum laws and strong nationalist rhetoric. This approach was incredibly successful, and the discourse around it has become hegemonic across the political spectrum and population, despite the inhumane treatment suffered by refugees in offshore centres.[11]

To illustrate the various ways in which the mainstreaming process has taken place in recent years, the US, French and British cases provide interesting insights. In each of these countries, mainstreaming has occurred in a distinctive fashion. In order to understand the true character of the issue, the holistic approach explored above must be applied in particular contexts.

Trump: Anachronistic evil or the new mainstream?

The election of Donald Trump has come to represent both the mainstreaming of the far and extreme right and the radicalisation of the mainstream. The notion of mainstreaming in the United States is

---

9   Robert Manne, 'Foreword', in Nadine Davidoff, ed., *Two Nations: The Causes and Effects of the Rise of the One Nation Party in Australia* (Melbourne: Bookman, 1998).

10   Aurelien Mondon, *A Populist Hegemony? Mainstreaming the Extreme Right in France and Australia* (Farnham: Ashgate, 2013); Andy Fleming and Aurelien Mondon, 'The Radical Right in Australia', in J. Rydgren, ed., *The Oxford Handbook of the Radical Right* (Oxford: Oxford University Press, 2018).

11   See David Marr and Marian Wilkinson, *Dark Victory: How a Government Lied Its Way to Political Triumph* (Crows Nest, NSW: Allen & Unwin, 2004). See also, Behrouz Boochani, *No Friend But the Mountains: Writing from Manus Prison* (Sydney: Picador, 2018), translated by Omid Tofighian.

complicated by the fact that there has been little space for a viable third or alternative far-right party due to the two-party dominance of the political system.[12] While the extreme right has stayed out of mainstream politics since the civil rights era, with the exception of David Duke, far-right ideas have entered the mainstream through individual figures such as Pat Buchanan, and media influencers including talk-radio personality Rush Limbaugh and Fox News commentators.

For many, and certainly in much of the public discourse, the election of Barack Obama in 2008 heralded a new step forward in post-racial and liberal politics in the United States and beyond. Racism, it was argued, was now the preserve of the past and of the extreme right. This idea was supported by the extreme-right response to the post-racial election when Thom Robb, national director of the Knights of the Ku Klux Klan, argued: 'It could mean a reawakening of our spirit and blood. Every time the television shows an image of Obama it will be a reminder that our people have lost power in this country.'[13] David Duke added: 'I believe tonight is a night of tragedy and sadness for our people . . . The country is not recognizable anymore.'[14] Duke referred to Obama as a 'visual aid' that was helping to attract interest and recruits.[15] The Southern Poverty Law Center (SPLC) reported a 4 per cent rise in hate groups in the period 2007–8, over 900 being currently active – a reversal of the decline experienced since 2000.[16] Other examples of racism

---

12   Exceptions to this were the nativist Union Party in the 1930s and Ross Perot's Reform Party in the 1990s. See David Bennett, *Demagogues in the Depression: American Radicals and the Union Party, 1932–1936* (New Jersey: Rutgers University Press, 1969); David Bennett, *The Party of Fear: From Nativist Movements to the New Right in American History* (New York: Vintage, 1990); Chip Berlet and Matthew Lyons, *Right-Wing Populism in America: Too Close for Comfort* (New York: Guilford, 2003); Sara Diamond, *Roads to Dominion: Right-Wing Movements and Political Power in the United States* (New York: Guilford, 1995).

13   Southern Poverty Law Center, 'In Their Own Words: Hating Barack Obama', *Intelligence Report*, 2009.

14   Ibid.

15   Stephanie Chen, 'Growing Hate Groups Blame Obama, Economy', CNN, 26 February 2009.

16   David Holthouse, 'The Year in Hate: Number of Hate Groups Tops 900', *Intelligence Report*, Spring 2009.

were a clear reminder of the past. Just days before the election, an effigy of Obama was hung in a mock lynching at the University of Alabama; and, hours after the election, a black church in Springfield, Massachusetts, was targeted by arsonists.[17]

In April 2009, US Homeland Security issued a report titled *Rightwing Extremism: Current Economic and Political Climate Fueling Resurgence in Radicalization and Recruitment*, warning of the rise of right-wing extremism.[18] Yet this was not limited to the extreme right. The Anti-Defamation League highlighted that conspiracy theories about Obama and the federal government had slipped into the mainstream.[19] One example of this was the 'birther' conspiracy, pushed by Jim Geraghty of the *National Review Online*, Donald Trump and Jerome Corsi, as well as Breitbart. It posited that Obama had been born in Kenya, and was thus not only an illegitimate president but a Manchurian candidate of sorts. This was bolstered by claims that he was also a Muslim, which were particularly powerful at a time when Islamophobia was spreading in the mainstream through both the far-right Stop Islamization of America and the liberal Islamophobia of Sam Harris and Bill Maher, who despite this continues to oppose Trump.

The Tea Party movement – taking its name from the rebellious anti-colonial Boston Tea Party – also played a key part in the mainstreaming of the far right and the radicalisation of the mainstream. Like Trumpism, it was represented as a 'populist' insurgency, as a symptom of or solution to the crisis in the traditional conservative movement and Republican Party. This fiscally conservative, anti-tax movement within the Republican Party, which opposed itself to the federal government, claimed to be a grassroots movement that represented and mobilised the social base of the party

---

17   Larry Keller, 'White Heat: Racist Backlash Greets New US President'. *Intelligence Report*, 2009. See also Winter, 'The Klan Is History', pp. 113–14.

18   United States Department of Homeland Security (Extremism and Radicalization Branch, Homeland Environment Threat Analysis Division), *Rightwing Extremism: Current Economic and Political Climate Fueling Resurgence in Radicalization and Recruitment*, 7 April 2009.

19   Anti-Defamation League, *Rage Grows in America: Anti-Government Conspiracies*, 16 November 2009.

to oppose Obama's policies.[20] It was later shown to be more akin to an 'astroturf' movement, propped up by funding from the Koch brothers' Americans for Prosperity and Freedomworks.[21] It was this precise movement in opposition to Obama, combined with an insurgent conservative base (notably within the establishment) and notions of white loss of power and privilege, couched in racism both overt and latent, that Trump mobilised in his campaign. He did so through a narrative of national decline and of a white working class that had been 'left behind' – in the process scapegoating Muslims and Mexicans, promising to build a wall on the border, trading in coded antisemitism, and appealing to white resentment and nativism. The idealised past implicit in his pitch to voters was condensed in his motto: 'Make America Great Again'. According to Henry Louis Gates, Jr, Trump's campaign and election 'clearly represented a backlash against the progress black people have made since 1965'.[22]

Liberalism, which was the target of Trump's rhetoric, would no longer be able to maintain the illusion of equality and colourblindness, or keep the illiberal at bay. Illiberal racism, so often eulogised, had returned to the mainstream emboldened. The SPLC argued that 'Trump's run for office electrified the extreme right, which saw in him a champion of the idea that America is fundamentally a white man's country.' He was endorsed by the Klan, the American Nazi Party, Aryan Nations, National Alliance, *Stormfront*, the *Daily Stormer*, Richard Spencer and David Duke – who he refused to disavow.[23] Duke would later say: 'We are determined to take our country back.

---

20   For more on the Tea Party movement, see Theda Skocpol and Vanessa Williamson, *The Tea Party and the Remaking of Republican Conservatism* (Oxford: Oxford University Press, 2012).

21   Brendan DeMelle, 'Study Confirms Tea Party Was Created by Big Tobacco and Billionaire Koch Brothers', *Huffington Post*, 11 February 2013.

22   Scott Timber, 'Henry Louis Gates on Trump: "That Election Clearly Represented a Backlash against the Progress Black People Have Made Since 1965"', *Salon*, 12 November 2016.

23   David Neiwert, 'Right-Wing Extremists Hail the Ascension of "Emperor Trump" as GOP Nominee', *Southern Poverty Law Center*, 6 May 2016; Peter Holley, 'KKK's Official Newspaper Supports Donald Trump for President', *Washington Post*, 1 November 2016; Alexis Okeowo, 'Hate on the Rise after Trump's Election', *New Yorker*, 17 November 2016; Sarah Posner and David Neiwert, 'Meet the Horde of Neo-Nazis, Klansmen, and Other Extremist Leaders Endorsing Donald Trump', *Mother Jones*, 21 September 2016.

We are going to fulfill the promises of Donald Trump. That's what we believed in, that's why we voted for Donald Trump. Because he said he's going to take our country back.'[24] The SPLC also reported a spike in hate-based harassment and attacks following the election, some of which were clearly linked to Trump's campaign.[25]

On the back of his campaign, the extreme right drew attention from the media, which offered a platform to the new 'alt-right', as if its leaders were important figures and represented a significant constituency. While the success of the alt-right's mainstreaming was partly a function of Trump's election, it also benefited from its less top-down organisational structure, based on a network of subcultures, platforms and movements. 'Red-pilling' became a key term in the alt-right universe. Taken from the film *The Matrix*, it refers here to the liberation of men from a life of delusion, particularly by feminism,[26] in line with its origins in what is commonly called 'the manosphere'. The radicalisation of the passive online 'lurker', as opposed to formal membership, can occur when an individual has their grievances affirmed, and becomes enculturated into a worldview that is increasingly extreme, reactionary, misogynistic and racist – in some cases, even fascist.[27] This process entails shifting what the alt-right, as well as political and social scientists studying such phenomena refer to as the 'Overton Window' – that is, modifying and expanding the range of acceptable options and ideas seen as publicly acceptable.[28] This is something that the alt-lite and wider liberal free-speech discourse

---

24   Hilary Hanson, 'Ex-KKK Leader David Duke Says White Supremacists Will "Fulfil" Trump's Promises', *Huffington Post*, 12 August 2017.

25   Hatewatch Staff, 'Update: More than 400 Incidents of Hateful Harassment and Intimidation Since the Election', *Southern Poverty Law Center*, 15 November 2016; Hatewatch Staff, 'Update: 1094 Bias Related Incidents in the Month Following the Election', *Southern Poverty Law Center*, 16 December 2016; Cassie Miller and Alexandra Werner-Winslow, 'Ten Days After: Harassment and Intimidation in the Aftermath of the Election', *Southern Poverty Law Center*, 29 November 2016; Aaron Winter, 'Brexit and Trump: On Racism, the Far Right and Violence', *Institute for Policy Research (IPR) Blog*, 2 April 2017.

26   Debbie Ging, 'Alphas, Betas, and Incels: Theorizing the Masculinities of the Manosphere', *Men and Masculinities*, May 2017.

27   Bharath Ganesh, 'What the Red Pill Means for Radicals', *Fair Observer*, 7 June 2018; George Hawley, *Making Sense of the Alt-Right* (New York: Columbia University Press, 2017).

28   Mike Wendling, *Alt-Right: From 4chan to the White House* (London: Pluto, 2018), p. 91.

also promote (and Trump has repeatedly tested with his rhetoric). The fact that the alt-right, and to a greater degree the alt-lite, has its origins in anti-feminist and misogynist subcultures and discourse, as Debbie Ging argues, shows the intersection between misogyny and racism, and challenges claims of liberalism on the part of its followers, activists and defenders – particularly liberalism relating to gender rights.

While its presence and strategy were mostly internet-based, an emboldened extreme right also held rallies in the wake of Trump's election. The most notable was the 'Unite the Right' rally on 12 August 2017, organised by alt-right webmaster Jason Kessler in Charlottesville, Virginia.[29] During Unite the Right, James A. Fields, a white supremacist affiliated with Vanguard America, drove a car into a crowd of counter-protestors, killing anti-fascist demonstrator Heather Heyer and injuring many more.[30] In response, Trump issued a statement, but failed to denounce the extreme right: 'We condemn in the strongest possible terms this egregious display of hatred, bigotry and violence on many sides, on many sides.'[31] A day later, faced with a growing backlash, Trump added: 'Racism is evil, and those who cause violence in its name are criminals and thugs, including the KKK, neo-Nazis, white supremacists, and other hate groups that are repugnant to everything we hold dear as Americans.' On 15 August, under questioning by journalists, he partially reverted to his original position, spreading the blame more widely and legitimising the rally in so far as it also was in defence of the statue of Robert E. Lee, declaring, in response to a question on whether he thought that what he calls 'the alt-left is the same as neo-Nazis':

> Those people – all of those people – excuse me, I've condemned neo-Nazis. I've condemned many different groups. Not all of those people were neo-Nazis, believe me. Not all of those people were

---

29   Aaron Winter, 'Charlottesville, Far-Right Rallies, Racism and Relating to Power', *openDemocracy*, 17 August 2017.

30   Hatewatch Staff, 'Alleged Charlottesville Driver Who Killed One Rallied with Alt-Right Vanguard America Group', *Southern Poverty Law Center*, 12 August 2017.

31   Ben Jacobs and Warren Murray, 'Trump Under Fire after Failing to Denounce Virginia White Supremacists', *Guardian*, 13 August 2017.

white supremacists, by any stretch. Those people were also there because they wanted to protest the taking down of a statue, Robert E. Lee ... So, this week it's Robert E. Lee – I noticed that Stonewall Jackson's coming down. I wonder, is it George Washington next week? And is it Thomas Jefferson the week after? You know, you really do have to ask yourself, where does it stop?

When he was told by a reporter that neo-Nazis had started it, Trump responded:

... you had some very bad people in that group, but you also had people that were very fine people, on both sides. You had people in that group. Excuse me, excuse me. I saw the same pictures as you did. You had people in that group that were there to protest the taking down of, to them, a very, very important statue and the renaming of a park from Robert E. Lee to another name.[32]

This explanation from Trump was a clear reference not just to the extreme right, but to the white Trump voter who was not a neo-Nazi, but had shared concerns about white America and its 'heritage' in the face of political correctness. In addition to sidestepping the racism at the heart the confederate statue defence, Trump was attempting to distance the latter from the former and legitimise his supporters and the rally. By doing so, he constructed a link between them, around an overlapping set of causes. Once in office, Trump consolidated, mainstreamed and institutionalised his extreme- and far-right support. He appointed Breitbart's Steve Bannon and white nationalist Stephen Miller to his administration. In November 2019, the SPLC revealed the extent of Miller's white nationalist politics and far right links. This included sharing links with VDARE which traffics in the white genocide and great replacement tropes and conspiracy theories, communication with alt-right figurehead Richard Spencer and Pamela Gellar of Stop Islamization of America, involvement in editing pieces that appeared in *American Renaissance*,

---

32   Angie Drobnic Holan, 'In Context: Donald Trump's 'very fine people on both sides' remarks (transcript)', *Politifact*, 26 April 2019.

and recommending or recommendation of *The Camp of the Saints* to Breitbart.[33] Trump also gave far-right radio show host Alex Jones a White House press pass, while referring to CNN as 'fake news', and appointed the former Alabama senator Jeff Sessions to the position of attorney general. When Sessions had been nominated as a federal district judge in the 1980s, he was seen by many – including Coretta Scott-King, who opposed the appointment in a letter to the Judiciary Committee – as a racist.[34] He had been accused by Thomas Figures – a black senior prosecutor who had served under him in the US attorney's office – of calling him 'boy'. He was also charged with making disparaging comments about civil rights organisations and positive ones about the Klan. In a 2015 Breitbart interview with Steve Bannon, Sessions expressed admiration for the 1924 Johnson-Reed Act.[35] He was therefore at home in an administration that had removed the civil rights page from the White House website,[36] and had been accused of degrading the Department of Justice's civil rights division and undermining civil rights protections.[37]

On 27 January 2017, Trump signed Executive Order 13769, 'Protecting the Nation from Foreign Terrorist Entry into the United States', which banned travel from seven Muslim countries; lowered the number of refugees admitted to the country; suspended the US Refugee Admissions Program; and halted Syrian refugee admissions. He also pushed for the construction of the Mexican border wall which had been a central feature of his campaign, precipitating the longest government shutdown in history. Although they have not always been successful, Trump's capacity to garner support for these ideas and policies has promoted them into the new mainstream.

While illiberal racism has increasingly encroached on the

---

33   Michael Edison Hayden, 'Stephen Miller's Affinity for White Nationalism Revealed in Leaked Emails'. *Hatewatch*, 12 November 2019.

34   Alexandra Wilts, 'Jeff Sessions: Man Once Deemed Too Racist to Be Judge Set for Confirmation as Trump's Attorney General', *Independent*, 8 February 2017.

35   Adam Serwer, 'Jeff Sessions's Unqualified Praise for a 1924 Immigration Law', *Atlantic*, 10 January 2017.

36   Janelle Ross, 'Civil Rights Page Also Deleted from White House Website', *Washington Post*, 20 January 2016.

37   MSNBC, 'Sessions Continues Perversion of DoJ's Civil Rights Division', 1 August 2017.

mainstream, some liberal limits remain. For example, Trump was opposed for separating refugee parents from their children at the border, a policy which Stephen Miller played a significant role in, and forced into a climbdown in 2018 – albeit after many had already suffered terrible consequences. In January 2019, Republican Senator Steve King, who had been elected on the Trump wave, faced a backlash from the Democrats and some Republicans when he asked: 'White nationalist, white supremacist, western civilization – how did that language become offensive?' and 'Why did I sit in classes teaching me about the merits of our history and our civilization?'[38] It was perhaps ironic that he should have received a backlash: not only was he elected as a known white nationalist, but his questions adopted the language of Trump. They also appeared to be an appropriation of the discourse of the more mainstream liberal IDW and free-speech activists's opposition to anti-racist critiques of western civilisation, the canon and enlightenment in higher education, and deriding those making accusations as being easily offended 'snowflakes'.

France and the rise and fall of the 'unabashed' right

As we have seen, the mainstreaming of the far right has a long history in France. It differs from our other case studies in that it is perhaps easier to track, since it has taken place in relation to one key organisation: the Front National. However, it would be mistaken to think that the FN has been solely responsible for the process. Instead, mainstream politicians and the media have played a key role in the situation in which France currently finds itself, whereby Marine Le Pen's renamed Rassemblement National (National Rally – RN) has become an almost normal contender for power. While some of the issues and events around FN/RN have already been touched upon in previous chapters, it is worth retracing key moments in its mainstreaming.[39] It was the left, and Socialist

---

38   Christina Zhao, 'Republican Senator from Iowa Joins in Condemning GOP Congressman Steve King's "Racist" Remarks', *Newsweek*, 1 January 2019.

39   This builds on more in-depth research available in Mondon, *Populist Hegemony?*; and Aurelien Mondon, 'The Front National in the Twenty-First Century: From Pariah to Republican Democratic Contender?', *Modern & Contemporary France* 22: 3 (2014).

president François Mitterrand in particular, who first helped prop up the FN in 1982, at a time when it was electorally irrelevant. Having turned to austerity politics, and facing bleak forecasts for the upcoming local elections, Mitterrand attempted to use the FN to split the right-wing vote, and thereby provided Le Pen with a platform on France's key political show on public television.[40] This lent the FN a degree of legitimacy that other parties of a similar size could only have dreamed of. It also allowed Le Pen to consolidate his leadership on the far right, and led a number of smaller extreme-right formations to join him and toe the line. While it would be simplistic to assign Mitterrand sole responsibility for the rise of the FN, it was at this stage, in the fertile context of austerity politics, that the far-right party began to register its first electoral breakthroughs.

Despite various scandals, particularly when Le Pen was sentenced for Holocaust denial following his repeated comments that the gas chambers were 'a detail of history', the FN gained increasing prominence in the late 1980s and 1990s. Its key campaigning issues, such as crime and immigration, entered mainstream political discourse. Bruno Mégret appeared to be winning his 'vocabulary battle' (see Chapter 1). Yet it was after he had left the party that the process reached its next key turning point. The 2002 presidential election created a crisis point in an already deeply disillusioned electoral environment, and the FN provided opportunistic politicians with a decoy from more pressing issues, such as the state of the economy. While the rise of the FN was not in fact the biggest lesson to take away from the election, the party nonetheless occupied much of the political discourse in the following five years. This atmosphere prepared the ground for the election as president, in 2007, of Nicolas Sarkozy, leader of the Union pour un Mouvement Populaire (Union for a Popular Movement – UMP).

Many voters now feared the return of fascism, flocking back to mainstream parties rather than abstaining or voting for smaller ones, and Sarkozy was thus able to count on increased participation.

---

40   E. Faux, T. Legrand and Gilles Perez, *La Main droite de Dieu. Enquête sur François Mitterrand et l'extrême droite* (Paris: Ed. du Seuil, 1994).

Turnout jumped from 71.6 per cent to 83.8 per cent. Yet, despite this unsurprising trend, which meant the FN was unlikely to be a threat, Sarkozy ran a campaign based on a sharp right-wing turn on both economic and social issues, bolstered by his recent authoritarian stint as minister of the interior. His focus on crime, national identity and immigration was particularly appealing to the many voters who had been seduced by Le Pen's discourse but felt that he would never be able to reach power. It was thus no surprise when, a few months before the election, Sarkozy declared, 'Yes, I am trying to appeal to the Front National electorate', and that he 'would go and get them one by one' if necessary.[41] This approach proved successful, and FN voters turned to Sarkozy in droves, leaving Jean-Marie Le Pen with 'only' 10 per cent of the vote. Surveys suggested that between 21 and 38 per cent of Le Pen's 2002 electorate had jumped ship. In the second round, two-thirds of Le Pen's voters transferred to the UMP candidate. The Lepéno-Sarkozystes surveyed showed that this shift was directly related to Sarkozy's borrowing of Le Pen's rhetoric and political themes.[42]

On the broader political scene, Sarkozy positioned himself as a torchbearer for an acute sense of nationalism, based on pride in a simplistic and glorified history and an unapologetic posture in relation to France's past, including colonisation. His denunciations of the 'intelligentsia' and their 'culture of repentance' were central to his discourse, and reminiscent of typical far-right strategies. For Sarkozy, France had made some mistakes, but 'not all French people were Pétainists', 'not all French people were colonists'.[43] This reactionary take on history coloured much of his presidency. In October 2007 in, a speech in Dakar, Senegal – a former French colony – Sarkozy argued that colonisation should not be blamed for the 'situation' in Africa, and that his audience should acknowledge 'the responsibility of the bloody wars Africans are waging among themselves, of genocides,

---

41 Nicolas Sarkozy, 'Nicolas Sarkozy répond aux lecteurs du Parisien, Entretien de Nicolas Sarkozy', *Le Parisien/Aujourd'hui en France*, 28 March 2006. Our translation.

42 Nonna Mayer, 'Comment Nicolas Sarkozy a Rétréci L'électorat De Le Pen'. *Revue Française de Science Politique* 57: 3–4 (2007).

43 Nicolas Sarkozy, 'Discours inaugural du congrès de l'UMP', UMP, 14 January 2010. Our translation.

dictatorships, fanaticism and corruption.[44] If things were bad on the continent, it was not because of the ongoing repercussions of colonialism, despite the wide range of evidence backing such claims;[45] it was because of the 'African man', who had not 'entered history enough', and whose 'mind-set does not leave space for human adventure or for the idea of progress': 'never [does the African man] venture towards the future.'[46]

For Sarkozy, 'undeniably, our worst betrayal [was] to have stopped being proud to be French'. If elected, he promised that he would not cease 'to affirm our pride in being French', and that this would be done through the creation of a new ministry in which national identity and immigration would be linked.[47] Throughout his campaign and presidency, Sarkozy drew a clear distinction between those who rightly felt proud to be French, and those who did not: Us and Them. He pushed the process of cognitive liberation to its extreme. Despite the looming financial crisis, Sarkozy believed urgency lay elsewhere: 'Our republican model is in crisis. This crisis is first and foremost a moral crisis . . . This moral crisis is a crisis of values, a crisis of landmarks, a crisis of meaning, a crisis of identity. The denigration of the nation is at the heart of this crisis.'[48] His understanding of the situation, and in particular his deployment of the idea of 'crisis', echoed traditional discourse on the far right: the focus on decadence, on one particular symbolic event as responsible for this situation, be it the Revolution, the Popular Front or May 1968. In line with far-right thinkers, it was thus no surprise that Sarkozy argued for an authoritarian solution based on ethno-exclusivist values and the singling out of the French people and French identity as superior. The subtle negation of the Revolution was present throughout

---

44 Nicolas Sarkozy, 'Discours à l'Université de Dakar Cheikh Anta Diop', Dakar, Senegal, 26 July 2007. Our translation. See also Nicolas Sarkozy, *La République, Les Religions, L'Espérance. Entretien avec Thibaud Collin et Philippe Verdin* (Paris: Editions du Cerf, 2004), p. 98.

45 For more detail, see Sadri Khiari, *La Contre-Révolution Coloniale en France. De de Gaulle à Sarkozy* (Paris: La Fabrique, 2009); François-Xavier Verschaves and Philippe Hauser, *Au Mépris des Peuples. Le Néocolonialisme Franco-Africain* (Paris: La Fabrique, 2004).

46 Sarkozy, 'Discours à l'Université de Dakar Cheikh Anta Diop'.

47 Nicolas Sarkozy, 'Mon Projet: Ensemble Tout Devient Possible', UMP, 2007. Our translation.

48 Nicolas Sarkozy, 'Discours à Caen', UMP, 2009. Our translation.

Sarkozy's campaign: it was not the Revolution or the Enlightenment that had brought human rights into being, but rather millennia of national identity: '2,000 years of Christian values'.[49] Sarkozy's conception of the nation and national identity was esoteric: France was a 'soul', a 'spiritual principle', 'a carnal soil to which one is bound by a mysterious link . . . that cannot be broken without losing part of oneself'. Sarkozy's conception echoed the concept of the *déracinés* ('uprooted') circulated by turn-of-the-twentieth-century far-right intellectual Maurice Barrès' – an author to whom he sometimes referred.[50]

Throughout his campaign and presidency, Sarkozy mainstreamed much of the discourse that had been more or less successfully kept to the margins by the anti-FN 'Republican Front'. Until then, mainstream parties had been cautious not to engage systematically with issues 'owned' by the FN, for fear of losing touch with an electorate that had become used to considering Le Pen as a monstrous figure. Sarkozy's impact was thus huge: his position as the leader of a mainstream political party lent an unprecedented sense of respect and legitimacy to Le Pen's ideas, in a similar way Trump would a decade later. It was no longer the pariah expressing such notions, but the main contender in the presidential election and leader of the Gaullist party, whose political tradition had mythically been born out of the fight against the Vichy regime and Nazi occupation.

By the end of his presidency, Sarkozy and his allies had shifted the line between what was acceptable and what was not – between what could be discussed and envisaged by the president, what was taboo, and what was the new normal. In his attempt to outbid the FN in promising that no debate would be out of bounds for his government, Sarkozy allowed for far-right discourse both to gain an increased amount of coverage and, more importantly, to become part of the republican and democratic sphere from which it had been excluded since the Second World War. While Sarkozy was successful in stealing the FN vote in 2007, his inability to satisfy the deeply divided parts of

49   Ibid.; Gérard Noiriel, *A Quoi Sert 'L'Identité Nationale'* (Marseilles: Agone, 2007), p. 88.

50   During his campaign, Sarkozy referred to Barrès as the one who 'wrote for the French youth the story of national energy'. Nicolas Sarkozy, 'Discours à Metz', UMP, 2007. Our translation.

his electorate during his time in power meant that many of his voters were left disillusioned.

Ten years later, Marine Le Pen appeared in an ideal position to propel her politics further into the mainstream. Since 2012, media commentators and politicians appeared to have uncritically accepted that Le Pen would reach the second round of the presidential elections, and that what remained to be decided was who she would face. Le Pen had received 17.9 per cent of the vote – almost 6.5 million votes – in 2012. This was a record for the party, which had since won the 2014 European election (thanks partly to widespread abstention). It broke another record in the 2015 regional election, when it received 6.8 million votes, but failed to win any single region. As is usually the case in France, the electoral system prevented the FN from winning in the second round, as the Socialist Party decided to withdraw in favour of the centre-right in areas where the FN posed a risk. Yet, as abstention was predicted to be as high if not higher than in 2002, it seemed unavoidable that, with a reservoir of more than 2 million votes compared to her father's best performance, and a much better image than his, Marine Le Pen had a clear path to the second round of the 2017 presidential election. Ten days before the first round, a poll conducted by Ipsos Steria for *Le Monde* indicated that only 66 per cent of respondents were certain to vote.

While it was certainly a shock, the reaction to Marine Le Pen's accession to the second round was much more tame and resigned than had been the case in 2002, and did not provoke mass demonstrations. This was a clear sign of how mainstream the party had become. However, the unexpected rise of Emmanuel Macron and his successful, albeit fragile capture of much of the uncertain vote led to the worst possible outcome for Le Pen, forcing her to face another outsider in the second round, rather than a member of the establishment. In fact, she was the one who now came across as the typical politician, having spent most of her life in electoral politics. Things went from bad to worse as her dreadful second-round campaign was punctuated by a debate in which an angry Le Pen demonstrated that she remained the candidate of the far right. She was defeated by a wider margin than expected: Le Pen received fewer than 11 million votes (33.9 per cent). While this was a new record for the party, it was clearly below what had been expected, and led to a number of complaints from prominent FN cadres regarding the strategy of the leadership. A further blow took place in the legislative elections, in which – despite increasing its number of parliamentarians from two to eight – the party performed rather poorly. The number of votes the FN received in the 2017 legislatives was in fact similar to previous years. As we have seen, however, the fate of a party at a particular election is much less important than whether the ideas it espouses are absorbed in mainstream discourse. Since his election in 2017, Macron has failed to provide a strong counter-narrative. Islamophobic debates around *laïcité* remain commonplace and Macron further mainstreamed far right ideas, most notably through an interview with far-right magazine *Valeurs Actuelles* in 2019.[51]

The UK, Brexit and racism

In the UK, a similar pattern emerged after the British National Party (BNP) managed to make some headway in local elections in the early 2000s, but has been even more marked since the rise of UKIP in the 2010s. While its success was certainly exaggerated, its impact was clear. It has not only reinforced the role of immigration as a key issue on the agenda; it also played a leading part in pushing David Cameron to call a referendum on Europe, and in the campaign that then ensued, in which immigration was a central issue.

In a sequence of events reminiscent of both France and Australia, the hype around UKIP has facilitated the adoption of immigration as a key political issue, and racist discourse has become a prominent feature on both left and right. Theresa May's 'Hostile Environment' policy and 'Go Home' vans, while she was at the Home Office under David Cameron's leadership, demonstrated how deeply entrenched anti-immigration discourse had become as a practical priority for the government.[52] This led to the establishment of inhumane and illegal

---

51   Bruno Cautrès, 'Emmanuel Macron, quelles valeurs actuelles ?', *The Conversation*, 6 November 2019.

52   See Goodfellow, *Hostile Environment*; Jones, Gunaratnam, Bhattacharyya, Davies, Dhaliwal, Forkert, Jackson and Saltus, *Go Home?*; Yuval-Davis, Wemyss and Cassidy, *Bordering*.

policies. The scandal over the treatment of the Windrush generation was therefore not an unfortunate mistake, but the product of a deliberate shift towards punitive politics that echoed the agenda of the far right. Nonetheless, this move was once again counterbalanced by some members of the Conservative Party, such as Cameron himself, who continued to pay lip-service to the benefits of immigration, albeit cautiously, and made sure to position himself in opposition to the illiberal far right 'loonies' and 'fruitcakes'.

More telling, perhaps, was the Labour Party's decision to enter a race to the bottom on the issue of immigration. This was clearest when Ed Miliband's 2015 campaign launched a set of five red mugs bearing their key policies. One of them proudly touted 'controls on immigration'. Miliband set out a number of proposals during the campaign which were clearly reminiscent of far-right pledges, such as promising to lower immigration drastically, 'bear down' on illegal immigration, and distinguish between 'British citizens and workers coming here from abroad'.[53] That Labour felt obliged to promote an issue on which it was certain to appear weaker than the right and far right was a testimony to the panicked state of the Labour leadership in 2015 – something which continues to haunt left-wing politics as demonstrated by Unite's Len McCluskey's comments over the need for a tougher approach on free movement during the 2019 campaign.[54] In the midst of widespread disillusionment with politics, which gripped much of the west, Labour caved to the pressure applied by narratives claiming that the party was haemorrhaging voters to UKIP, and that it was this constituency that it should try to retain. Ironically, Miliband was often derided by the media as 'Red Ed' – and portrayed by his opponents to the right as too radical a leader to follow in the footsteps of Third Way–proponent Tony Blair.

Political discussion in the UK since the 2015 general election has been dominated by Brexit. For more than three years, hardly a day went by without most newspapers headlining the upcoming exit, the impending doom, the inevitable betrayal, or the ultimate escape to

---

53   Patrick Wintour, 'Immigration Concerns Not Prejudiced, Says Ed Miliband', *Guardian*, 16 May 2014.

54   Larry Elliott, Severin Carrell and Heather Stewart, 'McCluskey sparks Labour backlash over tough line on free movement', *Guardian*, 13 November 2019.

freedom. Not only has Brexit hijacked political discussion in the media; it has also confiscated huge resources from the government, at a time when austerity politics have made them scarce in other key areas of society such as healthcare, education and policing. A recent UN report on poverty noted, according to the *Guardian*, that 'the UK government [had] inflicted "great misery" on its people with "punitive, mean-spirited, and often callous" austerity policies driven by a political desire to undertake social re-engineering rather than economic necessity' – a state of affairs exacerbated by the referendum and its aftermath.[55] A report by the Equality and Human Rights Commission pointed to similar failings, including extremely concerning trends towards dramatic increases in poverty.[56] The research found that 'the picture is still bleak for the living standards of Britain's most at-risk and "forgotten" groups of people, who are in danger of becoming stuck in their current situation for years to come'. Contrary to common assumptions hyped in the media, the 'left behind' were not the 'white working class', but all working-class people, and particularly women, racial and ethnic minorities, migrants and asylum seekers, and those with disabilities, who had long been at the sharp end of neoliberalism and reactionary democracy. For Imogen Tyler, 'Stigmatization operates as a form of governance which legitimises the reproduction and entrenchment of inequalities and injustices which impact upon us all. Indeed, the "selective and aggressive deployment" of strategies of social abjection is not only "constitutively injurious to the ideals of democratic citizenship" but has perverted the very meaning of democracy and citizenship.'[57]

---

55   Robert Booth and Patrick Butler, 'UK Austerity Has Inflicted "Great Misery" on Citizens, UN Says', *Guardian*, 16 November 2018.

56   *Is Britain Fairer? The State of Equality and Human Rights 2018*, Equality and Human Rights Commission, 2018.

57   Imogen Tyler, *Revolting Subjects: Social Abjection and Resistance in Neoliberal Britain* (London: Zed, 2013), p. 212 and Loic Wacquant, 'Crafting the Neoliberal State: Workfare, Prisonfare, and Social Insecurity', *Sociological Forum* 25: 2 (2010), p. 200. For more on austerity, stigmatisation and scapegoating in relation to race, class, gender and disability in Britain, see Tracey Jensen, 'Welfare Commonsense, Poverty Porn and Doxosophy', *Sociological Research Online* 19:3 (2014); Tracey Jensen and Imogen Tyler, 'Benefits Broods: The Cultural and Political Crafting of Anti-Welfare Commonsense', *Critical Social Policy* 35: 4 (2015); Alexandra Kokoli and Aaron Winter, 'What a Girl's Gotta Do: The Labour of the Biopolitical Celebrity in Austerity Britain', *Women and Performance:*

There is no doubt that the UK's exit from the EU will have very real consequences for people in both the UK and the EU, and that the chaotic nature of the negotiations have already affected many people. Yet, beyond the economic impact of this decision, the whole period, before and after the referendum, has had a deep impact on the mainstreaming of far-right politics in the UK, and has given a platform to political actors far beyond their electoral weight. As demonstrated by a report by Martin Moore and Gordon Ramsay on media coverage of the referendum campaign, while the economy was the most covered issue (7,028 articles), immigration was second (4,383 articles), far ahead of health, in third place (1,628 articles). Yet immigration became increasingly important as a theme during the campaign: its coverage trebled, and it became the most-covered issue on the front pages of newspapers. Unsurprisingly, given the state of politics and the media landscape in the UK, coverage of immigration was 'overwhelmingly negative', and specific nationalities were singled out, in line with what can be expected in a liberal-racist environment.[58] At a time when poverty was on the rise, and when people in many sections of the population started to feel the full extent of austerity measures which have depleted public services and social safety nets, it is hard not to see the referendum as a diversion from the political failings of mainstream parties. The use of the far right as a harbinger of an alternative future has furnished an excuse not to look at systemic issues rooted in the neoliberal politics espoused by both the UK and EU, and thus unlikely to be solved by the referendum.

This impression is compounded by the context within which the referendum was set up and conducted, which was bound to unleash nationalist forces. It placed the British far right in an incredibly strong position, as it had been campaigning on a populist

---

A *Journal of Feminist Theory – Special Issue: Texting Girls: Images, Sounds, and Words in Neoliberal Cultures of Femininity* 25: 2 (2015); Bassel and Emejulu, *Minority Women and Austerity*. For an analysis of Brexit and racism in relation to capitalism and the wider historical crisis, see Satnam Virdee and Brendan McGeever, 'Racism, Crisis, Brexit', *Ethnic and Racial Studies – Special issue: Race and Crisis* 10: 41 (2017).

58 Martin Moore and Gordon Ramsay, *UK Media Coverage of the 2016 EU Referendum Campaign*, Centre for the Study of Media, Communication and Power, May 2017.

anti-establishment and anti-EU platform for years, for which it had received disproportionate coverage. That the likes of Nigel Farage were given a prominent voice across much of the media, against a Remain campaign led by the British and European elite, was a godsend for far-right politics, as it made the Brexit position a popular one simply because of deep distrust for the establishment. Since the issue of immigration had been hyped as a key concern among British people for years, it was not surprising that this was one of the main issues debated during the referendum – and one which was far more amenable to discussion than more abstract or remote economic arguments, which were far harder to turn into binary debates. As both major parties had pledged to reduce immigration in the preceding years, UKIP and the more right-wing Conservatives were given free rein in positing themselves as the voice of 'the people', 'the left-behind' and 'the man on the street', despite clearly representing elite interests.

While the mainstreaming of the far right in France and the United States can be easily understood by focusing on particular actors – the FN/RN and Trump, respectively – the British case is more complex. UKIP, and Nigel Farage in particular, were allowed to play a particularly disproportionate role in the mainstreaming of racism in the UK, and especially during the EU referendum campaign itself. It is ironic that Matthew Goodwin, who has since played a part in hyping the importance of the far right in the UK, declared with Rob Ford in 2013 – before UKIP's first real breakthrough, in the 2014 EU election – that it had already received 'historically unprecedented levels of coverage for a minor party'.[59] This was confirmed by a study undertaken by Stephen Cushion, Richard Thomas and Oliver Ellis on the media coverage of the 2009 and 2014 European elections. The 2009 campaign received far less coverage, and the campaign was focused primarily on the expenses scandal, leaving less space to Eurosceptics. The 2014 campaign, on the other hand, saw disproportionate coverage given to UKIP and its main policy concerns. Cushion and his colleagues noted that,

59 Matthew Goodwin and Rob Ford, 'Just How Much Media Coverage Does UKIP Get?', *New Statesman*, 11 November 2013.

'whereas UKIP secured just 15 seconds' airtime in 2009, during the 2014 campaign on ITV and Channel 4 bulletins coverage of their party candidates collectively amounted to more than that of the other parties'.[60] It is therefore not surprising that the two issues most discussed in the coverage were immigration and being 'in or out of Europe', as UKIP was allowed to set the agenda by journalists looking for soundbites. As Cushion and his colleagues note, even though coverage of UKIP was mostly negative and challenging, and 'while Farage and UKIP might have been closely scrutinised, journalistic debates were largely contested on the party's ideological terrain'. This is fascinating when we consider that, of the 'major parties', only UKIP ran on a platform to leave the EU. It is also worth asking why UKIP was given a 'major party' status by Ofcom, while the Greens remained a 'minor party', despite having been rather successful in previous polls. This is particularly interesting, as it was this election which set in motion the EU referendum. This chicken-or-egg dilemma as to whether it is the far right, the people or those holding the keys to public discourse who drive the agenda will be discussed at more length in Chapter 4. Yet it is worth noting here that the mainstreaming of the idea of leaving the EU, and its ensuing legitimisation of radical anti-immigration and racist discourse, took place rather rapidly in the UK, despite Euroscepticism having always been present among Conservatives. Farage's access to the media did not stop with the 2014 EU election, or even with his resignation from UKIP's leadership. In fact, he has remained a prominent commentator, and continued to receive disproportionate coverage throughout the EU referendum campaign. He has also been increasingly present in the media commenting on broader issues central to the far right, such as terrorism. He has been regular guest on the BBC's *Question Time*, but was also given a slot on LBC radio, in addition to his regular columns in prominent newspapers. As Nesrine Malik has remarked, 'Impervious to plane crashes, seven failed attempts at election to parliament, and even his own

---

60   Stephen Cushion, Richard Thomas and Oliver Ellis, 'Interpreting UKIP's "Earthquake" in British Politics: UK Television News Coverage of the 2009 and 2014 EU Election Campaigns', *Political Quarterly*, 86:2 (2015).

resignations, Farage bellows from every medium about how Britain is intolerant of his views and how he receives so little airtime compared with mainstream politicians who are constantly muzzling him and muscling him off his podium.'[61]

The media platforming of the far right in Britain has been an ongoing issue – particularly in relation to the issues of immigration and Islamophobia. Former EDL leader Stephen Yaxley-Lennon (also known as Tommy Robinson) has been given numerous platforms by the media. For example, he was invited as a guest onto ITV's *Good Morning Britain*, following Darren Osbourne's attack on worshippers at the Muslim Welfare House in Finsbury Park in 2017, in which Makram Ali was killed. It was later revealed that Osbourne was one of his followers. He also received widespread coverage following a stunt which put at risk the trial of a number of men accused of sexual abuse, where he confronted them for being Muslim. When he was given a thirteen-month sentence for contempt of court at Leeds Crown Court, 15,000 people marched to 'free Tommy Robinson', in what became a widely covered event. The demonisation of Muslims and construction of them as a suspect community in terms of not only terrorism, but 'grooming gangs' by Robinson and others has become increasingly mainstream in the UK, and was notably indulged in by Sajid Javid in his role as Home Secretary. This has been greatly aided by Quilliam, a prominent 'counter-extremism' think tank with links to the government, which published a report in 2017 alleging that over 80 per cent of grooming gangs were Asian. This claim widened the issue beyond Muslims, but also foregrounded race and legitimised racism in addition to Islamophobia. While these statistics were powerfully rebutted by experts in the field, such as Ella Cockbain, it received intense coverage.[62] The process of mainstreaming was particularly well illustrated by former Tory minister Baroness Sayeeda Warsi, who described Quilliam members as 'a bunch of men whose

61   Nesrine Malik, 'Nigel Farage Is Not "Controversial" – He Is Toxic. Why Do We Keep Giving Him Airtime?', *Guardian*, 11 December 2016.

62   Ella Cockbain, 'When Bad Evidence Is Worse than No Evidence: Quilliam's 'Grooming Gangs' Report and Its Legacy', *Political Insight*, 20 March 2019. See also, Waqas Tufail, 'Rotherham, Rochdale, and the Racialised Threat of the "Muslim Grooming Gang"', *International Journal for Crime, Justice and Social Democracy* 4: 3 (2015).

beards are tame, accents crisp, suits sharp, and who have a message the government wants to hear'.[63]

Following the Finsbury Park attack, Hope Not Hate's Joe Mulhall pointedly argued: 'The reality is that in Britain there has been a creeping process of normalization of anti-Muslim rhetoric, with some mainstream media outlets such as the Daily Mail, the Sun, and the Daily Express and some politicians adopting positions not dissimilar to those promoted by anti-Muslim "counter-jihadists"'.[64] This situation has not escaped the UN special rapporteur on racism, E. Tendayi Achiume, who argued that Brexit, austerity and the hostile environment had 'made racial and ethnic minorities more vulnerable to racial discrimination and intolerance', and that anti-migrant and anti-foreigner rhetoric around the campaign had led to a 'normalisation of hateful, stigmatising discourse' even among high-ranking officials.[65] In its report Racial Violence and the Brexit State, the Institute of Race Relations argued that the boundaries between the mainstream and the far right were porous, citing the fact that perpetrators of hate attacks often repeat the same racist discourse used by the media, far-right activists and politicians, and government officials, such as references to 'Go Home' vans.[66]

CONCLUSION: MAINSTREAMING THE FAR RIGHT, RADICALISING THE MAINSTREAM

We have focused here particularly on discourse, rather than electoral politics as such. This allows us to take a more holistic approach to the process underpinning the mainstreaming of the far right, in which electoral success and failure are not the only legitimate indices of the spread of ideas within mainstream political discourse. As we have

---

63   Peter Oborne, 'Moral of Warsi: Tories Can't Cope with Muslims', Middle East Eye, 5 May 2017.

64   Joe Mulhall, 'Finsbury Park Attack: How Islamophobia Spreads from the Far-Right to the Media', Newsweek, 20 June 2017.

65   David Brown, 'Brexit, Austerity and "Hostile Environment" Have Made Britain Racist, Says UN Expert', The Times, 11 May 2018.

66   Jon Burnett, Racial Violence and the Brexit State, Institute for Race Relations, 2016. See also Aurelien Mondon and Aaron Winter, 'Normalized Hate', Jacobin, 17 August 2017.

demonstrated in our case studies, the electoral fate of a political party or movement is not always relevant if its ideas are pushed to the front and centre of public discussion. This is something the far right has managed to turn to its advantage, partly through a radical transformation of its strategy initiated in intellectual circles in the 1960s and 1970s. Building on and perverting Antonio Gramsci's theories on hegemony, far-right intellectuals in France, in particular, devised their own way out of the oblivion to which they had been consigned after the end of the Second World War, with the defeat of fascism and Nazism and establishment of the hegemony of liberal democracy. Their revival was based on the simple hegemonic principle that cultural power must precede political power – an insight that the alt-right has taken up in the United States, and Steve Bannon has put to use in his efforts on behalf of right-wing populist movements throughout the west.[67] In the UK, the demise of UKIP came only once its ideas had come to be ingrained in the Conservative party's discourse. Interestingly, at the time of writing, it appeared that Farage's Brexit Party could suffer the same fate as it has successfully managed to put pressure on Johnson to run on a hard Brexit platform. We can witness here how fuzzy the borders are between the illiberal and liberal as Johnson's move to the right eventually won him the support of Tommy Robinson during the 2019 campaign.[68]

As our three case studies show, there is no single way for the far right to mainstream its ideas. More importantly, however, it is not a task that is the sole preserve of the far right itself. Without a conducive context and the help of mainstream actors – politicians, the media and academics – the process is bound to be far less successful. Far-right ideas began to seep into the mainstream only when these actors perfected their strategy of discursive reconstruction, gaining increased impact in the media and on public discourse in the 1990s and 2000s. The second half of the 2010s seems to have heralded a new stage in this mainstreaming process, whereby the far right's ideas have come to be so normalised that their presence in government is no

---

67   See Dana Kennedy, 'The French Ideologues Who Inspired the Alt-Right', *Daily Beast*, 5 December 2016.

68   Jen Mills, 'Tommy Robinson endorses Boris Johnson to be prime minister', *Metro*, 15 November 2019.

longer a surprise – and is in fact increasingly common. We are often told that this is because it is what the people want – and that, since we are in a democracy, mainstream parties and the media have no choice but to cover and address issues prioritised by the far right. This approach has been given a scientific veneer, large swathes of academia joining the chorus about the importance of the far right and its pet issues such as immigration in contemporary politics. While there is no doubt that the far right and its politics are indeed of great concern for our societies, and for democracy in general, and thus certainly worthy of study, we argue in the next chapter that recent mainstream approaches to the topic have been problematic, serving the far right rather than impeding it.

CHAPTER FOUR

The Far Right, Populism and 'the People'

To understand how racism and far-right ideas and politics are mainstreamed and gain both prominence and legitimacy in public discourse and policy, we believe it is necessary to examine the ways in which they are framed and articulated as emanating from the 'people' or 'demos' through both populist constructions and constructions of 'populism'. Through the common overuse and misuse of the concept of populism to package and euphemise certain ideas, specifically around racism, we have witnessed the construction of the far right as representing the will of the 'people', and thus posited as an example of popular revolt, and even as a potential alternative to our current system. This is despite the fact that the far right is more often than not an extension of the logic of capitalism, inequality, exploitation and exclusion, rather than a radical response to it. This misrepresents the 'people' and democracy, and limits the critique of both liberal democracy and capitalism. It thus fails to address deep structural inequalities, as well as more specific institutional issues and wider power imbalances. Through a study of the concept of public opinion, the uses and misuses of populism and the demonisation of the working class, we will demonstrate here that the rise of the far right has been central to the advent of reactionary democracy.

FOLLOWING OR SHAPING THE PEOPLE? THE ROLE OF PUBLIC OPINION AND THE MEDIA

In recent years, the mainstreaming of racism and the far right has often been explained and legitimised through the desire of 'the people' for more reactionary authoritarian approaches to a range of social issues, from immigration to Islam. This is often articulated in terms of a particular construction, both racialised and classist, of 'the people'. Before turning to these narratives, it is important to understand how they have come to be advanced as if based on sound scientific principles of democracy, rather than deriving from the more passionate side of what used to constitute democratic debate. Indeed, the narratives which have allowed for the mainstreaming of the far right have increasingly been defended and supported using public opinion as the only index of democratic assent, elevated even above elections. The media, both left and right, regularly runs stories about immigration being a main concern of the electorate. While outlets do not agree on how this issue should be tackled, they have mostly accepted that voters will identify immigration (and the construction of the other) as a key concern. On the right, the media demands stronger measures from politicians and cheers tough promises of building walls, creating hostile environments, tightening border controls, stopping boats carrying migrants and refugees, and detaining and deporting people. On the left, journalists and pundits lament the ignorance of voters and plead for a more rational debate on immigration, usually based in instrumentalist, capitalist terms about how immigrants contribute more to the economy than they take, so that we finally get to 'know the facts'. While their view of the pros and cons of immigration vary, both sides seem to have accepted that it is indeed a key concern of the public, and thus dedicate countless articles, interviews and analyses to it. This was particularly clear during the 2016 EU Referendum campaign in the UK, when immigration received disproportionate coverage of a mostly negative character.[1] In France, the mainstream media is often reprimanded by the Audiovisual Council for providing too much airtime to the FN/RN, while the portrayal of certain communities has been overwhelmingly negative over the years. In the United States, despite his oft-proclaimed dislike for the 'mainstream media', Trump has also benefited from coverage that has given prominence to his key concerns, particularly on right-wing networks such as Fox.

Interestingly, while there are many calls to act on immigration across the political spectrum, very few public actors question their role in placing immigration (and the racist articulations which are almost always part of the debate) in the front and centre of people's

---

[1]   Martin Moore and Gordon Ramsay, *UK Media Coverage of the 2016 EU Referendum Campaign*, Centre for the Study of Media, Communication and Power (2017).

preoccupations. This oblivious approach rests on the contention that 'the people' are a simple collection of unadultered opinions, to be understood as an anthropomorphised source of ultimate wisdom whose pulse can be taken and its wishes directly articulated by politicians, the media and other elite actors. While this seems extremely naive, it is a common belief that public opinion guides elite actors, rather than the other way around. And yet the potential for the elite to manipulate public opinion has been widely acknowledged for a long time, albeit often simplistically. Edward Bernays was one of the key theorists of the potential of what he termed 'propaganda' in 1928, and was a huge influence on both the advertising industry and Joseph Goebbels. For Bernays, propaganda would serve to 'organise chaos' in nascent democracies. With the replacement of hereditary elites such as absolute monarchs by elected governments, Bernays found in the media the perfect tool to keep control over 'the masses'.[2]

Bernays took his cue from the rise of democracy, but also from the Industrial Revolution and the development of ever-easier means of communication: 'With the printing press and the newspaper, the railroad, the telephone, telegraph, radio and airplanes, ideas can be spread rapidly and even instantaneously over the whole of America.' A hundred years later, technology has continued to improve and make the world ever smaller, placing information within every citizen's reach, and its quantity and diversity ever more daunting. Political acumen is no easier for citizens to achieve today than it was a hundred years ago; we have no choice but to rely on mediated information to make political decisions over the fate of increasingly complex and interconnected matters. While this is not to say ordinary people are not active agents, it would be wrong to assume that our knowledge of the world, no matter our status in society, is not mediated by various factors, and that among them elite discourse is a powerful one.

Something similar is highlighted by Safiya Umoja Noble in *Algorithms of Oppression*, where she describes a campaign denouncing

---

2 Edward Bernays, *Propaganda, comment manipuler l'Opinion en démocratie* (Paris: Zones, 2007).

the prominence of sexist search results on Google. While the campaign targeted the right issues, it identified the wrong culprit:

> The campaign suggests that search is a mirror of users' beliefs and that society still holds a variety of sexist ideas about women. What I find troubling is that the campaign reinforces the idea that it is not the search engine that is the problem but, rather, the users of search engines who are. It suggests that what is most popular is simply what rises to the top of the search pile. While serving as an important and disturbing critique of sexist attitudes, the campaign fails to implicate the algorithms and search engines that drive certain results to the top.[3]

In our view, this campaign failed to hold the powerful to account, just as our media and politicians often fail to acknowledge their influence on the spread of ideas, whether good or bad.[4] This has obviously been exacerbated when such narratives oppose the powerful to those without access to public discourse in general. To put it simply, did the British 'people' want a referendum on the EU, or were they told they wanted one? Did all Trump voters vote for a white-supremacist leadership, or did they simply vote for the party they had always voted for? What happens when non-voters are taken into account? Does public opinion shape politics from scratch, or do politicians and the media shape public opinion? As Maxwell McCombs noted, 'most of the issues and concerns that engage our attention are not amenable to direct personal experience'; here he built on Walter Lippman's idea that 'the world that we have to deal with politically is out of reach, out of sight, out of mind'.[5] This means that our knowledge of the world beyond our very limited direct experience has to be mediated, and, while mediation can be performed by a number of sources (family,

---

3 Safiya Umoja Noble, *Algorithms of Oppression: How Search Engines Reinforce Racism* (New York: NYU Press, 2018).

4 For an in-depth analysis of the media policy failure with regard to populism, see Des Freedman 'Populism and Media Policy Failure', *European Journal of Communication* 33: 6 (2018).

5 Maxwell McCombs, *Setting the Agenda: Mass Media and Public Opinion* (London: Wiley, 2014).

friends, work, and so on), much of our political knowledge today is acquired through the media and the way in which politics is discussed through it, with certain actors having more powerful voices than others.

Of course, it is essential not to fall for conspiracy theories about a world governed or controlled by a small intellectual and economic elite here, as these are simplistic and often contain anti-Semitic tropes and can play in the hand of anti-Semites of all kinds. It is also important not to imply that the media can make people believe one thing or another. Instead, its impact is less direct, and is based on making certain issues more or less salient in public discourse: the media does not tell us what to think, but what to think about.[6] This is crucial as the logic behind the contemporary mainstreaming of the far right has been based on the simplistic idea that, for example, tougher immigration measures are 'what the people want', or that Islam is not compatible 'according to majority of people' of a given nationality. While the data, whether based on election outcomes or opinion polls, can only lead to selective interpretation, they often give the impression that it is the people qua demos who are driving the mainstreaming process, rather than the elite through its misguided perception, its inability to respond to current political crises or in defence of its narrow self-interest. This is a particularly pressing issue at a time when our governing elite has become increasingly disconnected from the rest of the population, and ever more unrepresentative, allowing so-called populists to claim to be representative of people.[7]

The role of the media and its continuing ability to shape the political discourse and agenda for good or bad is also key to the mainstreaming process. It is important to take account of this when trying to interpret what motivates voting behaviour, responses in opinion polls or vox-pop interviews. These effects were recently highlighted with the much-advertised rise of 'fake news'. There is some irony that this slippery and potentially unhelpful concept was originally popularised by the mainstream press, as if their status was

---

6   Bernard Cohen, *The Press and Foreign Policy* (Princeton: Princeton University Press, 1963), p. 13.

7   Peter Allen, *The Political Class: Why It Matters Who Our Politicians Are* (Oxford: Oxford University Press, 2018).

undeniably that of purveyors of *real* news. Obviously, we do not claim that the mainstream press peddles lies, and we would certainly not want to equate more serious news sources with straightforward propaganda outlets such as Breitbart, but it is again naive to assume that there is any such thing as straightforwardly 'real' news. In 1807, US president Thomas Jefferson was already lamenting:

> Nothing can now be believed which is seen in a newspaper. Truth itself becomes suspicious by being put into that polluted vehicle. The real extent of this state of misinformation is known only to those who are in situations to confront facts within their knowledge with the lies of the day. I really look with commiseration over the great body of my fellow citizens, who, reading newspapers, live & die in the belief, that they have known something of what has been passing in the world in their time; whereas the accounts they have read in newspapers are just as true a history of any other period of the world as of the present, except that the real names of the day are affixed to their fables.

This passage would not be out of place today in an opinion column in one of our major newspapers; indeed, the role of the news media in our democracy remains as important and contentious as ever. For Joshua Habgood-Coote, there are three compelling reasons why we should simply abandon the term 'fake news' (and its extension 'post-truth'):

> 'Fake News' and 'Post-Truth' are linguistically defective: they do not have stable public meanings, and it is not clear what is expressed by sentences that contain them.
>
> 'Fake News' and 'Post-Truth' are unnecessary: they do not add any useful descriptive resources to our language.
>
> 'Fake News' and 'Post-Truth' are propaganda: both 'fake news' and 'post-truth' have been weaponised for political ends, and are closely connected to bad ideology.[8]

---

8   Joshua Habgood-Coote, 'Stop Talking about Fake News!', *Inquiry: An Interdisciplinary Journal of Philosophy*, 11 August 2018.

The idea that there is now suddenly such a thing as 'fake news' stems from the fact that we generally believe that there must be real news. Yet this assumption is based on a simplistic understanding of the news, and in particular of news reporting. While a naive understanding of the news would be limited to journalists relating facts to us, the reality is very different, as only some facts and events can be reported on: 'journalists focus our attention and influence our perceptions of what are the most important issues of the day'.[9] This does not necessarily mean that journalists aim to manipulate or deceive their readership, but simply that they are limited by a number of factors, some of which are physical (logistical constraints of geography and time, for example), while others are ideological in nature (editorial guidelines, ownership, and so on). While it is true that the internet, and in particular social media, have had a huge impact on news creation and dissemination, and may have somewhat diluted or even democratised the process, the big news players (newspapers, network channels, and so on) remain gatekeepers of what is discussed by the wider population. Besides, as Safiya Umoja Noble demonstrates, Google, as a privileged purveyor of news on the web, is not unbiased. Algorithms that determine which piece of information and sites are privileged in searches are designed with particular interests in mind: 'Despite the widespread [belief] in the Internet as a democratic space where people have the power to dynamically participate as equals, the Internet is in fact organized to the benefit of powerful elites.'[10] This may change, as the internet develops further, especially if anti-monopolistic legislation is passed. Yet it will take some time, and currently, despite much talk of fake news, there is little evidence of the impact of such laws on politics. The rise of the far right, on the other hand, can be traced back to times when the traditional media were hegemonic, and played a large part in dictating what was salient in the national discussion: 'The public uses these salience cues from the media to organize their own agendas and decide which issues are more important. Over time, the issues emphasized in news reports become the issues regarded as most important by the public. The

---

9 McCombs, *Setting the Agenda.*
10 Noble, *Algorithms of Oppression*, p. 48.

agenda of the news media becomes, to a considerable degree, the agenda of the public.'[11]

This process of democratic mediation has more recently been dictated by the ubiquity of opinion polls in contemporary politics – both through media coverage of public polling and in the epistemic gatekeeping role played by psephology (the statistical study of elections and surveys) within political science – which has obscured the simple fact that there is no such thing as public opinion without its conscious construction by pollsters.[12] Nevertheless, we tend to anthropomorphise public opinion in public discourse, imbuing it with abilities such as the capacity to make up its mind, thereby rendering it more real: 'Pollsters have no qualms claiming that they have *found* the public *to have* a particular opinion, that the public *is* of a certain mind, and *has spoken, judged,* or *decided* an issue, and present quantitative measures in support of their claims.'[13] For Klaus Krippendorff this is crucial, as 'personification grants the public an independent mind whose capricious and often unreasonable nature can be dangerous for those who mess with it.'[14]

Thus, beyond widely covered issues of sampling and representation,[15] the construction of public opinion is based on a number of inaccurate, 'naively democratic' premises: that everyone can have an opinion; that all opinions are equal; and that the fact that an opinion can be elicited means a question was worth asking. The way in which public opinion is used in the coverage of politics, in particular, rarely takes account of the fact that the questions asked are not chosen in an objective or even neutral manner, but represent the interests of whoever commissions the polling company to conduct

---

11   McCombs, *Setting the Agenda*, p. 2.

12   Pierre Bourdieu 'L'opinion publique n'existe pas', *Temps Moderne* 318 (1973).

13   Klauss Krippendorff, 'The Social Construction of Public Opinion'. Annenberg School of Communication Departmental Paper, University of Pennsylvania (2005), p. 130.

14   Ibid.

15   As Alain Garrigou and Richard Brousse point out, 'To know what people think, we would only have to ask them. A rather naïve assumption. Do we really believe that surveys conducted in a rushed manner by poorly trained workers necessitating ten calls for one complete survey are a rigorous way to undertake an empirical study?' Alain Garrigou and Richard Brousse, *Manuel anti-sondages: La démocratie n'est pas à vendre!* (Paris: Editions la ville brûle, 2011), p. 22. Our translation.

the survey, or is likely to be willing to buy its results. As Pierre Bourdieu remarked almost fifty years ago, 'the simple fact of asking everyone the same question implies the hypothesis that there is a consensus about the problem, that is, an agreement about which questions are worth asking'.[16] Clearly, this does not mean the result will conform with the preferences of the questioner – only that it will focus on certain issues and obscure or ignore others: like the media, the pollster will not tell you what to think, but suggest what you should be thinking about – and will also, through various techniques, induce you to think about issues you have not considered before, and may have no need or desire to consider. Yet, through various prompts and a reliable fear of appearing ignorant, you will feel encouraged, or even compelled, to offer an opinion on something you have not weighed up at all, let alone evaluated carefully.

An example which highlights the way in which our understanding of politics and society is necessarily mediated for each of us, whatever our level of education or occupation, is the way in which people perceive issues in their everyday lives, as opposed to national or supranational ones. This is tested by the Eurobarometer survey. Like every survey, it is imperfect, but it is nonetheless widely trusted by academics and journalists. A simple test using this publicly available data raises some fascinating issues. The level of analysis we are interested in is the one most commonly attended to in elite discourse. What we demonstrate is how data available to those in control of public discourse can be used to push particular narratives while obscuring others. The data we have examined are not only publicly available, but its calculation and interpretation does not require any particular training. While the narratives privileged by elite discourse might be chosen unconsciously, this is not a valid excuse for what we see as a lack of accountability and the widespread ignorance of the impact such narratives can have on the people at the sharp end of inequality, oppression and discrimination. Our objective, therefore, is not to engage in in-depth quantitative measurement of public opinion, but to highlight the fact that the data easily available to and used by academics, journalists and politicians can be read in a number of ways. We do not intend to show that 'the people'

---

16   Bourdieu, 'L'opinion publique n'existe pas'. Our translation.

care about immigration, or that they do not, but instead to demonstrate that different narratives can be drawn from the data available, that some are privileged over others, and that this has consequences for public debate.

In a section of the Eurobarometer survey, respondents were asked a series of three slightly different questions:

- What do you think are the two most important issues facing (OUR COUNTRY) at the moment?
- What do you think are the two most important issues facing the EU at the moment?
- And personally, what are the two most important issues you are facing at the moment?

For each of these questions, respondents were asked to choose a maximum of two issues from among the following:[17]

- Crime
- Defence/Foreign affairs
- Economic situation
- The education system
- Energy
- Energy related issues
- The environment
- The environment, climate and energy issues
- Government debt
- Health and social security
- Healthcare system
- Housing
- Immigration
- (OUR COUNTRY)'s external influence
- Pensions
- Protecting the environment
- Public transport

---

17   Note that this selection varies slightly from year to year depending on particular events, but the main categories of interest are stable.

- Rising prices/ inflation/cost of living
- The state of Member states public finances
- Taxation
- Terrorism
- Unemployment
- Other (SPONTANEOUS)
- None (SPONTANEOUS)
- DK – Don't know
- Other (SPECIFY)

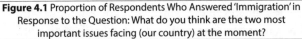

Figure 4.1 Proportion of Respondents Who Answered 'Immigration' in Response to the Question: What do you think are the two most important issues facing (our country) at the moment?

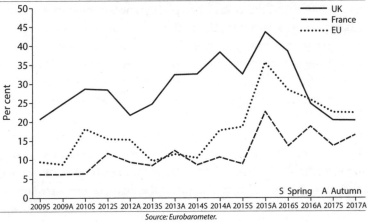

Source: Eurobarometer.

Figure 4.1 illustrates some interesting trends regarding the importance of immigration as an issue at the national level. We can see that it is consistently higher in the UK than in France or the EU as a whole, until the referendum on EU membership in June 2016. Following that vote, immigration as an important issue fell sharply, even falling below the EU average, which can be explained by the disproportionate focus on immigration as an issue during the campaign and the idea that Brexit would somehow fix it. We can also see that concern about immigration peaked in the autumn of 2015, at the height of the so-called 'refugee crisis', but fell sharply in the following surveys, once panic had receded. More importantly, in the UK, France and the EU as a whole, the proportion of respondents placing immigration among their top two concerns never reached 50 per cent – demonstrating that the issue was not high on the list of concerns of the majority of respondents.

In the EU, despite the widely advertised populist surge, the survey never identified immigration as the top issue of concern on average, while in spring 2015, during the 'refugee crisis', it became only the second-ranked issue, at 36 per cent. Throughout the period, unemployment remained the top issue, while the economic situation was ranked highly in the aftermath of the financial crisis, until 2012, as were inflation and the cost of living. In France, immigration ranked only second in a survey at the peak of the 'refugee crisis', in spring 2015. Yet it is worth noting that, at the national level, terrorism became the second-most-cited issue from Spring 2016, following a string of terrorist attacks, and has remained so up to the time of writing. Finally, the UK appears to have been an outlier, immigration being cited by respondents as the most important issue between autumn 2014 and spring 2016 – from UKIP's success in the European election until the Brexit referendum. Before that period, unemployment was the chief concern, and the economic situation was in second place for a number of years following the financial crisis. Following the referendum, health and social security rose to the top of key issues, while terrorism was in second place – and so it has remained up to the time of writing. As in France, this followed a string of domestic terrorist attacks.

When the same panel was asked what the most important issues were for them personally, there was a dramatic change in their responses. In Figure 4.2, immigration reached 10 per cent only once in the UK – at the height of the European referendum campaign – and never reached that threshold in the EU as a whole. In France, it barely reached 5 per cent. Compared to the national level, where immigration is thought of as a concern by almost half of all respondents, and might therefore justify headlines such as 'immigration: largest concern

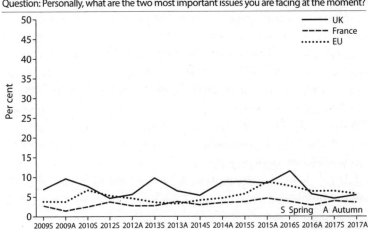

Figure 4.2 Proportion of Respondents Who Answered 'Immigration' in Response to the Question: Personally, what are the two most important issues you are facing at the moment?

Source: Eurobarometer.

among voters' of a particular nationality, a different reading shows that a maximum of one voter out of every ten feels it is a concern in their day-to-day lives. In the UK, the most important issue throughout the period studied was rising prices, with immigration appearing consistently among the issues of least concern – even during 2016. A similar pattern emerges in France, where immigration was usually among the least cited issues. In fact, until 2015, only terrorism ranked lower.[18]

In short, when respondents are asked about their country or about the EU as a whole, immigration always ranked very high as a concern, and might even represent the biggest concern for UK respondents. Yet when the very same people were asked about their own day-to-day lives, immigration vanished from the top of the list. Instead, issues given priority were more closely associated with the day-to-day concerns of most, whether immigrants or not: (un)employment, education, pensions, housing, and so on. While it might

---

18   Defence was also chosen less, but was only offered as an option until 2010.

be inferred that the respondents thought beyond their own immediate lives when asked to identify national or supranational issues of concern, and that this may have led to a variation in expressed priorities, we must also ask ourselves what informed them in making such assumptions about what mattered for millions of people in various countries and across Europe, and why there was such a disparity between the individual level, on one hand, and the national and supranational levels, on the other. Clearly, the difference did not derive from direct knowledge of their millions of co-citizens, regardless of their political expertise. As we have noted, in order for us to make decisions at a level beyond our reach and for the sake of our 'imagined community', we must rely on mediated knowledge.[19]

For Benedict Anderson, any nation is indeed an imagined political community:

> It is *imagined* because the members of even the smallest nation will never know most of their fellow-members, meet them, or even hear of them, yet in the minds of each lives the image of their communion . . . [I]t is imagined as a *community*, because, regardless of the actual inequality and exploitation that may prevail in each, the nation is always conceived as a deep, horizontal comradeship. Ultimately it is this fraternity that makes it possible, over the past two centuries, for so many million people, not so much to kill, as willingly to die for such limited imaginings.

That our political knowledge is mediated is not necessarily negative; in fact, it is essential in order to make any decision that pertains to the political future of our large communities, since one will never meet all their inhabitants or understand every aspect of the system. However, given what is at stake and the interests which stand to lose or gain from the democratic struggle, it is also possible that mediated knowledge can be manipulated – some information being highlighted, some obscured or downplayed. This does not mean that those pushing

---

19   Benedict Anderson, *Imagined Communities: Reflections on the Origin and Spread of Nationalism* (London: Verso, 2006).

for immigration to become a key concern are necessarily opposed to immigration or racist by intention; but the effort does serve a purpose, be it commercial (such as increasing the audience by offering lurid scare-stories) or political (such as diverting attention from more diffi-cult issues like the economy and inequality, and the powerlessness of the political elite in a capitalist system to address them). All of this partly explains why Eurobarometer's respondents express very differ-ent levels of concern regarding the same issues when they reflect upon their impact on their country or continent, as opposed to in their own everyday lives.

This raises broader questions about what the mainstream actually is, how it is created, and what effects it has. Selective use of data and ignorance of the way public opinion is constructed and can be influenced by elite discourse has had dramatic consequences, particularly in societies where democracy is almost uniquely associated with electoral primacy. In short, as Bourdieu noted, the most important function of opinion polls

> is perhaps to impose the illusion that a public opinion exists, and that it is simply the sum of a number of individual opinions. It imposes the idea for instance that in any given assembly of people there can be found a public opinion which would be something like the average of all the opinions or the average opinion. The 'public opinion' which is stated on the front page of newspapers in terms of percentages (60% of the French are in favour of . . .) is *a pure and simple artefact* whose function is *to conceal the fact that the state of opinion at any given moment is a system of forces, of tensions,* and that *there is nothing more inadequate than a percentage to represent the state of opinion.*[20]

This brings us to another caveat: even if opinion polls adequately reflected public opinion, it would be a mistake to argue that we are obliged to listen to it. In his book *The Perils of Perception*, based on decades of work in the field, Bobby Duffy demonstrates convincingly that our perceptions around what are often considered key political

---

20 Bourdieu, 'L'opinion publique n'existe pas'. Our emphasis and translation.

issues (immigration, religion, crime, the economy) are based on a number of shaky, mediated foundations.[21]

The question this raises is whether democracy can be limited simply to majoritarian elections when it is clear that the majorities concerned base their decisions on limited questions and skewed, ideologically loaded knowledge in a deeply inegalitarian setting, in which conservative hegemonic voices conduct most of the public discourse. In a political and media landscape which places great emphasis on Islam, immigration and horror stories, it is not surprising that, for example, people report immigration per centages way above the real levels. For example, when asked, 'What is the proportion of immigrants among your country's population?', the average guess for respondents in the United States was 33 per cent, compared to the reality of 14 per cent; in Great Britain, respondents give a figure of 25 per cent, inflating the reality of 13 per cent; and in France, 26 per cent rather than the real 12 per cent figure. Part of the fear that motivates this imaginary inflation of immigration levels is the result of the zero-sum argument too often pursued by the media and politicians, in which one immigrant means one job that is no longer available to 'local' people. While this idea has been widely debunked, it remains an incredibly potent one, as was demonstrated during the EU referendum campaign in the UK, in which immigration was hyped throughout.

When asked what kind of people respondents have in mind when they are prompted to think about immigration, it is also not surprising that 'refugees' and 'asylum seekers' are cited disproportionately, since they are regularly featured on the news and dehumanised as scapegoats by politicians and pundits.[22] While it would be simplistic to blame anti-immigration sentiment solely on elite manipulation of the agenda, the Australian case – in which John Howard, then prime minister, shamelessly scapegoated a few thousand asylum seekers, most of whom would eventually be found to have legitimate claims to refugee status – demonstrates how a moral panic can be created out of thin air, shifting the entire political agenda on issues like immigration. Between 1998 and

---

21   Bobby Duffy, *The Perils of Perception: Why We're Wrong About Nearly Everything* (London: Atlantic, 2018).
22   Ibid.

2001, approximately 12,000 people arrived by boat on Australian shores – an insignificant number compared to the quantity of migrants from Europe or the United States who regularly overstay their visas in Australia.[23] Yet it was those in the weakest possible position who would be used to reignite fears of invasion deeply rooted in the Australian national narrative. The focus on asylum seekers led to their extremely inhumane treatment. They were sent to camps on indefinite detention, and even transferred to third countries such as Nauru. Despite widespread international condemnation and clear misrepresentation and exaggeration of the issue for political ends, there is now a consensus in Australia around the 'tough' new approach to asylum seekers – an approach more recently being emulated by the EU.

Perceptions become even more skewed when the focus of public discourse turns to the size of Muslim populations. The average guess of respondents in the United States was that 17 per cent of the population was Muslim, while the reality was that it stood instead at only 1 per cent. The corresponding figures were, in the UK, 15 per cent as against 4.8 per cent, and in France 31 per cent as against below 10 per cent. These are extraordinary numbers, particularly for France, where respondents think that almost one out of every three people in their country is Muslim.[24] Recent geopolitical events, and particularly high-profile terrorist attacks, have placed Islam (and anyone loosely associated with it, accurately or otherwise) at the top of the agenda, making a loose community of over a billion people worldwide – in addition to those mistaken for belonging to it – into targets for

---

23 In 2000, 60,000 people were thought to have overstayed their visas in Australia; the largest groups were from the United Kingdom and the United States. As Peter Mares has noted, these groups, though just as illegal as boat people, were extremely rarely placed in detention, and were often given bridging visas to allow them time before their departure. Peter Mares, *Borderline: Australia's Response to Refugees and Asylum Seekers in the Wake of the Tampa* (Sydney: UNSW Press, 2002). Frank Brennan has highlighted the discrepancy between the detention of 308 unauthorised boat arrivals removed from Australia in 2001–02 and the almost 11,000 overstayers who were also removed without detention or media attention. Frank Brennan, *Tampering with Asylum: A Universal Humanitarian Problem* (St Lucia, Qld.: University of Queensland Press, 2003), pp. 112–13. For more detail, see Aurelien Mondon, 'An Australian immunisation to the extreme right?', *Social Identities* 18: 3 (2013); and David Marr and Marian Wilkinson, *Dark Victory: How a Government Lied Its Way to Political Triumph* (Crows Nest, NSW: Allen & Unwin, 2004).

24 Duffy, *Perils of Perception*.

opportunistic politicians. As we noted in previous chapters, Islamophobia has been a particularly convenient vector for the mainstreaming of liberal-racist arguments. It allows an other to be identified in contradistinction to the righteous west, in a sense replacing the old foe of Communism. This, in turn, legitimises more illiberal forms of racism, and Islamophobia in particular; indeed, the border between the two has become increasingly blurred.

What is true of opinion polls may certainly be extended to elections as processes that reinforce the status quo, supported by an apparatus (media, parties, state bureaucracy) dedicated to sustaining their position of power over others, and thus attempting to conceal the very possibility of alternatives, and by extension their viability. This also impairs our ability to imagine new futures – something essential to understanding the fundamental truth that our political circumstances are contingent in a variety of ways, and that we have the capacity to transform them.

MISCOUNTING 'THE PEOPLE': MAJORITY AS A DEMOCRATIC HORIZON

It is not only our perception of the news and political developments that has an impact on how we see the world, but also the way in which we understand politics and democracy. Today, democracy is widely equated with, and thus limited to, its liberal-capitalist form, and particularly one of its core elements: the numerical majority, measured through elections and informed increasingly by opinion polls. This is obviously rendered problematic by the factors mentioned above, related to agenda-setting and the true nature public opinion – and whether it can even be said to exist. The contingent and limiting relationship between voting, the majority and democracy further complicates this picture. As Josiah Ober pointedly noted,

> In modernity, democracy is often construed as being concerned, in the first instance, with a voting rule for determining the will of the majority. The power of the people is thus the authority to decide matters by majority rule. This reductive definition leaves democracy vulnerable to well-known social choice dilemmas, including Downs' rational ignorance and Arrow's impossibility theorem: If democracy

as a political system is reducible to a decision mechanism based on a voting rule, and if that voting rule is inherently flawed as a decision mechanism, then (as critics have long claimed) democracy is inherently flawed as a political system.[25]

This understanding of democracy has become hegemonic in the west, and is hardly challenged any longer. Leaving aside the accuracy of this definition and its desirability for our conclusion, and taking it for the moment at face value, we can nonetheless already point to some interesting problems in linking the rise of the far right, racism and nationalism to a democratic push. One of these issues arises when abstentions are taken into account.

Even though electoral abstention has become a growing concern in many established democracies, and it is common to hear politicians, pundits and the media lament poor voter turnout, very little academic attention has been paid to the phenomenon. Many scholars have written persuasively about why people may wish to abstain, but few have undertaken large-scale studies.[26] In 2007, Cécile Braconnier and Jean-Yves Dormagen noted that, before their own work, only two major studies had ever been published on the French case.[27] In the UK, no studies on such a scale appear to have been undertaken at all. As psephology has become an increasingly popular and well-funded field of research, with growing influence on policy-making and electioneering, the neglect of abstention might seem surprising, since those not voting – whatever their reasons – represent a large part of the electorate.

This is confirmed by a cursory search on Scopus, an academic database, which indicates that, from 2000 to 2018, 191 documents with the words 'abstention' and 'election' among either their title, abstract or

---

25   Josiah Ober, 'The Original Meaning of "Democracy": Capacity to Do Things, not Majority Rule', *Constellations* 15: 1 (2008).

26   See, among others, Wendy Brown, *Undoing the Demos: Neoliberalism's Stealth Revolution* (New York: Zone, 2015); Giorgio Agamben et al., eds, *Democracy in What State?* (New York: Columbia University Press, 2011); Alain Badiou, *De quoi Sarkozy est-il le nom?* (Paris: Nouvelles Editions Lignes, 2007); and Jacques Rancière, *La haine de la démocratie* (Paris: La fabrique éditions, 2005).

27   See, for example, Céline Braconnier and Jean-Yves Dormagen, *La Démocratie de l'abstention: Aux origines de la démobilisation éléctorale en milieu populaire* (Paris: Editions Gallimard, 2007).

keywords have been published in social sciences. A closer analysis demonstrates that most publications are concerned with voting rather than non-voting (two out of twenty in 2014 – the year when most articles were published). In much of academia, as in the mainstream discourse, abstention is thus usually mentioned in passing, and has hardly any impact on subsequent analysis, which remains focused on election results: whatever the level of abstention, the majority of votes or seats decides. While some academics have devoted their efforts to studying abstention and abstainers despite the difficulties, the interpretation of electoral results that most academics, the media and politicians generally take to be democratic benchmarks routinely ignores abstentions.

This would be surprising to anyone unfamiliar with our self-acclaimed democracies. Abstention encompasses – in the best case scenarios – one-fifth of the electorate in France and the UK, and up to half in major elections in the United States, though far more in second-order elections. This should highlight, despite the universal suffrage now enjoyed by liberal democracies, the distinctly partial nature of the model of democracy they observe in reality. While an exploration of the democratic credentials of universal suffrage is beyond the scope of this book, the contempt with which this growing phenomenon has generally been treated is certainly telling. Despite its scale and plethora of political meanings, it has become normal to ignore abstention, or to mention it only in passing, while at the same time uncritically reporting partial electoral results as the expression of popular sentiment, public opinion or 'the people'. Inevitably, when the media, politicians, and even academics talk about election results, they refer to the percentage of votes cast, habitually leaving aside the share swallowed up by abstention.

While some might argue that abstainers choose to remain uncounted, this justification falls apart when we consider blank and spoiled ballots. These usually suffer the same fate as abstention; their impact on the election is null, despite a rise in recent years across various democracies. While abstention is often simplistically considered a fault linked to laziness or low political knowledge or interest, the lack of recognition of blank votes and spoiled ballots appears counterintuitive, as those who have chosen this path recognise the system, participate in it, and yet remain uncounted. For a long time, the blank vote was ignored by parties from all sides of the spectrum who felt that acknowledging the phenomenon officially would encourage dissent. This culminated in France in 1852, when Napoleon III passed a law officially removing the blank vote from electoral results to prevent any contestation of his absolute power. This finally changed in 2014, when blank votes were once again formally counted in France, but remained separate from the official results. In the 2017 presidential election, more than 11 per cent of the votes were blank or void in the second round between Emmanuel Macron and Marine Le Pen. In the UK, the Electoral Commission states that unmarked ballot papers are automatically rejected, meaning that, if someone wants to vote for no one, they are simply unable to do so – or, more precisely, will be counted with other 'mistakes'. In the United States, where rules vary by state, the *Washington Post*'s analysis of the 'undervote' in thirty-three states and DC in 2016 highlighted the fact that more than 1.75 million voters – representing 2 per cent of the vote, compared with just over 750,000 in 2012 – had decided not to vote in the presidential contest, even though they had submitted a ballot in other contests on the same day.[28] Indeed, both sides highlight the inherent restriction of the voice and power of the people that is characteristic of representative democracy: while citizens are given a stake in decision-making and governance through their vote, it is limited by the rules under which that vote takes place and the alternatives put forward and promoted.

While these rules have become part of a common-sense understanding, they provide a skewed view of the electorate and of democracy, understood as majoritarian decision-making. The following example illustrates this.

A referendum takes place, and the headline that follows reads: 'Proposition A wins with 52 per cent of the vote'. Should you read this headline only, as most people do, you could be forgiven for assuming that the proposition had received majority support. Should you read further, you might find that turnout was 72 per cent, indicating that over a quarter of citizens had decided not to

---

28 Chiara Superti, 'The Blank and Null Vote: An Alternative Form of Democratic Protest', manuscript, Harvard University, 2016.

turn up to vote, for whatever reason. While it would be wrong to assume they had all decided to stay home to make a political statement, the same stricture would apply to the claim that they were all politically apathetic, lazy, or whatever other condescending adjective is commonly attached to non-voters. Thus, would it not be more accurate to include the abstention rate in the headline: 'Proposition A elected with 37.44 per cent of the vote, while 28 percent abstain'? While our democratic systems are built on ignoring abstention, would it not be more representative to include it in the electoral picture? Otherwise, we must presumably conclude that these people who decide to abstain are not to be included in 'the People'. While voting is often wrongly seen as a duty rather than a right, should we expect someone to vote against their will in a democracy? And, if they do not, should we not still include them in some appropriate manner?

As many readers will have guessed, the electoral results used above are those of the 2016 EU referendum in the UK. Imagine the difference in narrative between: '52 per cent of the British people vote for Brexit' and '37.4 per cent of the British people vote for Brexit; 28 per cent decide not to take part'. The vote for Brexit would still win, but its victory would be far less convincing. Imagine the same adjustment to the presentation of the result of the 2016 US presidential election: 'Donald Trump elected with 26.7 per cent of the vote'. This headline would have resonated differently from the ones trumpeting the astounding victory Trump was then able to boast about. Three-quarters of US voters did not vote for Trump. As we show in our case studies, this discrepancy is even starker when we narrow our focus on various social and demographic characteristics, because certain social, age and ethnic groups tend to vote less than others. Of course, this argument about who is to be counted could be pushed even further, since all we have mentioned here are actual citizens who are registered and able to vote. This still leaves out millions of people uncounted on the basis of arbitrary restrictions relating to registration, age, nationality, criminal record, and so on.

We do not argue that those currently excluded from ballot counts should necessarily be included, or that those who abstain do so out of a political motivation and would not, for example, vote for racist parties if obliged to cast their ballots. We simply question the narratives advanced to justify incredibly important decisions. Equally, we do not believe that compulsory voting, which applies in Australia for example, represents a solution; the option of abstaining should not be removed, particularly in an authoritarian or punitive manner. Moreover, the limited options for political representation within the current democratic system would probably mean that any such measure would be used to enforce 'democratic' consent and legitimacy for the parties of the status quo. While there is no denying that those who win election contests do get to implement their politics and policies in our liberal-democratic system, this fact does not circumscribe what kinds of statement can be made about groups within society, and their voting patterns. We argue that ignoring abstention has two main consequences:

1. In post-democratic societies, where abstention is generally high, basing electoral analysis on the total number of votes as opposed to the number of registered voters tends to exaggerate results, and thus gives more power to the winner or to parties that happen to rise in the polls.

2. Ignoring abstention impairs analysis of voting patterns within sections of society. As Table 4.1 shows, abstention in the 2014 European elections was not evenly spread and – as is common between various countries and types of election – some categories, such as younger voters and those from lower social classes, tend to abstain more than their (older and wealthier) counterparts. In France, Braconnier and Dormagen found a correlation between the rate of electoral participation in Paris and the price of property per square metre; abstention was clearly not spread equally throughout the population.[29] This effect is compounded by the number of people unregistered or improperly registered voters, who were to be found predominantly in more deprived areas. This was sometimes – most notoriously in the United States – a result of active voter suppression.

---

29 Braconnier and Domargen, *Démocratie de l'abstention*.

	Voters (per cent)	Non-voters (per cent)
Gender		
Men	45	55
Women	41	59
Social class		
Self-employed	52	48
Managers	53	47
Other white-collar	44	56
Manual workers	35	65
House persons	37	63
Unemployed	31	69
Retired	50	50
Students	37	63

Table 4.1. Voters and non-voters in the European Elections in 2014. *Source: EU, 2015.*

THE WORKING-CLASS, POPULISM AND THE FAR RIGHT

In recent years, the working class has made a return to the forefront of political discourse.[30] It is no longer represented through the lens of class struggle, however, but instead argued to have turned to the far right in something more akin to a race struggle. This notion is based on the spurious or partial, and often ideological reading of data, and has a serious impact on the way in which the public views the working class, inequality and democracy. In October 2016, as the US election loomed, Nigel Farage wrote in an opinion piece in the *Sunday Telegraph*:

> The similarities between the different sides in this election are very like our own recent battle. As the rich get richer and big companies dominate the global economy, voters all across the West are being left behind.

---

30 This section is derived in part from Aurelien Mondon and Aaron Winter, 'Whiteness, Populism and the Racialisation of the Working Class in the United Kingdom and the United States', *Identities, Global Studies in Culture and Power*, 26:5 (2018). See also Aurelien Mondon, 'Limiting Democratic Horizons to a Nationalist Reaction: Populism, the Radical Right and the Working Class', *Javnost/The Public: Journal of the European Institute for Communication and Culture* 24: 3 (2017).

The blue-collar workers in the valleys of South Wales angry with Chinese steel dumping voted Brexit in their droves. In the American rust belt, traditional manufacturing industries have declined, and it is to these people that Trump speaks very effectively . . .

Statements of this kind were not limited to far-right politicians claiming political support from the working class, but were common in much political commentary in both the UK referendum and US election campaigns. For the *New Statesman*, Trump and Brexit represented 'a working-class revolt'. In March 2016, Fox News called Trump 'the working-class candidate'. In the UK, the *Daily Express* talked about a 'working-class revolution' on the day of the referendum, and right-wing libertarian *Spiked!* claimed: 'The Brexit vote was a revolt against the establishment', its editor arguing that 'Britain's poor and workless have risen up'. In the *Guardian*, John Harris claimed that 'Britain is in the midst of a working-class revolt', while Dreda Say Mitchell compared the anger felt by Remain voters to the way 'working-class people feel'. In the *New York Times*, David Brooks referred to Trump's election as a 'revolt of the masses', while Nate Cohn claimed that Trump had 'won working-class whites'. The same tendency can be seen in the work of scholars and analysts, some of whom we discussed in Chapter 3.

According to Robert Ford and Matthew Goodwin, support for Brexit was to be found within the working-class 'left-behind' who feared a loss of order and identity in 'a more diverse and rapidly changing Britain', championed by a homogenised and mythologised socially liberal elite.[31] As we have noted, J. D. Vance argued that Trump's support and success could be understood by looking at the economic and cultural crisis of the white working class and underclass in rural America,[32] while Arlie Hochschild suggested that Trump offered a 'solution' for white, native-born, heterosexual men who were the 'left behinds' of the celebration of other identities associated with the 1960s and 1970s.[33]

---

31   Robert Ford and Matthew Goodwin, 'Britain After Brexit: A Nation Divided', *Journal of Democracy* 28: 1 (January 2017).

32   J. D. Vance, *Hillbilly Elegy: A Memoir of a Family and Culture in Crisis* (London: Harper, 2017).

33   Arlie R. Hochschild, *Strangers in Their Own Land: Anger and Mourning on the American Right* (New York: New Press, 2016), p. 230.

The argument that Brexit was a white working-class revolt became so widely established that, for some, accusations of racism and far-right activism during and after the campaign were to be condemned as automatically 'classist'. The assumption of classism in criticism of Brexit and Trump support was of course informed by the notion that these were 'left behind' working class votes, as well as their populist framing as 'the people' vs the elites. This sense of abandonment was reinforced and given extra power by Hillary Clinton's patronising and insulting reference to Trump supporters as 'deplorables' in a 2016 speech: 'You know, to just be grossly generalistic, you could put half of Trump's supporters into what I call the basket of deplorables . . . Right? . . . They're racist, sexist, homophobic, xenophobic – Islamophobic – you name it'. The term would continue to be used to prove the contempt political elites have for 'the people' and support the rationale for the votes. In addition to numerous articles, Spiked! even produced a film titled *Deplorables: Trump, Brexit and the Demonised Masses.*[34]

In terms of racism specifically, since the assumption was that the working class was white, criticism was often taken to imply a form of (post-racial) reverse racism. *Spiked!* editor Brendan O'Neill claimed that the bigotry was directed by the elites against the demos, arguing that 'Brexit Voters are not thick, not racist: just poor', and that 'Britain's poor and workless have risen up'. In response to the rise in hate crime, Luke Gittos claimed that 'the onset of panic has revealed how the very publications and commentators who once claimed to stand up for the working class in fact view working-class people as a violent, racist horde'.[35] Yet, although these and other commentators appeared to be defending working-class people, the link between Brexit, the working class and racism was in fact constructed in these very analyses. By assuming that the working class voted for Brexit, accusations that Brexit was racist could only be about the working class. While one could say this is not the only conclusion that can be drawn from this, the assumption that the working class is racist was also part of the narrative by many of these actors when they explained working class support for Brexit in terms of the 'Left Behind' thesis which pointed

---

34   Spiked!, *Deplorables: Trump, Brexit and the Demonised Masses* (2019).
35   See Winter, 'Brexit and Trump'.

to working class anti-immigrant sentiment as a main factor. They thereby revealed their class prejudice and exonerated themselves as both actors in shaping public discourse and, in some cases, far-right legitimisers.

While this narrative was clear and widespread, the nature of 'the working class' was rarely defined, or took various shapes – though most frequently white and 'native'. Of course, the representation and use of the working class as 'the people' is not new. It was mostly derived from the mythologised nature of this particular group and its role in politics since the industrial revolution. As Selina Todd notes, in the twentieth century, and specifically after the Second World War, 'the working class became "the people", whose interests were synonymous with those of Britain itself'.[36] In a trend that was obviously not limited to the UK, the working class became imbued with a peculiarly democratic quality, for a long time rightly praised for many of the social advancements that had taken place in the west, often won through huge self-sacrifice.

Yet the working class was also constantly feared by the elite, which complained about the 'rule of the mob' as it struggled to retain its privileges. For many commentators, this changed in the second part of the twentieth century: 'the "respectable" working class had ended in the 1960s; by the 1980s people had been made lazy by welfare, greedy by consumerism or arrogant by trade unionism ... But the stories of ordinary people remind us it was never quite like that: there was no golden age.'[37]

Falling victim to this simplification and away from its traditional emancipatory meaning, the conception of the working class identified with the far-right vote has taken on a different meaning, in which it is no longer the beating heart of democracy but has instead become synonymous with white reaction. The elite, seen as out of touch and contemptuous, is still targeted through populism. Yet the real enemy is clearly the

---

36   Selina Todd, *The People: The Rise and Fall of the Working Class, 1910–2010* (London: John Murray, 2015), p. 1. For Todd, 'Class is a relationship defined by unequal power, rather than a way of life or an unchanging culture. There can be no "ideal" or "traditional" working class. Instead, there are individuals who are brought together by shared circumstances and experiences' (p. 7).

37   Ibid., p. 5.

other, whether immigrants, Muslims, refugees or their allies. In this discourse, it is them, not the elite, who threaten jobs and resources. The construction of a 'white working class' is therefore a displacement of rightful anger in the form of a struggle in which the enemy is defined only by race, ethnicity or foreign nationality, rather than by class. By operating what has been described by Miri Song as a culture of racial equivalence, this post-racial narrative promotes a notion of white victimhood and negates any notion of white privilege.[38]

Our argument is not that the working class should be seen uncritically as a vessel for emancipatory politics, as is too often claimed by some on the left. This claim is simplistic. It ignores the forces at play in different contexts and the ways in which the nature and composition of the working class can be perverted and diverted by powerful social narratives. Yet we hope to highlight the particular narrative which has been privileged in much of elite discourse, which equates the working class with the rise of the far right. This will allow us to understand the ideological underpinnings of this manoeuvre, which places the blame squarely on the voiceless, cynically divided along racial lines, thereby deflecting attention from those responsible for the current sociopolitical situation.

The case studies below demonstrate that such claims are not only untenable in light of the data, but also ideologically loaded in such a way as to have serious impacts on the very nature of democracy. Before turning to these case studies, it is important to clarify that our use of the concept 'working class' is based on elite narratives about the working class. We do not intend to account comprehensively for the political preferences and potentials of the working class, but rather to highlight the fragility – even in its own terms – of the elite discourse that frames the working class as the key base of support for the far right.

Make the American Working Class Great Again?

It is true that an analysis of exit polls conducted by Edison Research for the National Election Pool points to strong performance by Trump

---

38   Miri Song, 'Challenging a Culture of Racial Equivalence', *British Journal of Sociology* 65: 1 (2014), pp. 107–29.

among poorly educated white men (see Tables 4.1, 4.2).[39] Compared to the data from 2012, the shift in the vote by income level is also striking, showing a much smaller gap between the two main candidates within the two lowest income categories. Here already, however, it must be noted that Hillary Clinton, the Democratic candidate, still received a majority of the vote in these categories, traditionally associated with the working class. Yet what is interesting, and conspicuously absent in much of the media coverage about the 'white working-class revolt', is the comparison between Trump's level of support and that of previous Republican candidates. While Trump did appeal to poorer voters in larger numbers than Mitt Romney or John McCain, his performance was similar to that of George W. Bush, suggesting that Trump's victory may not in fact have represented the widely advertised working-class breakthrough.

Equally, this was not the first time the 'populist' appeal to white working-class traditional Democratic voters has been mobilised. In 1980, and later in 1984, Ronald Reagan famously mobilised so-called 'Reagan Democrats'. These were moderate white working-class residents of the industrial and post-industrial, so called 'Rust Belt', states, who had traditionally voted for the Democrats. Reagan targeted and mobilised this bloc, bringing it over to the Republicans with his narrative of renewal ('Morning Again in America'), rhetoric of the 'Silent Majority', and conservative outlook on cultural issues such as abortion, race (as governor of California, Reagan had a history of opposing civil rights and the Black Panthers), immigration, national security (particularly during the Cold War and in the wake of the Iranian Revolution), and economic issues. Reagan not only promised to avoid the crises which beset the 1970s under Carter (such as the oil crisis), but managed to lend a democratic tone to his advocacy of free markets and trickledown economics. One illustrative case is that of Macomb County, Michigan – a county highly populated by white, unionised auto workers, 63 per cent of whose voters had turned out for John F. Kennedy in 1960.[40] In 1984, Reagan won 66 per cent of the county's

---

39   Jon Huang, Samuel Jacoby, Michael Strickland and K. K. Rebecca Lai, 'Election 2016: Exit Polls', *New York Times*, 8 November 2016.

40   Stanley B. Greenberg, *Middle Class Dreams: Politics and Power of the New American Majority* (New Haven: Yale University Press, 1996).

electorate. This constituency allowed Reagan to be seen as the president of the white working class while he oversaw mass deindustrialisation and the farm crisis that led to the revival of the far right. And this strategy was not new. Richard Nixon, whose 'Silent Majority' concept was used by Reagan, had already created a 'Southern Strategy', which appealed to racism and fears about the impact of civil and voting rights amongst white voters, and notably white conservative Democrat voters.[41]

	Size of category in 2016	2016		2012		2008		2004	
		Clinton	Trump	Obama	Romney	Obama	McCain	Kerry	Bush
Under $30,000	17	53	41	63	35	65	32	6	40
$30,000 – $49,999	19	51	42	57	42	55	43	50	49
$50,000 – $99,999	31	46	50	46	52	49	49	44	56
$100,000 – $199,999	24	47	48	44	54	48	51	42	57
$200,000 or more	10	47	49	44	54	52	46	35	63

Table 4.2. Per cent vote in presidential elections according to income. *Source: NYT/ Edison Research.*

While income levels of voters already provide reason to question the hegemonic narrative around Trump's breakthrough, the same is true in relation to education. Romney and McCain did particularly poorly against Obama within the least educated voter categories, making Trump's appeal within these categories seem like a real breakthrough. However, Trump's performance appears far less

41   Chip Berlet and Matthew Lyons, *Right-Wing Populism in America: Too Close for Comfort* (New York: Guilford, 2003); Sara Diamond, *Roads to Dominion: Right-Wing Movements and Political Power in the United States* (New York: Guilford, 1995); Michael Omi and Howard Winant, *Racial Formation in the United States: From the 1960s to the 1990s* (New York: Routledge, 1994).

exceptional when compared to that of George W. Bush in 2004 (see Table 4.3).

	Size of category in 2016	2016		2012		2008		2004	
		Clinton	Trump	Obama	Romney	Obama	McCain	Kerry	Bush
Some college/ associate degree	32	43	52	49	48	51	47	46	54
College graduate	32	49	45	47	51	50	48	46	52
Postgraduate study	18	58	37	55	42	58	40	55	44
High school graduate	18	45	51	51	48	52	46	47	52
No high school diploma				64	35	63	35	50	49

Table 4.3. Per cent vote in presidential elections according to level of education. *Source: NYT/ Edison Research.*

Finally, Trump's performance with white voters was certainly strong, but does not appear to have been significantly different from that of previous Republican candidates (see Table 4.4).

	Size of category in 2016	2016		2012		2008		2004	
		Clinton	Trump	Obama	Romney	Obama	McCain	Kerry	Bush
White	70	37	58	39	59	43	55	41	58
Black	12	88	8	93	6	95	4	88	11
Hispanic/ Latino	11	65	29	71	27	67	31	53	44
Asian	4	65	29	73	26	62	35	56	44
Other	3	56	37	58	38	66	31	54	40

Table 4.4. Per cent vote in presidential elections according to race. *Source: NYT/ Edison Research.*

There is no denying, however, that Trump managed to appeal to more less-educated white men than his predecessors. While Bush and Romney attracted the votes of 61 per cent of the whites without a college degree, and McCain 58 per cent, Trump won the support of 67 per cent in that category. Yet the narrative of Trump's 'break-through' is nuanced further by Konstantin Kilibarda and Daria Roithmayr's analysis of the 'myth of the rust belt revolt', which demonstrates that Clinton in fact lost more white working-class votes compared to Obama than Trump gained compared to Romney in 2012.[42] It is also worth noting that Trump also won the majority of white professional males with a college education, and over 40 per cent of white professional females with a college education, pointing further to race, specifically whiteness, over class as a factor. This insight is supported by a Public Religion Research Institute survey showing that Trump's appeal could be better explained by a fear of cultural displacement (such as the loss of white, male, Christian privilege) shared by whites across classes, than by real or feared economic displacement.[43]

Interestingly, responses to supplementary questions in the exit poll suggest that, beyond the traditional Republican electorate of middle- and upper-class conservatives, Trump managed to appeal to an electorate demographically similar to the one that has underpinned the resurgence of the far right in Europe. This particular segment feels insecure about its future, even though it remains in a relatively privileged position, and is more interested in issues such as immigration and terrorism than the economy. Therefore, rather than a radical shift of the working class towards Trump, what has taken place is the development of a typical, 'European-style' far-right electorate.

While this is certainly a concerning development, the size of this portion of the electorate is marginal, and would not have been sufficient for Trump to win had the Democrats managed to retain

---

42   Konstantin Kilibarda and Daria Roithmayr, 'The Myth of the Rust Belt Revolt', *Slate*, 1 December 2016. See also John Henley, 'White and Wealthy Voters Gave Victory to Donald Trump, Exit Polls Show', *Guardian*, 9 November 2016.

43   Niraj Chokshi, 'Trump Voters Driven by Fear of Losing Status, Not Economic Anxiety, Study Finds', *New York Times*, 24 April 2018.

their share of the vote. Another key finding is that the largest share of Trump's electorate does not appear to differ in composition from the traditional Republican electorate since the Reagan era, and resembles the profile of Bush's voters in particular. This means that Trump's victory represents more the confirmation of a trend that emerged with Nixon – characterised by the increasing normalisation of racism in American politics and the resurgence of the far right – than a real break from politics as usual.

FN/RN as The Working-Class Party?

The French case points to some similar trends. It is common to read that the FN/RN has taken a more 'social' turn under Marine Le Pen's leadership. While there is no doubt that the party has evolved in its approach to economic issues, away from its outright neoliberal stance in the 1980s, this strategy has been slower, and more subtle and rhetorical, than is usually recognised.[44] Similarly, the focus on former left-wing bastions is not new, and the party had its first breakthrough in 1983 in local elections in Dreux, in northern France, where it won 16 per cent of the vote. Nonetheless, much of the economic discourse emanating from the FN/RN today does indeed appear to target the working class, and the fact that the party and Marine Le Pen herself have been relatively successful in the industrial Nord-Pas-de-Calais, in particular, tends to confirm that trend.

Yet a closer look at opinion surveys and the FN electorate demonstrates that the link between the working class and the FN was not as direct or strong as is often assumed, and that this disproportionate focus leads to an incomplete understanding of the appeal and support base of the party. Nonna Mayer already demonstrated in 2002 that the role of class in the vote for the FN was murkier than was commonly thought. Contradicting the theory of 'leftwing lepenism' (*gaucho-lepénisme*),[45] Mayer argued

---

44 See Sylvain Crépon, Alexandre Dézé and Nonna Mayer, eds, *Les faux-semblants du Front National* (Paris: Les Presses de Sciences Po., 2015).

45 Nonna Mayer, *Ces Français qui votent Le Pen* (Paris: Flammarion, 2002); Pascal Perrineau, *Le symptôme Le Pen; radiographie des électeurs du Front national* (Paris: Fayard, 1997).

that the FN did not draw its support from former left-wing work-ing-class voters, but rather from those alienated from previous forms of political socialisation, whom she called the *ninistes* ('neither-nors'). Florent Gougou's analysis of working-class voting patterns in France demonstrated further that the shift in pattern away from the left was to be taken with caution, and that, while the FN benefited from this realignment, other factors had to be taken into account, such as abstention and the generational divide.[46] Gougou's analysis also suggests that, like UKIP, the FN has gener-ally done better in working-class communities where the right already had a hold, while workers in traditionally left-wing communities appear to have chosen abstention.

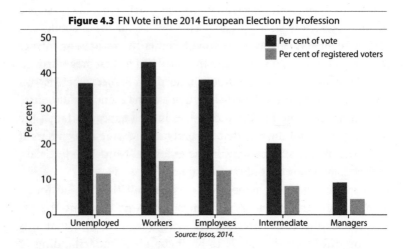

Figure 4.3 FN Vote in the 2014 European Election by Profession

Source: Ipsos, 2014.

Gougou's call for caution when studying the working-class vote in France is vindicated by an analysis of surveys conducted after the 2014 European election, when the FN claimed to have become the 'largest party in France'. As Figure 4.3 shows, surveys suggest that the FN vote comes predominantly from voters who are part of the

46   Florent Gougou, 'Les mutations du vote ouvrier sous la Ve république', *Fondations* 1: 5 (2014).

unemployed, worker or employee categories (37 per cent, 43 per cent and 38 per cent, respectively), compared to 20 per cent for intermediate professions and 9 per cent for the managerial class. Yet when abstention is taken into account, the disparity becomes much less impressive, the FN garnering registered votes in the following shares: 11.5 per cent for the unemployed, 15 per cent for workers, 12.2 per cent for the unemployed, 8 per cent for middle management (*intermédiaires*) and 4.2 per cent for the managerial class. While the FN vote in this calculation remains predominantly anchored in what is commonly understood as the broad working class, the difference between the share of the largest segment of the vote in the first calculation – 34 percentage points between workers and managers – falls below 11 percentage points when the registered vote is counted.

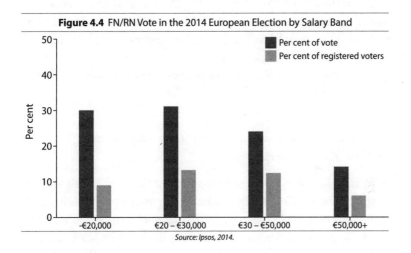

Figure 4.4 FN/RN Vote in the 2014 European Election by Salary Band

Source: Ipsos, 2014.

However, more nuance can be incorporated into this calculation by taking salaries of respondents into account (see Figure 4.4). In this case, it is those in the middle categories of the salary range who appear to have voted predominantly for the FN, rather than the poorest. This is confirmed by the research undertaken by Nonna Mayer in France, according to which the portion of the lower classes

who turn to the FN are those with something to lose (skilled workers, independents, shopkeepers, and so on). This significantly alters
the narrative of the FN as the party of the working class, as only 9
per cent of those on the lowest incomes voted for Le Pen's party,
compared to 13 per cent of those earning between €20,000 and
€30,000, and even 12.2 per cent for those earning between €30,000
and €50,000. The difference between the lowest and highest earners
is a mere 2 percentage points once registered voters (and thus
abstentions) are taken into account.

Nonetheless, it is the party's claim of being a champion of the
working class which placed its leader in an ideal position in 2017,
when Le Pen was able to present herself as the candidate of the
people against the elite. If not for Macron's surprise candidature and
success, she would have been in an excellent position to reap not
only the benefits of her party, through its reconstruction, but also
those produced, often inadvertently, by much of the media and
other politicians, through their careless association of the far-right
party with 'the people'. While Le Pen had demonstrated the limit of
her appeal once again – particularly in her return to more unadorned
far-right strategies – this fact attracted very little comment. A deeply
entrenched myth remained mostly unchallenged.

The British Working Class: Reactionary, Xenophobic and Drawn to Right-Wing Populism?

In the UK, the rise of UKIP and the so-called 'revolt on the right' have
commonly been linked to the working class and its predisposition for
turning to populist alternatives. Yet the claim made most forcefully by
Goodwin and Ford – namely that UKIP is 'the most working-class
party' – is not only untenable, but damaging.[47] Most obviously, the
'working class', understood in socioeconomic terms continues to vote
predominantly for Labour and the Conservatives (see Table 4.5).
Moreover, it is clear from the rhetoric of political campaigns that the
common representation of the working class and their interests and

---

47   Rob Ford and Matthew Goodwin, *Revolt on the Right: Explaining Support for the Radical Right in Britain* (Abingdon: Routledge, 2014).

politics is not framed in socioeconomic terms, but in terms of whiteness, racism and xenophobia.

The alleged sentiments of the working class on issues like immigration and multiculturalism are tacitly validated, and then framed as the source of its disenfranchisement, in preference to socioeconomic factors. According to Goodhart, the increased diversity produced by mass immigration has threatened social solidarity for those attached to their locality and traditions, who he refers to as 'somewheres' – in contradistinction to the rootless, socially liberal, middle-class, cosmopolitan 'anywheres'.[48] What is omitted from this analysis is the socioeconomic dimension of working-class inequality, regardless of race and settled status. Where internal differences occur, they are often due to the racism and racial inequality suffered disproportionately by working-class BME people. Goodhart's narrative privileges instead notions of culture, reinforcing fears of difference, ignoring socioeconomic realities, and foregrounding racial and ethnic differences as the cause of inequality for the – especially white – working class. As a result, it not only legitimises racism, but also limits our under-standing of structural and socioeconomic inequalities, and our ability to develop emancipatory responses to address them. For the Runnymede Trust, the racialisation of the working class and the focus on white interests ignores the wider diversity of the working class and the inequality faced by black and minority ethnic communities, migrants and refugees, who form a large part of it,[49] as they have done historically.[50] Such

---

48 David Goodhart, *The British Dream: Successes and Failures of Post-War Immigration* (London: Atlantic, 2013); David Goodhart, *The Road to Somewhere: The Populist Revolt and the Future of Politics* (London: C. Hurst, 2017).

49 Omar Khan and Faiza Shaheen, *Minority Report: Race and Class in Post-Brexit Britain*, Runnymede Trust/CLASS, 2017.

50 See Satnam Virdee, *Race, Class and the Racialised Outsider* (Basingstoke: Palgrave, 2014); Jagdish Patel, '"Both Racism and Anti-Racism Were Present in the Making of the English Working Class"': An Interview with Satnam Virdee', *Media Diversified*, 18 November 2015. This is also the case in the United States, but is often ignored in analysis of Trump and the white working class. See Aurelien Mondon and Aaron Winter, 'Whiteness, Populism and the Racialisation of the Working Class in the United Kingdom and the United States'; Noel Ignatiev, *How the Irish Became White* (London: Routledge, 1995); Matthew Frye Jacobson, *Whiteness of a Different Colour* (London: Routledge, 1998); David

divide-and-rule politics have constructed a framework of zero-sum competition for representation and reduced resources between the 'indigenous' white working class and 'others'. Yet socioeconomic inequality and related issues (poverty, lack of social mobility, low wages, poor housing and inadequate institutional representation), predominantly represented as white working-class problems, 'cut across racial groups', with ethnic minorities suffering the brunt of austerity politics.[51]

Such claims about working-class support for far-right politics, reported across much of the media, become even more implausible when the role of abstention, and in particular its spread among the working class, is taken into account. The understanding of class in British surveys is often based on the 'social grades' taken from the National Readership Survey, in which A, B and C1 represent the middle class and C2, D and E represent the working class. As Mark Rubin and his colleagues argue, this categorisation is obviously far from precise, as it ignores differences between individuals and the impact that numerous factors – such as geography, and personal, national and local history – have on behaviour.[52] This definition is obviously problematic, considering the points made about public opinion above. Yet the label itself is simply misleading, since it ignores those at the bottom who have truly been left behind, but are routinely ignored by those who assert the salience of the 'white working class'.

Despite the problematic data available, our aim is to show that – using the very tools used to create the narratives we hope to challenge – electoral analysis uncovers some important findings regarding the selection of certain narratives over others. In 2015, in its best-ever performance in a general election, UKIP received 12.7 per cent of the

---

Roediger, *The Wages of Whiteness: Race and the Making of the American Working Class* (New York: Verso, 1999).

51   Omar Khan, 'Who Cares About the White Working Class?', *Huffington Post UK*, 21 March 2017. See also Runnymede Trust, *The 2015 Budget Effects on Black and Minority Ethnic People*, Runnymede Trust (July 2015). Bassel and Emejulu, *Minority Women and Austerity*.

52   See Oliver Heath and Matthew Goodwin, 'The 2017 General Election, Brexit and the Return to Two-Party Politics: An Aggregate-Level Analysis of the Result', *Political Quarterly* 88: 3 (2017).

vote. Table 4.5 provides a breakdown of the results as they would traditionally be taken up in much of the media, that is, without abstention taken into account.

	Con	Lab	LD	UKIP	Greens	Other
AB	45	26	12	8	4	5
C1	41	29	8	11	4	7
C2	32	32	6	19	4	7
DE	27	41	5	17	3	7

Table 4.5. GE2015 results shown in per cents.

Social classes are taken from the National Readership Survey (2008). A = higher managerial, administrative and professional; B = intermediate managerial, administrative and professional; C1 = supervisory, clerical and junior managerial, administrative and professional; C2 = skilled manual workers; D = semi-skilled and unskilled manual workers; and E = state pensioners, casual and lowest-grade workers, and unemployed with state benefits only.

Source: Ipsos MORI 2015.

Table 4.5 shows that UKIP seems to have been particularly appealing to categories C2 and DE. Yet, as we have made clear, UKIP has not functioned as the pre-eminent working-class party, since the Conservative and Labour parties continue to have far greater appeal than the far-right party in these occupational categories. When abstention is taken into account, the narrative of UKIP as the party representing the working class collapses altogether. As demonstrated by Figure 4.5, once all registered voters are accounted for, the gap between categories DE and C2, on one hand, and categories C1 and AB on the other becomes much narrower, and UKIP's performance within these categories is far less impressive. Obviously, this also ignores all unregistered voters and non-citizens who nonetheless have a stake in the community, pay taxes, or, as residents, are simply affected by the decisions made by politicians.

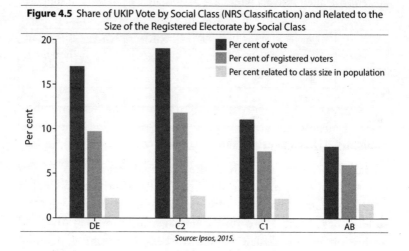

Figure 4.5 Share of UKIP Vote by Social Class (NRS Classification) and Related to the Size of the Registered Electorate by Social Class

Source: Ipsos, 2015.

Another issue with the reporting of electoral results is that it tends to assume that each of the four social categories specified is equal in size, so that AB, C1, C2 and DE are each worth one-quarter of the electorate. This is inaccurate, and the sizes of these classes vary dramatically. As the third column of Figure 4.5 shows, when related to the electorate as a whole, the size of UKIP's DE and C2 vote amounted respectively to 2.2 per cent and 2.5 per cent of the total electorate, while UKIP's C1 and AB vote amounted to 2.2 per cent and 1.6 per cent of the electorate, respectively. Thus, when abstention and the size of respective social classes are taken into account, DE and C2 together account for 55 per cent of UKIP's vote, while C1 and AB account for 45 per cent. If the data are understood in this way, UKIP not only ceases to seem like the main working-class party, but loses its character as a working-class party altogether.

This conclusion is supported by the work of Geoffrey Evans and Jonathan Mellon, which is based on much more sophisticated data analysis:

Working class voters are a little more likely to support UKIP than other classes, but there is stronger support among the self-employed and business owners, who were Mrs Thatcher's hard-core support-ers, not Labour's. Even within the working class, the strongest UKIPers are the lower supervisory category, who are not the disad-vantaged semi- and unskilled workers that have been thought to provide the core of UKIP support.[53]

The narrative around the 2016 European Union referendum is similarly misleading. According to Danny Dorling, 'of all those who voted for Leave 59 per cent were middle class (A, B and C1), and 41 per cent were working class (C2, D and E)'.[54] Claims that Brexit was a working-class revolt are further undermined by a geographical study of the vote. Among people who voted Leave, 52 per cent lived in the southern half of England. For Derek Sayer, the discrepancies between the results in Scotland and Northern Ireland, which both voted overwhelmingly for Remain (by 62 per cent and 55.8 per cent, respectively), and Wales and England, which both favoured Brexit (by 52.5 per cent and 53.4 per cent, respectively) increase the need for a more nuanced approach, since 'there is no consistent correla-tion with income levels across the regions that might help explain these disparities in class terms'.[55] Were it simply a question of class qua income, for example, Scotland and Northern Ireland, whose gross disposable household income (GDHI) is lower than the UK average, would have been fertile ground for Brexit. Based on similar data, Wales, whose GDHI is lower than all of the English regions, returned a stronger Remain vote (albeit with a Brexit majority). Out of the top ten Leave districts, only two could be considered working class in the most general understanding of the term, the other eight being either found in rural areas or in depressed seaside and fishing towns.

---

53   Geoffrey Evans and Jonathan Mellon, 'Working Class Votes and Conservative Losses: Solving the UKIP Puzzle', LSE blog, 30 April 2015.

54   Danny Dorling, 'Brexit: The Decision of a Divided Country', *BMJ*, 6 July 2016, p. 354.

55   Derek Sayer, 'White Riot – Brexit, Trump, and Post-Factual Politics', *Journal of Historical Sociology* 30: 1 (2017).

While analysis of the vote already provides us with a number of qualifications to the hegemonic narrative placing the blame for the Brexit decision squarely on irrational working-class voters, the inclusion of abstention as a variable weakens such generalising claims even further. Unfortunately, the Ashcroft poll, which we use in our analysis, does not provide estimates of abstention by social class, but applying the data available for the 2015 general election regarding participation (see above), while not a perfect match, raises some interesting questions – the most obvious being the neglect of abstention as an important variable in our democracies.[56] The following results were therefore calculated assuming a similar rate of abstention within each election, but adjusted according to their overall turnout (27.8 per cent versus 33.9 per cent). Taking abstention into account renders the difference between social classes far less convincing, since the DE and C2 groups register a lower turnout than C1 and AB, causing the gap between C2 (42.3 per cent) and AB (35.2 per cent) to narrow from 21 percentage points when taking only the number of votes into account to just 7 percentage points when taking abstention into account. With this calculation, the difference between C1 (38.3 per cent) and DE (39.8 per cent) becomes marginal, thus refuting the working-class nature of the vote. This differential between classes is further undermined when taking account of the size of each of these social classes within the entire population (see Figure 4.6): AB (9.5 per cent) and C1 (11.1 per cent) become the largest sources of Leave voters, above both C2 (9 per cent) and DE (9 per cent). This more nuanced picture further undermines the claim that the poor, the working classes, or ordinary people rose up against the well-off elite.

56   Lord Ashcroft, 'How the United Kingdom Voted on Thursday … and Why', lordashcroftpolls.com, 24 June 2016.

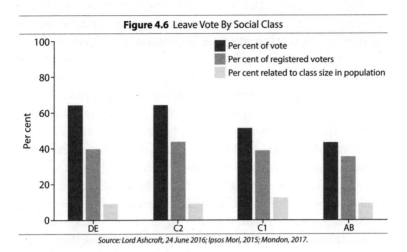

Figure 4.6 Leave Vote By Social Class

Source: Lord Ashcroft, 24 June 2016; Ipsos Mori, 2015; Mondon, 2017.

Some attention has also been paid to the pattern of voting in the EU referendum within BAME communities.[57] Although it does challenge the 'white working-class' Brexit narrative, we do not expand on it here, as the focus of this section is white working-class support. Moreover, according to the Runnymede Trust, ethnic minority voters backed Remain by a significant margin regardless of income;[58] meanwhile, votes from within these communities are often invoked by Brexiters, along with claims about allowing Commonwealth immigration instead of EU immigration after Brexit, in order to rebut accusations that Brexit has been chiefly a white and/or racist project. The argument relating to Commonwealth immigration could also be explained as an attempt to broaden its support base, evoking a nostalgia for empire that also played a role in more elite Brexit campaign discourses.[59]

---

57 Neema Begum, *Race and the Referendum: An Intersectional Analysis of Ethnic Minority and White Voting Behaviour in the 2016 EU Referendum*, Bristol, PhD Dissertation, University of Bristol, 2020.

58 Khan and Shaheen, *Minority Report*.

59 See Charlie Bayliss, 'Empire 2.0: UK to "Improve Trade Links with African Commonwealth Nations" after Brexit', *Sunday Express*, 6 March 2017.

As our three case studies show, widely available data suggest that more than one narrative can be proposed regarding support for the far right among the working class. Nonetheless, a particular angle has been widely adopted across elite discourse, and we argue that this has had two major consequences: a) it has legitimised the far right and its politics as representative of 'the people'; and b) it has promoted the vilification of the people qua working class, and, in turn, of what the working class represents in our collective democratic consciousness. Of course, we do not seek to deny that part of the working class supports the far right, or that some may have switched from a formerly left-wing allegiance to what would once have been considered a mortal enemy. However, revealing the complexity of the vote for the so-called populist right has allowed us to place it back within its historical and socioeconomic contexts, and to underline the fact that its recent rise is not only itself limited, but is only one among many symptoms of dysfunction within liberal democracies.

POPULISM, POPULIST HYPE AND THE HATRED OF THE PEOPLE

When we study populism, we talk about populism, we articulate meanings in language and discourse, and language is never innocent.

Yannis Stavrakakis

'Populism' is today ubiquitous in public discourse. In November 2018, the *Guardian* launched an 'investigation into the rise of a global phenomenon', with the collaboration of over thirty academics. While it is clear that scholars hoped they would be able to share their research with a wider audience, the *Guardian* took a clearly opportunistic approach, with hip designs and clickbait headlines. On the first day of this investigation, the main articles warned us that 'one in four Europeans votes populist' without telling us quite what populism was or how difficult it is to define, let alone place parties and leaders in neat boxes. More strikingly, perhaps, an article asked candidly: 'Why Is Populism Suddenly All the Rage?', while its standfirst stated obliviously: 'In 1998, about 300 *Guardian* articles mentioned populism. In 2016, 2,000 did. What happened?' Journalists who had been working with experts for weeks had never considered that part of the answer as to why populism was 'all the rage' might have lain in that very stand-first: agenda-setting was not part of their remit; they were mere purveyors of news, with no political role to play and no intended effect to generate through their work. Things deteriorated on the second day, when no less than four articles dedicated to Steve Bannon's failed European adventure led the website. As the former Breitbart editor struggled to gain any ground in Europe, and was gradually dropping off the radar, the Guardian felt it appropriate to lend him a hand with some catchy headlines: 'Steve Bannon: I Want to Drive a Stake through the Brussels Vampire'; 'Bannon's Europe Plan'. Should you have read further than the headlines, you would have discovered that he had become largely irrelevant at this stage, craving attention as his grand plans collapsed. Yet how many of us read past the headlines of so many articles? The Guardian later published an interview with Hillary Clinton, whose headline declared: 'Europe Must Curb Immigration to Stop Rightwing Populists'. If you can't beat them, join them.

These are just examples from one outlet. More widely, hardly a day passes without the media warning us about the next populist threat. Hardly an election goes by without so-called populist parties shaping the campaign, even though their performance is more often than not below expectations. Since the Brexit vote and the election of Donald Trump, which took place in close succession and were widely hyped as populist revolts, most elections are seen through the prism of 'populism'. In 2017, it was the Dutch who were set to deliver with another populist earthquake. An opinion piece in the Washington Post even asked whether 'the "Dutch Trump" [would] win next week's election in the Netherlands', while BBC news warned: 'Dutch Populist Geert Wilders Is Scenting Victory'. On 15 March, while his one-man-party PVV finished second, this remained a poor performance, in which it took only 13.1 per cent of the vote. While this was no doubt concerning, it was nonetheless far from what Wilders had expected, and in fact 2.3 percentage points below his 2010 result, despite his much enhanced public profile. Unsurprisingly, while international interest was huge before the election, the spotlight on Dutch politics quickly faded, and you could soon have been forgiven if you did not know who won the election and went on to govern the country.

A similar event took place in Sweden in 2018. The *Wall Street Journal* predicted 'a populist surprise in Sweden' two days before the election, while the *Guardian* warned of the 'danger ahead'. Here again, while the Sweden Democrats did achieve an increase of 5 percentage points in their share of the vote compared to the previous election, the Social Democrats, who had been leading a rather unpopular coalition, managed to stem the tide, despite the campaign being fought over immigration and the so-called 'refugee crisis' – demonstrating that voters remained for the most part immune to the far right's framing of these issues. The Sweden Democrats ultimately polled worse than predicted; again, most are now unaware of the current situation in Sweden, since interest in the country's politics has vanished now that the populist wave, created in and by the media, has receded, if only temporarily. In Germany, something similar took place. While we have been told that the main story is all about the AfD, the impressive rise of the Greens has been mostly ignored.

The metaphor of the populist wave is actually fairly accurate in describing the phenomenon, albeit not in the sense it is commonly used. The media tend to picture this wave as generated by 'populist parties' themselves, and fuelled by the support of disgruntled masses (usually the white working class), crashing against the banks of liberal democracy in election after election. Catastrophising headlines are common, referring to natural disasters and evoking war (earthquakes, the people's army, and so on). Yet the wave is in fact not created primarily by the far right or its supporters, whose performance is uneven and whose agendas vary widely. While they may increase in certain cases, they usually remain in the minority across the board, more often than not polling closer to 10 per cent than 50 per cent, particularly when abstention is taken into account. Instead, the wave, such as it is, is created by media frenzy and fuelled by opportunistic mainstream politicians and pundits – warmly welcomed by the far right.

This focus on populism is not limited to the media, or to politicians who claim to be populists themselves or attack their opponents for being populists. Academics have also played their part, developing a huge volume of literature on the topic.[60] While many colleagues have approached the issue in a real attempt to understand the present conjuncture, the neoliberalisation of higher education and the 'sexiness' of the topic have attracted a flock of more opportunistic scholars, whose work has only served to obscure real efforts to flesh out not only what populism is, but also how it functions. These academic entrepreneurs often move from one topic to another engaging with the field in a cursory manner; and yet, with their expert status and often well-oiled PR machine, they do great damage to the fields they ravage, and have a dramatic impact on public discourse. In the most extreme cases, this approach has been used to push the clear liberal-racist agendas discussed earlier.

Our aim here is not to engage with the academic debates on populism – something we and others have done elsewhere, at great length, and which is not directly relevant to this book.[61] Instead, we have addressed the way in which populism is discussed more generally, and the impact it has on the wider public discourse. Yet we should first make clear what we believe populism is, as this will inform how we talk about the discourse around it. We understand populism as a discourse centred on a construction or constructions of 'the people' against a similarly constructed 'elite'. Parties that are explicitly far right, far left, socialist, nationalist, racist – or subscribe to any other ideology – can also be populist, but none is populist by definition. They can be said to be populist to the extent that they rely in their discourse on the construction of a people against a real or perceived elite. 'The people' can thus be inclusive (the poor, 'the 99 per cent') or exclusive (white men, British people based on nationality or race). Populism is thus neither good nor bad, and it cannot be used on its own to explain any political phenomenon: there is no such thing as a populist party.[62]

---

60 See Cristóbal Rovira Kaltwasser, Paul A. Taggart, Paulina Ochoa Espejo and Pierre Ostiguy, eds, *Oxford Handbook of Populism* (Oxford: Oxford University Press, 2017), p. 9.

61 For one of the most thorough and accessible overviews of the state of the art, discussing key theoretical debates, see Giorgos Katsambekis, 'The Populist Surge in Post-Democratic Times: Theoretical and Political Challenges', *Political Quarterly*, 88: 2 (2016), pp. 1–9.

62 Benjamin De Cleen, Jason Glynos and Aurelien Mondon, 'Critical Research on

What we have witnessed in much of the coverage of the 'populist wave' in the West has been the almost exclusive association of the term 'populism' with the far right. While in other parts of the world, such as Latin America, populism has been more commonly associated with left-wing politics, in Europe and North America it has predominantly been linked to racist parties and movements such as the FN/RN, UKIP and the Republican Party under Donald Trump. This link is problematic for two main reasons: it legitimises the far right and its ideas and delegitimises the people as central to the democratic process. The etymology of the term 'populism' suggests that populists may represent the true wish of the 'people'. When linked to the far right, this means that the people come to be represented as an irrational mass which turns to authoritarian solutions in times of crisis (political, civilisational and economic – real or perceived). This understanding is in fact reminiscent of John Stuart Mill's theory of democracy, Gustave Le Bon's theories of the crowd, and Bernays's use of political propaganda as a necessary tool for democratic subjugation.[63] In a logical but perverse development, the far right thus acquires a legitimate façade denied to it since the end of the Second World War, when it was classified under the terms 'fascist', 'extreme right', 'radical right' and 'far right'.

As Annie Collovald noted fifteen years ago, the populist classification is not only 'blurrier, but also less stigmatising than the ones it is meant to replace, such as fascism or extreme right.'[64] While its electoral and popular base of support in fact remains marginal, the discursive link created between the 'people' and the far right through the term 'populist' has helped transform the claims it defends into popular demands. This has, in turn, legitimised its racist and exclusionary ideals, laundering them as popular and democratic demands through the skewed interpretation of the rise of the populist right. Furthermore, 'the people' for the populist right and far right is often

---

Populism: Nine Rules of Engagement', *Organization* 25 : 5 (2018).

63   Gustave Le Bon, *Psychologie des foules* (Paris: Les Presses universitaires de France, 1963); Edward Bernays, *Propaganda: Comment manipuler l'opinion en démocratie* (Paris: Zones, 2007).

64   Annie Collovald, *Le populisme du FN: Un dangereux contresens* (Bellecombe-en-Bauges: Ed. du Croquant, 2004). Our translation.

represented by elites such as in the case of Le Pen, Trump, former stockbroker Farage or old Etonian Prime Minister Boris Johnson. This is sustained despite actions demonstrating low faith in 'the people' such as when Johnson prorogued (discontinued) an elected Parliament in August 2019 in order to allow his Brexit package to pass without a vote and opposition. In the following campaign, Farage decided not to run for election or stand 317 of his Brexit Party candidates in seats where it could split the Tory vote in the 12 December 2019 election.[65]

Together with the process of legitimisation of the parties and their ideas, a concurrent process of delegitimisation has occurred with regard to the concept of the 'people'. Beyond its potential as a term legitimising the far right, populism has been used by the social and political elite to imply what Jacques Rancière has described as the supposed ungovernability of democracies.[66] The rise of the far right has become the perfect excuse to explain the inability of mainstream parties to gather consequent and consistent support during elections: the 'people' and their irrational and irresponsible behaviour are to blame for the rise of 'extreme' parties. While the use of populism to describe the far right has reduced the stigma which has marginalised them for decades, the creation of a link – albeit a semantic one – between such parties and the 'people' has transferred blame for the situation onto the latter. What appears as menacing in the far right is thus no longer its ideas per se, but its role as 'the voice of the people'. The link between the irrational and shameful vote for the far right and the people in general, through the term 'populism', has allowed governing elites to feel more secure in their position: 'if the people have become more authoritarian and reactionary, it is because of their own ignorance and naivety', not because those who are meant to represent the people have failed in their task.[67] This, in turn, has justified the increasing prevalence of the notion that the sole

---

65 Paul Sandle, 'Brexit Party leader Nigel Farage will not run in UK election', Reuters, 3 November 2019; Kate Proctor and Graeme Wearden, 'Brexit party will not contest 317 Tory-won seats, Farage says', *Guardian*, 11 November 2019.

66 Rancière, *La haine de la démocratie*.

67 Collovald, *Le populisme du FN*, pp. 74–5.

purpose of elections is the transfer of approval to those who are judged – or judge themselves – qualified to lead the people, leaving the *demos* with no choice or power (*kratos*).

The media panic caused by the recent rise of the populist right can be partly explained by reference to the psychoanalytical concept of 'theft of enjoyment' in a loose fashion. Our own enjoyment exists in relation to that of others. If the enjoyment of others is seen as taking away from our own, a powerful emotional response becomes inevitable. This theft of enjoyment is central to the electoral performance of the far right, inasmuch as its supporters feel that their enjoyment of their nation, land, and so on, has been stolen or spoiled by immigrants or other races. Yet such a feeling is not limited to far-right voters; in our view, it is also central to the reaction elicited by the far-right vote and its exaggeration. In voting for irrational, racist and xenophobic options, the populist-right voter throws the contingency of the concept of liberal democracy into full daylight, highlighting the boundaries between acceptable and unacceptable choices. In this case, others (those voting for the 'populist right') derive irrational enjoyment from their democratic freedom as they vote for seemingly radical options. However, by enjoying this freedom, they infringe on our enjoyment of our understanding of democracy, whereby one's choice is unlimited so long as it remains within clear boundaries (defined around fuzzy, changeable and often contradictory values): in short, so long as it is limited.[68]

In our view, even the rise of left-wing forms of populism, in southern Europe in particular, has served to obscure the situation more than to diversify the political spectrum. Left-wing alternatives to the status quo have thus been positioned alongside far-right parties under the populist umbrella, and thus immediately and irremediably tarnished. This move has also exaggerated their radicalism, as it has created a new political dichotomy between populists on one side, whether of left or right, and anti-populists on the other. The latter often describe themselves as defenders of liberalism

---

68   Jason Glynos and Aurelien Mondon, 'The Political Logic of Populist Hype: The Case of Right-Wing Populism's "Meteoric Rise" and Its Relation to the Status Quo', *Populismus Working Paper Series*, no. 4 (2016).

against all forms of authoritarianism and irrational politics. This, of course, ignores the fact that liberalism has its share of responsibility for the rise of authoritarian politics, both historically and in the present, as we hope to have shown. Nonetheless, the use of populism to describe parties on the left and right opposing the status quo has allowed liberals to create a diversion away from their own failures, as well as to reinforce their hegemony by hyping false or limited alternatives. While parties such as Syriza, Podemos, France Insoumise, and even Labour under Jeremy Corbyn and the movement of support for Bernie Sanders within the US Democratic Party, have been called 'populist' and presented as a threat in most of the mainstream media, these alternative movements have in fact offered moderate reforms within the hegemonic system, rather than proposing a real challenge to the status quo.

It is therefore no surprise that many have tried recently to link the so-called populist left and right, as against the liberal hegemony, as part of a thesis framing them as two sides of the same (threatening) coin. In an opinion piece about Labour's position on Brexit in September 2018, Rafael Behr, a *Guardian* columnist, claimed that 'on Europe, Labour's left is revealing its affinity to the alt-right'. The same equivalence has been drawn in France between France Insoumise's Jean-Luc Mélenchon and the FN/RN's Marine Le Pen. As early as 2011, Plantu, one of France's most famous mainstream cartoonists, drew both reading from the same speech, describing them as representing 'the rise of neopopulisms'. In the US, *Newsweek* argued that 'Bernie Sanders voters helped Trump win'. It is for this reason that we need to highlight the issue of the socioeconomic analyses and policies presented by the left, and how they differ from those offered by the right by focusing on the hegemony, structures, institutions and processes of capitalism as the source of inequality – which also affects immigrants and people of colour – as opposed to immigration and 'race'. Where the right legitimises the presumed racism of the targeted base, this manoeuvre must be challenged not because it represents populism or a threat to liberal democracy, but as racism.

This notion that there is a 'populist vote' strengthens a tendency towards democratic repression when alternatives are sought beyond the current hegemonic order, whether on the left or right. In 2005,

Chantal Mouffe rightly stated that it was 'the lack of an effective democratic debate about possible alternatives that [had] led in many countries to the success of political parties claiming to be the "voice of the people"'.[69] What she was criticising was the apparent unanimity in the state of politics, or what Rancière has described as the 'politics of consensus'.[70] For Mouffe, popular sovereignty – the democratic symbol par excellence – has now been superseded by the values of the market, and is 'usually seen as an obsolete idea, often perceived as an obstacle to the implementation of human rights'. In western democracies, human rights have routinely been used to support the claim that the 'democratic' system works for the general good, beyond partisan factions: if human rights are a product of liberalism, the system is above all suspicion.[71] The absence of antagonism in contemporary politics and the rejection of this supposed final stage of history by a vast portion of the population have been central to the resurgence of the far right. The misuse of the category of populism and the hype of the threat it represents – as the only alternative to the establishment, as wholly unacceptable – has allowed the systemic failures of liberalism to go unremarked within public discourse, impeding the emergence of real alternatives.

---

69 Chantal Mouffe, 'The "End of Politics" and the Challenge of Right-Wing Populism', Francisco Panizza, ed., *Populism and the Mirror of Democracy* (London/New York, Verso, 2005), p. 51.

70 Rancière, *La haine de la démocratie*. Our translation.

71 Robert Meister, *After Evil: A Politics of Human Rights* (New York: Columbia University Press, 2010).

Against Reactionary Democracy: Courage and Accountability

In recent years, the far right has become ubiquitous as a topic of discussion in contemporary politics across the west and beyond. It has developed in various ways, from the reconstruction of traditional extreme-right parties such as the Front National in France, to its adaptation through multiple forms in the UK – from the fascist National Front to UKIP, the Brexit Party and the EDL. In the United States, we have witnessed a shift in the politics of the Republican Party, allowing a loose coalition of far-right and extreme-right activists and ideologues to have a direct impact on presidential power. This phenomenon, of course, has extended far beyond these three national cases. Nonetheless, in each we have witnessed a mainstreaming of far-right ideas against immigrants, Muslims and the other in general. While each case deserves detailed attention in its own right, there are a number of heuristic elements we can draw from the current situation in order to understand this phenomenon more fully. First of all, we developed a framework within which we could achieve a better grasp of how racism has evolved since the Second World War, and later during the 'post-racial' period. This is an essential step in developing an understanding of the reach of racism and the productive interplay between its various articulations, but also of the role played by the mainstream in its concealment and perpetuation. It is important to recognise that this mainstreaming process originates not only from the successful or popular politics of far-right parties and movements. Instead, a dual process has been necessary in which discursive elites (such as the media, politicians and academics) have played a key role in legitimising certain ideas. Finally, we argue that the scale of far-right support has been exaggerated. This does not mean that the far right is not a threat, but that, if we are to combat it, we must understand not only its true character, but also the historical, social and political contexts in which it operates. We reject the argument that the far right is solely responsible for the resurgence of racism. We also reject the claim that the solution to the rise of the far right lies in placating or emulating it. We do not believe, like Hillary Clinton, that 'Europe must curb immigration to stop right-wing populists', or, with Tony Blair, that migrants must be required to integrate in order to stop the 'far-right bigotry on the rise'. This kind of discourse can only further legitimise racism and the far right.

Our central claim is that the far right would not, by itself, have been able to achieve such success, either electorally or ideologically. While the far right should not be left off the hook, we have argued here that we need to shift the responsibility for the situation towards those who too often claim to be mere bystanders, despite their strong capacity to shape public discourse. This conclusion is partly dedicated to these people – among whom, as academics, we must count ourselves. We believe that power over discourse comes with a responsibility to act: at this stage, inaction equals acquiescence, and ultimately complicity. These recommendations should also be of use to anyone serious about the fight against racism and the far right. Anti-racist action must target racism's illiberal forms decisively on the ground; but we must not lose sight of the more structural power relationships and inequalities which have fed on such ideas. Our aim is not to be prescriptive about how to lead the fight, but to provide a basis upon which to build the more holistic approach which is urgently required.

STOP HYPING THE FAR RIGHT

The far and extreme right sell. They provides entertainment through drama or horror – something the media embraces, encourages, and sometimes even helps to create. In some cases, platforming extreme, and especially more acceptable, far-right actors or their ideas serves to distract from the more mundane, liberal, coded racism in our structures, institutions and policies. It also distracts from more pressing issues in our daily lives, drawing attention instead to extraneous, fantasised threats. Of course, the far right is part of our political landscape, and we do not argue that it should not be studied, discussed and combatted. But we must stop pretending that our elite are detached spectators merely analysing or creating policy around the desires of 'the people'. As we have shown, such gestures do not merely paint an inaccurate picture; they also wilfully ignore their own roles as shapers of narrative and public discourse, thus allowing them to shirk their responsibilities. It is lazy, cowardly and harmful, and those in power (both political and discursive) must be held accountable.

For the media, this requires more careful and less sensationalist coverage, and greater precision in the use of terminology. While comprehensive media reform, in addition to radical political reform, is necessary if we are to achieve a more democratic system, journalists must also reflect on the impact of the stories they run and their role as influencers on, if not generators of, public discourse and narratives. While reporting on the far right is vital, it is not the only story; other alternatives to the status quo should be covered appropriately and proportionately. Similarly, electoral results and public opinion surveys must be reported more carefully, making clear their many imperfections with respect to democracy. We do not necessarily argue that a strategy of no-platforming the far right is the correct one; but, giving it an unchallenged or inflated platform in media coverage is a political choice which will tend to lead to its normalisation. We must move beyond the idea that objective and unbiased coverage of the news requires the invocation of false equivalences. Just as we do not need a climate sceptic to contribute to a debate on climate change, or a revisionist in a debate on the Holocaust, we do not need to hear from racists in a discussion on immigration. This would also necessitate a more careful use of language, avoiding the euphemisation pursued by the far right itself. Steve Bannon and Marine Le Pen are not simply or primarily 'populist'; Richard Spencer is not 'a dapper white nationalist'; Nigel Farage does not represent 'the people'; fascists are not 'alternative' or 'hipsters'. None have the support of a 'silent majority'.

Politicians also bear a large measure of responsibility for our current predicament. As discussed in Chapters 3 and 4, the mainstreaming of the far right is not simply or even predominantly the result of popular demand or the savviness of the far right itself. For politicians, this has manifested in short-term, opportunistic strategies such as borrowing ideas and discourses that appear to counter the rise of the far right, possibly denting its support at first, but ultimately legitimising their ideas as a credible alternative. This has been particularly useful to the far right at a time when mainstream politics is deeply distrusted, and when the convergence of the centre-left and right has left no outlet for discontent with a system that seems increasingly dysfunctional. The populist hype has thus also been a symbol of the powerlessness, venality and cowardice of our political class and its lack of imagination in dealing directly and honestly with the many crises we are facing. That is not to say the wider population has no role or agency in this, and are merely influenced and impacted by it, but they are evoked in claims of 'popular demand', to justify 'solutions' or as scapegoats for problems in a system without a full range of parties, positions, visions and alternatives to choose from. That is our focus and concern here. Instead of developing necessary radical mid- to long-term visions, requiring radical political reforms, parts of our political elite have used the far right and its focus on immigration and racism as short-term fixes for electoral gain. For this, history will judge today's politicians; but this is of little comfort to the millions whose lives have been severely impacted in the meantime.

Finally, the academic popularity of the far right as a topic of study has also led to some serious issues. Certain scholars already working in the area serve effectively as gatekeepers, while others have jumped on the bandwagon, exploiting the renewed interest in the far right, hype its importance without always reflecting on the impact of their work. In some cases, this has led to the misrepresentation of the true significance of the far right, giving it an unprecedented profile and platform, not only within scholarship, but in media and policy circles. Ideological claims have been advanced suggesting that dealing with the threat of the far right requires either tighter securitisation or stricter immigration controls – or both. To be clear, our aim is not to protect our turf against newcomers, or promote ourselves. We simply call for responsibility, reflexivity and accountability – particularly from gatekeepers who have the ear of the media and political establishments. We can no longer shy away from our role as shapers of public discourse, hiding behind pseudo-objective, positivist scientific arguments; our domain of study cannot be abstracted from our experience and position in society. Failure to acknowledge and take proper account of this fact represents the real threat to impartiality, high-quality research and the development of novel ideas. We would also encourage newcomers to the field to engage with it thoroughly, going beyond niche interests and methodologies. This means engaging in an interdisciplinary manner with history, ideology and theory beyond the hegemonic canon.

RACISM EVOLVES AND ADAPTS: IT IS NOT EXHAUSTED BY ITS ILLIBERAL ARTICULATIONS

Despite the wealth of evidence in the field, it has been far too lazily accepted in mainstream discourse that racism is a thing of the past and that, when it rears its ugly head, it is only in extraordinary and idiosyncratic circumstances. Acts of clear illiberal racism are denounced by all, including the far right itself, seemingly placing everyone within in the non-racist camp. In the wake of the Christchurch mosque attacks in 2019, both Generation Identity and Renaud Camus, the author of 'Great Replacement' theory, who had clearly had an influence on the perpetrator, were given a platform – on the BBC in the case of the former – and allowed to declare almost unchallenged that their ideas had nothing to do with the attack. In this context, it has become common to hear opportunistic politicians, pundits and academics pretend that being Islamophobic is not racist, since they argue that their claims concerned religion or culture. Others have complained about anti-white racism, and even the possibility of white minoritisation or decline, borrowing directly from the far- and extreme-right playbook. This phenomenon is partly a product of a misunderstanding on the part of a self-righteous liberal mainstream of the way in which racism persists in our societies. It has been exploited by the far right and its acolytes, and has led to a situation in which it is now impossible to describe anyone as racist, no matter how clear their intent. Ironically, those who are quick to call the left 'snowflakes' have been especially precious about being tagged with a term which applies to them so appropriately (see Chapter 3).

In our view, it is not enough simply to claim not to be racist on the basis that one does not subscribe to the most illiberal, biological forms of racism. Moreover, being *non*-racist is not enough either. In societies where racism is and remains systemic, we have no choice but to be anti-racist if we do not want to be on the side of inequality and oppression.[1] We believe that real emancipatory and egalitarian politics can only unfold in a setting where racism is seen in a holistic manner that recognises its deep roots, multiple forms and transforming or adaptive character, and where all are acknowledged, resisted and opposed. This is hardly a radical demand.

The term 'racist' whether applied to a person, party or institution is indeed insulting, and properly so. And it can be applied to elite actors in the mainstream. If it is applied justifiably, we should not shy away from using it or fall for counter-claims that the targets of racism and anti-racists are easily offended snowflakes, who are denying 'free speech' to the privileged and powerful and their cowardly position against equality.

RACISM IS NOT (ONLY) IN THE OTHER

The resurgence of far-right politics, and of more obvious or brazen forms of racism, has often been blamed on an other. As we have seen, the far right itself has often been used as a decoy to distract attention away from the mainstream's own use of racism and from systemic abuses. It has also been useful for politicians lacking imagination to blame their lazy rightward turn on the far-right alternative and their hyped 'popular' support. But the persistence of racism does not rely on the far or extreme right. While far- and extreme-right racism is often more obviously violent and less palatable to our 'post-racial' sensibilities, it is not solely responsible for the plight of racialised minorities who suffer on a daily basis from racist violence – whether physical, economic or symbolic – unleashed upon them precisely by the liberal states which claim to stand against racism and the far right. It is not the place here to discuss whether liberalism is bound to be racist or support systemic racist discrimination, but only that it has so far failed to live up to its own supposed ideals, despite having convinced us that this is the case and that we live indeed after evil.

---

1   Ibram X. Kendi makes a powerful argument along similar lines in Ibram X. Kendi, *How to be an anti-racist* (London: Penguin Random House, 2019).

This diversionary tactic is linked to what we described in the previous chapter as the 'theft of enjoyment' felt by the self-righteous liberal centre. In this setting, 'far-right voters' are blamed for damaging what would otherwise be a perfect, tolerant, liberal society. Of course, this narrative is based on a rose-tinted vision of liberal societies in which minorities are treated equally and according to merit – something which has clearly never been the case. There is a more perverse side to this question, as the other blamed for the theft of our enjoyment is usually to be found among the working class, with all its associated meanings. While we are not denying that parts of the working class have indeed turned to the far right, we demonstrated in Chapter 4 that the real phenomenon involved has been dwarfed by a narrative that has been exaggerated and simplified. Not only is it not tenable as an argument; it has also served the far right and its allies, lending their ideas democratic credence. The self-righteous liberal centre thus does exactly what the far right does with immigrants and other racialised minorities: it essentialises a mostly voiceless and powerless cohort within the population, using and abusing it while propping up systemic inequalities and injustice.

We believe it is urgently necessary to stop shifting the blame in this way – to take a closer look at our current political system to see whether it is fit for the purpose of underpinning a fair and equal society, an objective that is a long way off by most standards. This cannot be done without taking a sober look not only at our economic system, but also at where power lies – at who can more readily create public narratives and sustain them through state power and its policed and militarised complex.

THE FAR RIGHT IS NOT THE (ONLY OR INEVITABLE) ALTERNATIVE

The extent of popular support for the far right is far from clear (see Chapter 4). It certainly does not justify the disproportionate coverage and treatment these parties have received, and the way in which their ideas have been mainstreamed by opportunist politicians, pundits and academics, with the help of poor journalistic practice. This discursive hype has meant that the far right and its ideas have been posited as the alternative to the status quo – an enviable position in a context where there are high levels of distrust towards establishment politicians and the elite in general. This distrust is often legitimate, since politicians have often proved disconnected, untrustworthy and unaccountable – but also because liberal democracy has failed to achieve social justice across western societies, while continuing to inflict harm on those outside the west through economic and military hegemony. Challenges to this hegemony by other nation-states and potential superpowers have meant that rights hard won by social movements and financed by the fruits of former imperial domination have become increasingly threatened by politics of austerity and the desire to prop up the capitalist economy, even at the expense of peoples' livelihoods and well-being.

Offering the far right the role of the alternative to this system is not only empirically problematic, but dangerous. The far right and the current mainstream in its liberal form are not structurally antagonistic, as we are often told. Liberalism is not in essence a bulwark against the far right, and the far right is not a mortal threat to liberalism in its current capitalist hegemonic version: the borders between them are porous and fuzzy; they are in effect mutually supportive. Racism and liberalism were not mutually exclusive in the past, and they are no more so today. This can be seen in the many countries where the far right has reached various degrees of power, sometimes through its own means and sometimes through the dissemination of their ideas by mainstream parties and political actors. Racism did not need the resurgence of the far right to become part and parcel of our liberal societies; but its resurgence has nevertheless strengthened the hold of systemic racism on our society. While the myth of our societies as post-racial made it easier for us to ignore the continuation of systemic racism, the far right, and particularly the associated resurgence of illiberal racism, have made it easier to downplay challenges to systemic racism on the basis that 'real' racism is 'out there', and that we must all rally in defending liberalism against it. The inflation of this imminent threat has caused discussion of the role of capitalism and liberalism in the perpetuation of injustice based on race, class and gender to be derided as peripheral; instead of attending to these phenomena, we must instead band together uncritically behind a united liberal front, whatever costs and compromises that might entail.

Not only should we challenge the assumption that the far right is an alternative to the status quo, rather than recognising the uncomfortable fact that it is an integral part of it, we should challenge the very nature of the liberal hegemony and its role in perpetuating a system based on structural racism, as well as other forms of injustice, oppression and discrimination. It is irrelevant whether we think that liberalism as such is bound to be racist; what matters is to ensure a critical approach, based on a knowledge of its history up to the present and its intricate links with oppressive politics. It is essential that we take a more critical look at the status quo, and explore radical alternatives. As we have seen in recent years, this will be a long struggle, as even the moderate left-wing alternatives represented by figures such as Jeremy Corbyn in the UK, Jean-Luc Mélenchon in France and Bernie Sanders in the United States have often proved too much for the liberal mainstream even to contemplate. At times, their possible success has in fact created more outrage than the progress of the far right itself.

BROADEN POLITICAL HORIZONS; RETURN TO MORE EMANCIPATORY FORMS OF DEMOCRACY

As Jacques Rancière pointedly noted in 2005:

> We do not live in democracies. Neither, as certain authors assert . . . do we live in camps. We live in States of oligarchic law, in other words, in States where the power of the oligarchy is limited by a dual recognition of popular sovereignty and individual liberties. We know the advantages of these sorts of States as well as their limitations.[2]

We have certain rights – though they are limited, and protest is heavily policed. We are able vote in elections that are mostly fair – although this usually only leads to the reproduction of the same interests that are already represented and defended within the system. We can participate in public life, although our success in influencing its direction will often depend on our financial power and connections. Perhaps more importantly for our purposes,

---

2   Jacques Rancière, *Hatred of Democracy* (London: Verso, 2007), pp. 73–4.

Rancière stresses that, no matter how limited these rights and free-doms may be, they were not granted as part of an original liberal package, but had to be wrested through struggle, and have required constant defence and enactment against the powerful, against the mainstream, and against liberalism itself – particularly in its capital-ist, neoliberal manifestations.

These limitations of liberal democracy – and the failure to address them in recent years, in the face of looming or deepening crises – have been facilitated by mainstream narratives, and by a lack of courage on the part of liberal politicians. In our view, we must therefore take a more radical approach towards politics and democracy.

Our aim here has not been to be prescriptive about what is to be done. But it would be remiss of us to lament the failures of the main-stream to tackle the rise of the far right and of racism more generally without reflecting upon the broader context and possibilities. As we have reiterated throughout this book, we believe that the far right and racism can be successfully combated only through a comprehensive political strategy. We believe that this requires a deep rethinking of our current understanding of democracy, and a return to considering radi-cal emancipatory forms of politics. Our politics should not be based on the defence of a status quo against the potential dangers of alternatives, wherever they come from. It must be based on a comprehensive chal-lenge to every and any injustice, and to all racial, gender, political and economic power structures, rather than taking a piecemeal approach.

To even consider implementing a comprehensive strategy, it is thus necessary to distinguish between electoral and ideological successes when attempting to understand the mainstreaming of the far right and racism. While everyday grassroots anti-racist action remains as essential as ever, the left has reached a point where it must develop a broader response, reaching beyond the far right itself. This approach must tackle the activation of racism by and within the mainstream, as well as the roots of the continual and pervasive presence of racism in our societies' structures and institutions, relying on critical, intersectional and historical approaches. This means that we must understand racism as part of a broader system of oppression which cannot be divorced from emancipatory struggles regarding class, gender and all forms of injustice.

Our understanding of 'the people' must therefore be reconnected to more radical, diverse and emancipatory understandings of politics and democracy. We must challenge purely electoral politics and the necessity to count and divide people, as well as the link between majority and democracy. We must return to an uncountable understanding of the demos, in which politics are for all or not at all. Since the future, shaped by climate change and resource scarcity, will require us to take an ever more globalised approach, considering the people as one, without others or exceptions, this will be the only way in which we can ensure we will not travel down the otherwise inevitable path towards oppression, exploitation and the potential return of fully-fledged fascist politics.

Emancipatory politics will never come from the top, as the powerful will always resist the loss of their status. As Stuart Hall remarked back in 1998, when referring to Tony Blair and his Third Way politics, 'it needs to be clearly said that a project to transform and modernise society in a radical direction, which does not disturb any existing interests and has no enemies, is not a serious political enterprise.'[3] Grassroots movements the likes of which are currently simmering across the globe will therefore be essential in this struggle. However, in a world increasingly globalised, but where wealth and power is held in ever fewer hands, the democratic struggle cannot simply be placed on the shoulders of those at the sharp end of injustice and oppression and there is a particular role to play for those in various positions of power, those able to influence and shape public discourse and narratives. For them, it is essential to acknowledge that their compliance and passivity can only mean upholding an unjust status quo and thus places them squarely on the side of oppression. Democracy can only thrive in a society rid of privileges, and it is thus essential that all forms of oppression are both clearly delineated and combated indiscriminately, not as a matter of priorities. Democracy must be anti-racist, as it must be anti-sexist and anti-classist, and against any and every form of oppression and where they intersect. Any less is cowardly. Any less is reactionary.

---

3   Stuart Hall, 'The Great Moving Nowhere Show', *Marxism Today*, November/ December 1998.

Index